Marketing Value Metrics

Marketing Value Metrics

A new metrics model to measure marketing effectiveness

Malcolm McDonald,
Peter Mouncey and
Stan Maklan

KoganPage

LONDON PHILADELPHIA NEW DELHI

First published in Great Britain and the United States in 2009 by Kogan Page Limited as *Marketing Accountability*
Second edition published in 2014 as *Marketing Value Metrics*

2nd Floor, 45 Gee Street	1518 Walnut Street, Suite 1100	4737/23 Ansari Road
London EC1V 3RS	Philadelphia PA 19102	Daryaganj
United Kingdom	USA	New Delhi 110002
www.koganpage.com		India

© Malcolm McDonald and Peter Mouncey, 2009
© Malcolm McDonald, Peter Mouncey and Stan Maklan, 2014

ISBN   978 0 7494 6897 2
E-ISBN 978 0 7494 6898 9

British Library Cataloguing-in-Publication Data

A CIP record for this book is available from the British Library.

Library of Congress Cataloging-in-Publication Data

McDonald, Malcolm.
  [Marketing accountability]
  Marketing value metrics : a new metrics model to measure marketing effectiveness / Malcolm McDonald, Peter Mouncey, Stan Maklan. – [Second edition].
    pages cm
  Revision of the authors' Marketing accountability.
  ISBN 978-0-7494-6897-2 (paperback) – ISBN 978-0-7494-6898-9 (ebook)   1. Marketing–Management.
2. Marketing–Cost effectiveness.   I. Mouncey, Peter.   II. Maklan, Stan.   III. Title.
  HF5415.13.M369159 2014
  658.80072–dc23
                                                                            2014026470

Typeset by Graphicraft Limited, Hong Kong
Print production managed by Jellyfish
Printed and bound by CPI Group (UK) Ltd, Croydon, CR0 4YY

CONTENTS

Introduction

1.1 Cheerleaders for the demise of the strategic marketing function

The challenge, and the opportunity, could not be greater for the marketing profession. The major opportunity is to focus on the role played by marketing capabilities in delivering profitable, long-term growth as opposed to the current frenzy to prove the effectiveness of promotional expenditure. Financial Management, which has dominated the boardroom for too long, has been rumbled. Exotic debt instruments, excessive leverage, 'right sizing' and excessive focus on cash, can no longer be relied on for the sustainable growth America and Europe need to pay off their debts. Over the next few years, as economies recover from the recession, you can expect an avalanche of management writing about innovation and growth; and the prescriptions will include the usual list of change management attributes: commitment, leadership, longer-term planning, investment in people, customer focus and more. A consensus will emerge for a complete reversal in the direction of the marketing function within businesses if we are to have a future. This political and economic discourse coalesces around a twin track prescription: 1) find new markets for high-value goods and services that people around the world wish to buy; and 2) establish branded positions in the supply chains to capture sufficient wealth from innovative new offers. If these are not the foci of marketing within business, the authors are at a loss to suggest what is. But this is not marketing's focus today, nor what it measures.

Regrettably, the marketing community seems bent upon travelling down a path of collective self-destruction. For the past 20 years we have successfully promoted an overly critical and defeatist view of our profession: convincing ourselves (and others) that marketers are often wasteful, self-indulgent, innumerate or detached and therefore deservedly lacking in influence. We accuse ourselves of not speaking the language of the board as the reason for our limited and decreasing presence at the top table: 'language of the board' is code for applying simple financial-based metrics to track the contribution of marketing in achieving business goals.

The discourse that we as marketers have promoted, rather too well, is that our contribution must be subject to different measures than other functions, a seductive but ultimately self-defeating strategy for us and our employers. We delight in writing that marketing presents its outcomes using measures such as brand equity, preference, awareness, hits and eyeballs. Top executives don't know (or believe) how to convert, for example, brand equity to 'real' equity; advertising may build awareness but senior management are unconvinced about the marginal return on media versus alternate uses of money. Without precise answers to these questions, marketers are said to engage in expensive self-indulgence. What the board wants to see is the return on investment – show me the money! Not surprisingly, boards have bought into the 'one number you need to know' philosophy, such as enshrined in the Net Promoter Score™, to cut through the clutter of metrics by which marketers clamour to be judged, and provide a simple measure of marketing effectiveness. But the level of investment in marketing; today's highly competitive international markets; the multi-layered strategies necessary to stimulate loyalty through enhanced customer experiences; the growing complexity of multichannel opportunities to reach consumers, surely deserve, and need, more than one measure of performance? If we wish to ensure that our marketing strategies are as effective as possible, we must be able to identify the right levers to pull to keep the train on the tracks and achieve our corporate goals.

Marketers supposed inability to identify the bottom-line impact of marketing spending is contributing to its demise. Marketing functions are hollowed out: strategic, central marketing groups are dispersed into business unit support functions (Verhoef *et al*, 2009) to provide tactical sales support 'close to the customer' (Webster, Malter and Ganesan, 2005). This has resulted in a situation where often there is no one person or function responsible for taking a strategic overview, creating a long-term vision or spotting discontinuity and inconsistencies in the promises made to consumers. Yet, the complexity of today's multichannel, experience-led marketing surely requires more, rather than less, control and central planning. Marketing directors have no automatic right to sit on the boards of companies where strategic decisions are made. Marketing's sphere of influence is increasingly limited to executional details (Verhoef *et al*, 2009). Not to worry, research suggests that it does not matter if the chief marketing officer is absent from the board, as long as the company is 'market oriented' (Verhoef *et al*, 2009); concerns about the role of marketing are therefore conveniently dismissed as posturing by vested interests. It is surprising that the marketing profession appears to lead the discourse that because marketing is everyone's responsibility, we should not worry about the seemingly irreversible decline of the central, strategic marketing function. It is as if our job is somehow done once a company declares it is market orientated or customer focused. For too long we have seemingly presided over, and welcomed, the demise of the marketing function as a measure of our success, the logical culmination of over half a century's effort spent in building marketing into a key business function, taught as a discrete topic within all the world's leading business management schools.

Therein lies a dangerous and self-destructive fallacy; one that we don't observe in other business areas. We have never heard that because prudence is everyone's business, we don't need a strategic finance function, or that because customers are everyone's concern, we don't need a strong sales function. While indifferent to the demise of the marketing function, board directors still expect marketing to lead breakthrough innovation (Verhoef *et al*, 2009) and commentators criticize British businesses for failing to convert British innovation into world-beating brands. We worry (rightly) as British branded businesses are bought by foreign firms because branch-plant Britain will not develop the global marketing capabilities we need to rebound economically. It also leaves companies potentially out of touch with the needs of consumers, and the structure of markets in emerging economies, the likely source of key future revenue.

1.2 More than a sum of its parts

We challenge the dominant discourse as both misinformed and misdirected. Misinformed merely rankles, misdirected is far more dangerous as it deflects focus from sustainable growth.

Popular wisdom promotes the mistaken view of marketing practice and scholarship as unconcerned with accountability. For at least 20 years, the prestigious Marketing Science Institute has promoted this agenda with great success. Marketing's most renowned scholars regularly publish compelling, evidence-based research linking marketing investment directly to share price (Srinivasan *et al*, 2009; Rao and Bharadwaj, 2008) or linking intermittent marketing outcomes, such as customer satisfaction, to shareholder value (Fornell *et al*, 2006; Anderson, Fornell and Agarwal, 2004; Rust *et al*, 2004). Technological advances allow firms to construct dashboards, managerially friendly, visual representations that integrate disparate databases to link marketing activity to the bottom line or other strategic objectives (Pauwels *et al*, 2009). Scholars have invested huge effort in developing ever more sophisticated models of consumer behaviour, and the software sector in this era of 'big data' has invested even more in database design, data integration and mining tools that generate individualized customer treatments cost effectively. Mobile phone companies deploy sophisticated predictive modelling to the call centre operator to improve the efficacy of offers made over the phone. Tesco's much discussed ClubCard programme enjoys coupon redemption 10 to 12 times the industry norm of untargeted offers, increasingly matched by competitors in the UK market such as Sainsbury's. If the evidence is compelling, quality research is being published and practice is improving, then why do we continue to critique marketing as unaccountable?

We believe that there are institutional factors (Townley, Cooper and Oakes, 2003; Greenwood and Hinings, 1996) at play that will not be solved regardless of how good the science of marketing measurement becomes. Marketing accountability is discussed purely as a rational search for evidence, ignoring issues of legitimacy and power. We accept, without empirical evidence, that merely having the right metrics will improve marketing decision making and accountability. Yet, we have ample evidence 'that marketing pays' but this evidence, and the metrics contained therein, are ignored because assessing marketing in real-world situations is difficult. Moreover, the marketing function has lost legitimacy so that its proposed measures lack credibility. Good measures are therefore necessary but not sufficient. To solve the issue of marketing accountability, to ensure business does not starve itself of the funds needed to identify and capture global markets, we must address issues of legitimacy and application of metrics. Yet, despite repeated pleas to understand the real-world context of accountability, we fixate on ever better measures, more sophisticated methods and better data-sets. By defining accountability as a purely technical issue, we avoid a more fundamental critique of what is happening: how we are pulling apart the strategic marketing function that we need to generate innovation led growth.

If the accusation that we are not accountable is often misinformed, we are more concerned that it is misdirected. The 'the language of the board' argument in practice directs managers and scholars to search for a magic formula (Ambler and Roberts, 2006) that ties spending on marketing activities to a limited number of financial ratios (eg RoI) or discounted cash flows (eg NPV, EVA). Indeed, when we ran a Cranfield-Industry club on marketing accountability, the focus of our members was to find the water-tight measure 'to convince the Finance Director'. Implicit in this discourse is a definition of marketing limited to its operational, short-term related, activities: advertising, promotion, web pages, social media etc. Marketing is scoped as a function that does things that should be ultimately tied to measured financial contribution. Not to dispute that such tactical activities can and should be assessed commercially (and strategically), however, that definition of the role of marketing, its competency and remit, will not enable business to find and exploit new markets profitably across the world. It is a definition of marketing more commensurate with 1990s financial theory than the highly dynamic global market environment we face.

1.3 Assessing the right things for the future

Oddly, marketing's critics never ask for an assessment of its unique contribution to the firm's ability to secure profitable growth: understanding customers' unmet needs, market/customer segmentation, competitive analysis, product portfolio analysis and managing marketplace risk. Accountability has been focused on matching expenditure to generating cash flow and income – understandable, but limited.

Perhaps marketing and advertising were synonymous in the 1960s and 70s when consumerism was growing, media became ubiquitous and most companies wanted to diversify and grow internationally. As market growth cooled in the 1970s and early 80s, maximizing shareholder value was the new mantra of the Anglo-Saxon business model, generating cries to justify advertising and promotion spending. Suddenly marketing, the rock-stars of the go-go 60s, became 'out of touch', self-indulgent and even irrelevant. The new discourse mirrored a new economic reality. As that reality changes again towards growth and global competition, so must the rhetoric. What companies need to assess and measure is the *quality* of marketing's insight, the extent to which new opportunities are being identified, competitive strategies understood and contingencies for marketplace risk developed. Successful identification and exploitation of new opportunities will have a far greater impact on business sustainability and profitability over the long run than optimizing the last dollar of advertising alone. This is not to suggest that marketing should not continue to build upon the huge advances it has made in matching spending to outcome; but a focus on the RoI of promotional spending does not address the strategic issue of marketing measurement and accountability.

Failure to focus on the role played by marketing capabilities in delivering profitable long-term growth is by far a bigger risk to firms than suboptimal promotional spending at the margin.

Even if the reader is not convinced by the need-for-growth arguments we present above, not many will argue that marketing has a strategic role to play ensuring the firm adapts to ever changing customer needs and market conditions. Here we draw upon a wealth of literature exploring why successful firms often fail to respond effectively to market changes. Let us use the example of the rapid changes in mobile data. Microsoft dominated desk-top computing for many years with a seemingly unassailable position due to its dominant share and commensurate ability to set standards. Nokia had built an extremely strong position in mobile devices (phones to most people). Both had all the ingredients for successfully building mobile data platforms well before Apple launched iPhone and Google introduced Android. Apple and Google had little experience in mobile data, no distribution arrangements with mobile carriers or any reputation in the area; Microsoft had already launched Windows-based mobile phone solutions. Yet, in 2007 Apple established a new segment for consumer easy-to-use mobile data through the iPhone, then iPad, to dominate the mobile data market. Google quickly launched Android and in less than two years overtook Apple, outselling it 2:1 at the time of drafting this chapter. In a period of less than five years, the new entrants have taken the dominant position in mobile data (phones and tablets) with something approaching 70 per cent of the market. At least some of the 'fault', if one is sitting in Microsoft or Nokia, is due to a lack of strategic marketing. The starting point for the incumbents was clearly not with the customer experience, the 'it just works' mantra of Apple. They had mobile data solutions that were simply nowhere near as good, intuitive or 'magical' – to use a Steve Jobs expression. They failed to incorporate the customer experience in their product development, anticipate the huge latent demand for mobile data ('done right'), the segments to whom this would appeal, the speed of adoption, the consumerization of corporate IT (channel change) and ultimately the risk to their businesses. Roll back the clock to when it was clear that Apple would launch a phone and ask: was a comprehensive grip on the RoI on marketing activity what was most needed by either Microsoft or Nokia? Was strategic marketing influencing decision making at these two technology giants sufficiently?

Business leaders wishing to make their marketing function accountable should demand answers to three fundamental questions – and in this order:

1 For what should their marketing function be accountable?

2 To whom?

3 And how should this be measured?

We observe that the dominant practice is to start with the last question about measurement and work up from there. Remember: RoI is king, we must speak the language of the board if we are to be taken seriously. By starting with RoI, we infer that marketing is about a series of expenditures and as such, responsible to share-holders through the instrument of short- to medium-term cash flow analysis.

1.4 A new perspective on the accountability of marketing

This book presents a different logic, in fact a 180-degree change in our concept of accountability. We argue that marketing should be accountable for creating new markets and extracting a sustainable flow of profit from them. It is therefore account-able to both customers and shareholders in equal measure for without a market/customer focus, there is no possibility of sustainable profit. All of which leaves us with the question of how to measure whether marketing is achieving this role. The measures we ask top executives to ask of their marketing functions include:

1 How well are we identifying customer needs and translating this into compelling promises?

2 To what extent are we identifying opportunities to serve needs better than competitors?

3 Have we segmented our markets/customers intelligently so as to make informed choices about where we are competing now and into the future with appropriate strategies for each segment?

4 Are we taking sustainably profitable positions in the supply chains in which we compete through partnerships, brand and developing unique capabilities that generate sustainable advantage?

5 Is our scanning of the environment sufficiently good to identify risks to the sustainability of our marketing plans?

6 Have we taken sensible measures to prepare for those risks?

7 Most importantly, do we empower marketing to co-ordinate the roles of other functions necessary to delivering the promises made to consumers and ensure that these other areas fully support the strategy, prioritize their resources accordingly, ensure the promise is delivered and accept the need to be measured on their contributory performance?

This book is not a compendium of measures; a 1001 metrics you might find useful when defending your budget against a mythical ogre-like finance director. We write for leaders, and aspiring leaders, of marketing. We ask you to consider taking up what is the biggest economic challenge facing our societies, generating the sustainable growth to overcome our economic crisis. Marketing must lead this process by identifying opportunities, generating attractive global offers and ensuring that we occupy the commanding heights of the supply chains. Marketing accountability is no longer about justifying the budget, it is about promoting innovation, building influence in the firm, leading growth and ensuring the voice of the customer is heard throughout the firm.

1.5 The structure of this book

At the core is a model, developed and tested at Cranfield School of Management, that helps organizations identify, firstly, the key strategies necessary within a marketing strategy to achieve corporate goals, and secondly, the measures necessary to track performance. As mentioned above, this is not the 1001 marketing metrics you'll ever need – we take a much wider perspective, recognizing that while the marketing team is responsible for developing the marketing strategy, delivery of this strategy will be dependent upon the actions of others, both inside and external to the organization. All of these activities need metrics. So, for example, if the overall strategy requires a more informed call centre team, then the process for achieving this needs to be agreed; targets set and performance measured. Whatever is implied in the promise made to customers within the marketing strategy needs to be identified, actions agreed and metrics set. If the marketing team are at the helm, responsible for delivering whatever has been agreed in the plan, then they need the information at their fingertips to check that the ship is on course, and what corrective action is necessary if it appears that someone, somewhere, is compromising the way forward. So, in addition to the core model, you will find other tools described that can help keep the ship off the rocks.

In the early chapters we describe what is meant by strategic marketing planning (Chapter 2); introduce a three-level marketing accountability framework (Chapter 3) and discuss the importance of due diligence in linking the impact of marketing to shareholder value (Chapter 4). We then summarize the core metrics model, and describe the methodology for implementing the model (Chapter 5). In subsequent chapters (6–9) we describe in detail the key steps within the model process, in identifying strategies and associated metrics. As the model is dependent on data, we include a chapter describing strategies for improving data quality (Chapter 10). We then follow with three chapters, each covering a relevant special topic. Chapter 11 is co-authored with Professor Wilson covering measures for customer experience and multichannel marketing, two of the most prominent areas of customer marketing theory. Chapter 12 is written by Robert Stratton, Vice President Analytics, MarketShare, a specialist company in assessing the value of social media. Brand and customer equity is co-authored with David Haigh, Chairman of one of the world's most respected brand valuators, Brand Finance. Finally, we have two appendices: one covering econometric modelling (Appendix 1) and the second describing seven key business questions, or financial measures, which marketers need to be familiar with (Appendix 2).

References

Ambler, T and Roberts, J (2006) Beware the Silver Metric: Marketing performance measurement has to be multidimensional, *Marketing Science Institute Working Paper Series*, *06-113*, pp 1–13

Anderson, E W, Fornell, C and Agarwal, S (2004) Customer Satisfaction and Shareholder Value, *Journal of Marketing*, **68**, pp 172–85

Fornell, C, Mithas, S, Morgeson, F V I and Krishnan, M S (2006) Customer Satisfaction and Stock Prices: High returns, low risk, *Journal of Marketing*, **70** (1), pp 3–14

Greenwood, R and Hinings, C (1996) Understanding Radical Organizational Change: Bringing together the old and the new institutionalism, *The Academy of Management Review*, **21** (4), pp 1022–54

Pauwels, K, Ambler, T, Clark, B, LaPointe, P, Reibstein, D, Skiera, B and Wiesel, T (2009) Dashboards as a Service: Why, what, how, and what research is needed?, *Journal of Service Research*, **12** (2), pp 175–89

Rao, R and Bharadwaj, N (2008) Marketing Initiatives, Expected Cash Flows, and Shareholders' Wealth, *Journal of Marketing*, **72** (1), pp 16–26

Rust, R, Lemon, K and Zeithaml, V (2004) Return on Marketing: Using customer equity to focus marketing strategy, *Journal of Marketing*, **68** (1), pp 109–27

Srinivasan, S, Pauwels, K, Silva-Risso, J and Hanssens, D M (2009) Product Innovations, Advertising, and Stock Returns, *Journal of Marketing*, **73** (January), pp 24–43

Townley, B, Cooper, D J and Oakes, L (2003) Performance Measures and the Rationalization of Organizations, *Organization Studies (01708406)*, **24** (7), pp 1045–71

Verhoef, P C, Leeflang, P S H, Natter, M, Baker, W, Grinstein, A, Gustafsson, A and Suanders, J (2009) *A Cross-National Investigation into the Marketing Department's Influence within the Firm*, Cambridge, pp 1–27

Webster, F J, Malter, A J and Ganesan, S (2005) The Decline and Dispersion of Marketing Competence, *Sloan Management Review*, **46** (4), pp 35–43

Strategic marketing planning – a brief overview

02

For those readers totally familiar with strategic marketing planning, please proceed to Chapter 3, although we do recommend that readers spend time on this chapter.

Summary

In order to explore the complexities of developing a winning marketing strategy plan, this chapter is written in three parts. The first describes the strategic marketing planning process itself and the key steps within it. The second part provides guidelines for the marketer that will ensure that the input to the marketing plan is customer focused and considers the strategic dimension of all of the relationships the organization has with its business environment. The third part provides 12 guidelines for world-class marketing.

2.1 Introduction

Research into the efficacy of formalized marketing planning has shown that marketing planning can make a significant contribution to commercial success. The main effects within organizations are:

- the systematic identification of emerging opportunities and threats;
- preparedness to meet change;
- the specification of sustainable competitive advantage;
- improved communication among executives;
- reduction of conflicts between individuals and departments;

- the involvement of all levels of management in the planning process;
- more appropriate allocation of scarce resources;
- consistency of approach across the organization;
- a more market-focused orientation across the organization.

However, although it can bring many benefits, a strategic marketing plan is mainly concerned with competitive advantage – that is to say, establishing, building, defending and maintaining it.

In order to be realistic, it must take into account the organization's existing competitive position, where it wants to be in the future, its capabilities and the competitive environment it faces. This means that the marketing planner must learn to use the various available processes and techniques that help in making sense of external trends and in understanding the organization's traditional ways of responding to these.

However, this poses the problem regarding which are the most relevant and useful tools and techniques, for each has strengths and weaknesses and no individual concept or technique can satisfactorily describe and illuminate the whole picture. As with a jigsaw puzzle, a sense of unity emerges only as the various pieces are connected together.

The links between strategy and performance have been the subject of detailed statistical analysis by the Strategic Planning Institute. The Profit Impact of Market Strategy – PIMS – (Buzzell and Gale, 1997) project identified, from 2,600 businesses, six major links. From this analysis, principles have been derived for the selection of different strategies according to industry type, market conditions and the competitive position of the company.

However, not all observers are prepared to take these conclusions at face value. Strategy consultants Lubatkin and Pitts (1985), believe that all businesses are unique, and are suspicious that something as critical as competitive advantage can be the outcome of a few specific formulae. For them, the PIMS perspective is too mechanistic and glosses over the complex managerial and organizational problems that beset most businesses.

What is agreed, however, is that strategic marketing planning presents a useful process by which an organization formulates its strategies, providing it is adapted to its environment.

2.2 Positioning marketing planning with marketing

In 2003, a Cranfield doctoral thesis (Smith, 2003) proved a direct link between organizational success and marketing strategies that conform to what previous scholars have agreed constitutes strategy quality, which was shown to be independent of variables such as size, sector, market conditions and so on.

This thesis linked superior performance to strategies with the following qualities:

- homogeneous market segment definition;
- segment-specific propositions;
- strategy uniqueness;
- strength leverage and weakness minimization;
- creation of internal and external synergies;
- provision of tactical guidance;
- alignment to objectives;
- alignment to market trends;
- appropriate resourcing;
- clear basis of competition.

Let us first position strategic marketing planning firmly within the context of marketing itself. Marketing is a process for: defining markets; quantifying the needs of the customer groups (segments) within these markets; determining the value propositions to meet these needs; communicating these value propositions to all those people in the organization responsible for delivering them and getting their buy-in to their role; playing an appropriate part in delivering these value propositions to the chosen market segments; and monitoring the value actually delivered. For this process to be effective, organizations need to be consumer/customer driven.

A map of this process is shown in Figure 2.1. This process is clearly cyclical, in that monitoring the value delivered will update the organization's understanding of the value that is required by its customers. The cycle is predominantly an annual one, with a marketing plan documenting the output from the 'understand value' and

FIGURE 2.1 Map of the marketing process

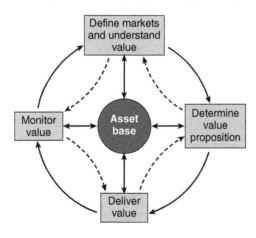

'Determine value proposition' processes, but equally changes throughout the year may involve fast iterations around the cycle to respond to particular opportunities or problems.

It is well known that not all of the value-proposition-delivering processes will be under the control of the marketing department, whose role varies considerably between organizations. The marketing department is likely to be responsible for the first two processes, 'Understand value' and 'Determine value proposition', although even these need to involve numerous functions, albeit coordinated by specialist marketing personnel. The 'Deliver value' process is the role of the whole company, including product development, manufacturing, purchasing, sales promotion, direct mail, distribution, sales and customer service. The marketing department will also be responsible for monitoring the effectiveness of the value delivered.

The various choices made during this marketing process are constrained and informed not just by the outside world but also by the organization's asset base. Whereas an efficient new factory with much spare capacity might underpin a growth strategy in a particular market, a factory running at full capacity would cause more reflection on whether price should be used to control demand, unless the potential demand warranted further capital investment. As well as being influenced by physical assets, choices may be influenced by financial, human resources, brand and information technology assets, to name just a few.

Thus, it can be seen that the first two boxes are concerned with strategic marketing planning processes (in other words, developing market strategies), while the third and fourth boxes are concerned with the actual delivery in the market of what was planned and then measuring the effect.

Input to this process will commonly include:

- the corporate mission and objectives, which will determine which particular markets are of interest;
- external data such as market research;
- internal data that flow from ongoing operations.

Also, it is necessary to define the markets the organization is in, or wishes to be in, and how these divide into segments of customers with similar needs. The choice of markets will be influenced by the corporate objectives as well as the asset base. Information will be collected about the markets, such as the market's size and growth, with estimates for the future.

The map is inherently cross-functional. 'Deliver value proposition', for example, involves every aspect of the organization, from new product development through inbound logistics and production to outbound logistics and customer service.

The map represents best practice, not common practice. Many aspects of the map are not explicitly addressed by well-embedded processes, even in sophisticated companies.

Having put marketing planning into the context of marketing and other corporate functions, we can now turn specifically to the marketing planning process and how it should be done. We are, of course, referring specifically to the 'Determine value proposition' box in Figure 2.1.

For the purpose of this book, it is important to understand that the 'Monitor value' box is not a separate step in strategy making, and what needs to be monitored and the frequency of measurement will depend totally on a deep understanding of the other three boxes, which we will now proceed to explain.

2.3 The marketing planning process

Most managers accept that a formal system and process for marketing planning is beneficial. Accordingly they need a system that will help them to think in a structured way and also make explicit their intuitive economic models of the business. Unfortunately, very few companies have planning systems that possess these characteristics. Those that do tend to follow a similar pattern of steps.

Figure 2.2 illustrates the several stages that have to be gone through in order to arrive at a marketing plan. This illustrates the difference between the process of

FIGURE 2.2   The 10 steps of the strategic marketing planning process

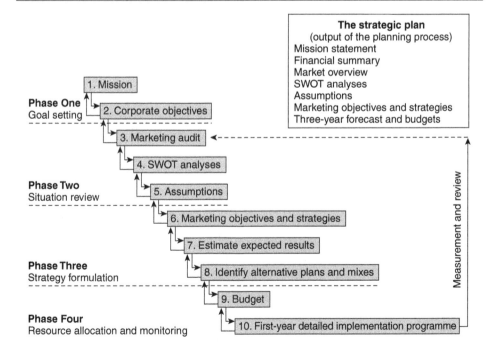

marketing planning and the actual plan itself, which is the output of the process, which is discussed later in this chapter.

Each of the process stages illustrated in Figure 2.2 will be discussed in more detail in this chapter. The dotted lines joining up stages 5–8 are meant to indicate the reality of the planning process, in that it is likely that each of these steps will have to be gone through more than once before final programmes can be written.

2.4 How formal should this process be?

Although research has shown these marketing planning steps to be universally applicable, the degree to which each of the separate steps in the diagram needs to be formalized depends to a large extent on the size and nature of the company. For example, an undiversified company generally uses less formalized procedures, since top management tends to have greater functional knowledge and expertise than subordinates, and because the lack of diversity of operations enables direct control to be exercised over most of the key determinants of success. Thus, situation reviews, the setting of marketing objectives and so on are not always made explicit in writing, although these steps have to be gone through.

In contrast, in a diversified company, it is usually not possible for top management to have greater functional knowledge and expertise than subordinate management; hence planning tends to be more formalized in order to provide a consistent discipline for those who have to make the decisions throughout the organization.

Either way, there is now a substantial body of evidence to show that formalized planning procedures generally result in greater profitability and stability in the long term and also help to reduce friction and operational difficulties within organizations.

Where marketing planning has failed, it has generally been because companies have placed too much emphasis on the procedures themselves and the resulting forecasts rather than on generating information useful to and consumable by management. Let us now look at the marketing planning process in more detail, starting with the mission statement.

2.4.1 Step 1 Mission statement

Figure 2.2 shows that a strategic marketing plan should begin with a mission or purpose statement. This is perhaps the most difficult aspect of marketing planning for managers to master, because it is largely philosophical and qualitative in nature. Many organizations find their different departments, and sometimes even different groups in the same department, pulling in different directions, often with disastrous results, simply because the organization hasn't defined the boundaries of the business and the way it wishes to do business.

Here, we can see two levels of mission. One is a corporate mission statement; the other is a lower-level, or purpose, statement. But there is yet another level, as shown in the following summary:

- *Type 1: 'generic'* – usually found inside annual reports designed to conform with institutional norms, but limited practical use for operational (marketing) strategy;

- *Type 2: the real thing* – a meaningful statement, unique to the organization concerned, which 'impacts' on the behaviour of the executives at all levels;

- *Type 3: a purposeful statement (or lower-level mission statement)* – appropriate at the strategic business unit, departmental or product group level of the organization.

We construct below that which we believe to be a generic-type mission statement, regrettably of a type all too common. It states rather obvious goals of all businesses, such as meeting customer needs, and rarely inspires employees. While institutionally we understand the pressures for conformity (DiMaggio and Powell, 1983; Scott, 1995), nonetheless, there is a need for a mission statement that inspires and directs.

The generic mission statement

Our organization's primary mission is to protect and increase the value of its owners' investments while efficiently and fairly serving the needs of its customers. [Name of organization] seeks to accomplish this in a manner that contributes to the development and growth of its employees, and to the goals of countries and communities in which it operates.

The following should appear in a mission or purpose statement, which should normally run to no more than one page:

- *Role or contribution:*
  - profit (specify); or
  - service; or
  - opportunity sought.

- *Business definition* – define the business, preferably in terms of the benefits you provide or the needs you satisfy rather than in terms of what you make.

- *Distinctive competences* – these are the essential skills/capabilities resources that underpin whatever success has been achieved to date. Competence can consist of the possession of one particular item or the possession of a number of skills compared with competitors. If, however, you could equally well put a competitor's name to these 'distinctive' competences, then they are not distinctive competences.
- *Indications for the future:*
  - what the firm will do;
  - what the firm might do;
  - what the firm will never do.

2.4.2 Step 2 Setting corporate objectives

Corporate objectives usually contain at least the following elements:

- the desired level of profitability;
- business boundaries:
  - what kind of products will be sold to what kinds of markets (marketing),
  - what kinds of facilities will be developed (operations, R&D, information systems, distribution, etc),
  - the size and character of the labour force (personnel),
  - funding (finance);
- other corporate objectives, such as social responsibility, corporate image, stock market image, employer image, etc.

Such a corporate plan, containing projected profit and loss accounts and balance sheets, being the result of the process described above, is more likely to provide long-term stability for a company than plans based on a more intuitive process and containing forecasts that tend to be little more than extrapolations of previous trends. This process is further summarized in Figure 2.3.

2.4.3 Step 3 The marketing audit

Any plan will be only as good as the information on which it is based, and the marketing audit is the means by which information for planning is organized. There is no reason why marketing cannot be audited in the same way as accounts, in spite of its more innovative, subjective nature. A marketing audit is a systematic appraisal of all the external and internal factors that have affected a company's commercial performance over a defined period.

FIGURE 2.3   The role of marketing in the context of business and corporate planning

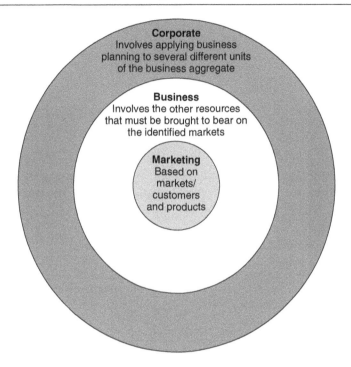

Given the growing turbulence of the business environment and the shorter product life cycles that have resulted, no one would deny the need to stop at least once a year at a particular point in the planning cycle to try to form a reasoned view of how all the many external and internal factors have influenced performance.

Sometimes a company will conduct a marketing audit because it is in financial trouble. At times like these, management risks treating the wrong symptoms, most frequently by reorganizing the company. But such measures are unlikely to be effective if there are more fundamental problems that have not been identified. Of course, if the company survived for long enough, it might eventually solve its problems through a process of elimination. Essentially, though, the argument is that the problems have first to be properly defined. The audit is a means of helping to define them.

2.4.3.1 Two kinds of variable

Any company carrying out an audit will be faced with two kinds of variable. There is the kind over which the company has no direct control, for example economic and market factors. Secondly, there are those over which the company has complete control, the operational variables, which are usually the firm's internal resources.

This division suggests that the best way to structure an audit is in two parts, external and internal. Table 2.1 shows areas that should be investigated under both headings. Each should be examined with a view to building up an information base relevant to the company's performance.

TABLE 2.1   Conducting an audit

External audit	Internal audit
Business and economic environment	Own company
Economic political, fiscal, legal, social, cultural, technological	Sales (total, by geographical location, by industrial type, by customer, by product)
Intra-company	Market shares
The market: total market, size, growth and trends (value volume)	Profit margins, costs
Market characteristics, developments and trends; products, prices, physical distribution, channels, customers, consumers, communication, industry practices variables, product management, price, distribution, promotion	Marketing information research
Competition	Marketing mix operations and resources
Major competitors	Key strengths and weaknesses
Size	
Market share coverage	
Market standing and reputation	
Production capabilities	
Distribution policies	
Marketing methods	
Extent of diversification	
Personnel issues	
International links	
Profitability	

Many people mistakenly believe that the marketing audit should be a final attempt to define a company's marketing problems or, at best, something done by an independent body from time to time to ensure that a company is on the right track. However, many highly successful companies, as well as using normal information and control procedures and marketing research throughout the year, start their planning cycle each year with a formal, audit-type process of everything that has had an important influence on marketing activities. Certainly, in many leading consumer goods companies, the annual self-audit approach is a tried-and-tested discipline.

Where relevant, the marketing audit should contain life cycles for major products and for market segments, for which the future shape will be predicted using the audit information. Also, major products and markets should be plotted on some kind of matrix to show their current competitive position.

The next question is: what happens to the results of the audit? Some companies consume valuable resources carrying out audits that produce very little in the way of results. The audit is simply a database, and the task remains of turning it into intelligence, that is, information essential to decision making.

A market overview, which appears prominently in the actual strategic marketing plan, should spell out clearly:

- what the market is;
- how it works;
- what the key decision-making points are;
- what the segments are.

Market definition is fundamental to success and must be made in terms of need sets rather than in product/service terms. Thus, Gestetner failed by defining its markets as 'duplicators', and IBM almost failed by defining its market as 'mainframes'. Accordingly, a pension is a product, not a market, as many other products can satisfy the same or similar needs – Kodak and Nokia being recent examples. Table 2.2 lists hypothetical markets in the financial services sector.

Figures 2.4 and 2.5 show the marketing books market in the UK. The first shows the market 'mapped' solely as marketing books. The second shows the market mapped in terms of the broader market definition of knowledge promulgation, from which it can be seen that new competitors and distribution channels come into play. Thinking and planning like this certainly had a dramatic effect on the marketing strategy of the major publisher involved.

Figure 2.6 is a generic market map, which shows how a market works from suppliers to users, and, like a balance sheet, it must 'balance', in the sense that, if 5 million radiators are made or imported, 5 million radiators must be distributed, 5 million radiators must be installed, and the decision about which radiators are to

TABLE 2.2 Some market definitions (personal market)

Market	Need (online)
Emergency cash ('rainy day')	Cash to cover an undesired and unexpected event (often the loss of/damage to property)
Future event planning	Schemes to protect and grow money that are for anticipated and unanticipated cash calling events (eg car replacement/repairs, education, weddings, funerals, health care)
Asset purchase	Cash to buy assets they require (eg car purchase, house purchase, once-in-a-lifetime holiday)
Welfare contingency	The ability to maintain a desired standard of living (for self and/or dependants) in times of unplanned cessation of salary
Retirement income	The ability to maintain a desired standard of living (for self and/or dependants) once the salary cheques have ceased
Wealth care and building	The care and growth of assets (with various risk levels and liquidity levels)
Day-to-day money management	Ability to store and readily access cash for day-to-day requirements
Personal finance protection and security from motor vehicle incidents	Currently known as car insurance

be installed must be made by someone. It is the purpose of the market map to spell all this out quantitatively.

It is at key decision points that market segmentation should take place. A segment is a group of customers or consumers that share the same (or approximately the same) needs. This step is crucial, for it is upon the key segments from the market map that SWOT analyses should be completed.

Market segmentation is crucial for success in markets, so this topic is explained in detail in Chapter 6.

FIGURE 2.4 Market map for marketing books in the UK

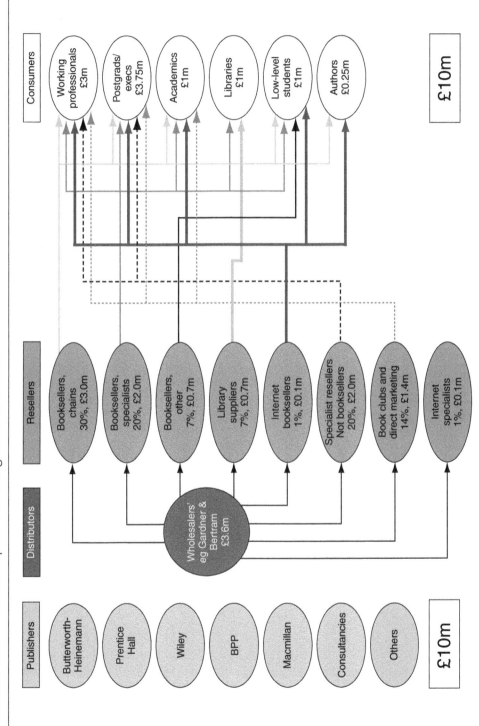

FIGURE 2.5 Expanded market map for knowledge promulgation

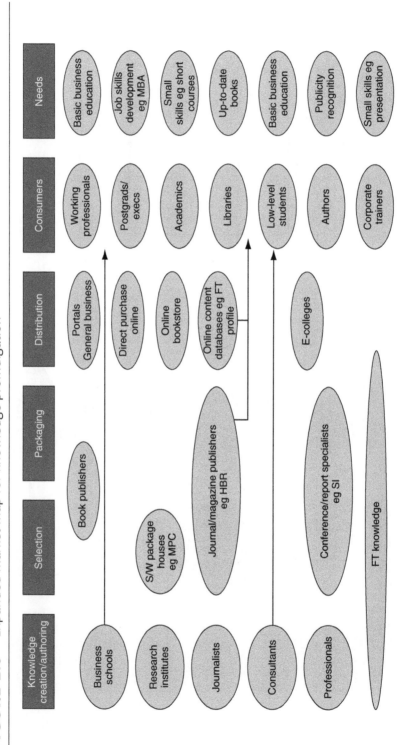

FIGURE 2.6 Generic market map

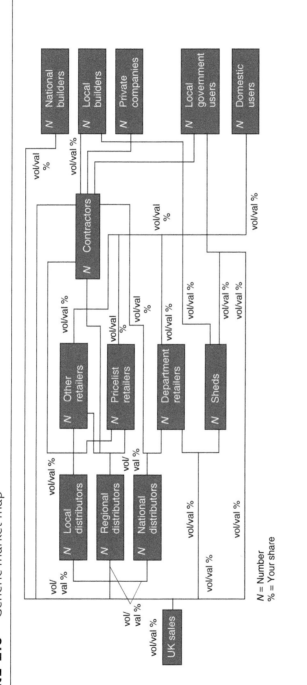

N = Number
% = Your share

2.4.4 *Step 4 SWOT analyses*

The only remaining question is: what happens to the results of the audit? Some companies consume valuable resources carrying out audits that bring very little by way of actionable results.

Indeed, there is always the danger that, at the audit stage, insufficient attention is paid to the need to concentrate on analysis that determines which trends and developments will actually affect the company. While the checklist demonstrates the completeness of logic and analysis, the people carrying out the audit should discipline themselves to omit from their audits all the information that is not central to the company's marketing problems. Thus, inclusion of research reports, or over-detailed sales performance histories by product that lead to no logical actions whatever, only serve to rob the audit of focus and reduce its relevance.

Since the objective of the audit is to indicate what a company's marketing objectives and strategies should be, it follows that it would be helpful if some format could be found for organizing the major findings. One useful way of doing this is in the form of a number of SWOT analyses.

> A SWOT is a summary of the audit under the headings of an organization's strengths and weaknesses in relation to competitors as they relate to opportunities and threats in their environment.

A SWOT should be conducted for each segment that is considered to be important in the company's future. These SWOT analyses should, if possible, contain just a few paragraphs of commentary focusing on key factors only. They should highlight internal differential strengths and weaknesses vis-à-vis competitors and key external opportunities and threats. A summary of reasons for good or bad performance should be included. They should be interesting to read, contain concise statements, include only relevant and important data, and give greater emphasis to creative analysis.

To summarize, carrying out a regular and thorough marketing audit in a structured manner will go a long way towards giving a company a knowledge of the business, trends in the market, and where value is added by competitors, as the basis for setting objectives and strategies.

2.4.5 *Step 5 Assumptions*

Let us now return to the preparation of the marketing plan. If we refer again to the marketing planning process, and have completed our marketing audit and SWOT analyses, assumptions now have to be written.

There are certain key determinants of success in all companies about which assumptions have to be made before the planning process can proceed.

It is really a question of standardizing the planning environment. For example, it would be no good receiving plans from two product managers, one of whom believed the market was going to increase by 10 per cent, while the other believed the market was going to decline by 10 per cent.

An example of assumptions might be: 'With respect to the company's industrial climate, it is assumed that:

- Industrial overcapacity will increase from 105 per cent to 115 per cent as new industrial plants come into operation.
- Price competition will force price levels down by 10 per cent across the board.
- A new product in the field of x will be introduced by our major competitor before the end of the second quarter.'

Assumptions should be few in number and, if a plan is possible irrespective of the assumptions made, then the assumptions are unnecessary.

2.4.6 Step 6 Marketing objectives and strategies

The next step in marketing planning is the writing of marketing objectives and strategies, the key to the whole process.

An objective is what you want to achieve. A strategy is how you plan to achieve your objectives.

Thus, there can be objectives and strategies at all levels in marketing. For example, there can be advertising objectives and strategies, and pricing objectives and strategies.

However, the important point to remember about marketing objectives is that they are about products, services, offers and markets only. Common sense will confirm that it is only by selling something to someone that the company's financial goals can be achieved, and that advertising, pricing, service levels and so on are the means (or strategies) by which we might succeed in doing this. Thus, pricing objectives, sales promotion objectives, advertising objectives and the like should not be confused with marketing objectives.

Marketing objectives are derived from Ansoff's famous matrix (Ansoff, 1957) and categorized as one, or more, of the following:

- existing products for existing markets;
- new products for existing markets;
- existing products for new markets;
- new products for new markets.

They should be capable of measurement; otherwise they are not objectives. Directional terms such as 'maximize', 'minimize', 'penetrate', 'increase', etc are acceptable only if quantitative measurement can be attached to them. Measurement should be in terms of some, or all, of the following: sales volume; sales value; market share; profit; and percentage penetration of outlets (for example, to have 30 per cent of all retail outlets stocking our product by year 3).

Marketing strategies are the means by which marketing objectives will be achieved and have traditionally been built around the four Ps, as follows:

- *product:* the general policies for product deletions, modifications, additions, design, branding, positioning, packaging, etc;
- *price:* the general pricing policies to be followed by product groups in market segments;
- *place:* the general policies for channels and customer service levels;
- *promotion:* the general policies for communicating with customers under the relevant headings, such as advertising, sales force, sales promotion, public relations, exhibitions, direct mail, etc.

The four Ps can be criticized as overly product-centric, whereas more of our modern economies are represented in services. Recognizing the need to modify the marketing mix, many services marketers have embraced Booms and Bitners' extension to seven Ps (1981) with the following 'new Ps' of the marketing mix: *people, process* and *physical evidence.*

2.4.7 Step 7 Estimate expected results, and Step 8 Identify alternative plans and mixes

Having completed this major planning task, it is normal at this stage to employ judgement, analogous experience, field tests and so on to test out the feasibility of the objectives and strategies in terms of market share, costs, profits and so on. It is also normally at this stage that alternative plans and mixes are considered, if necessary.

2.4.8 Step 9 The budget

In a strategic marketing plan, these strategies would normally be costed out approximately and, if not practicable, alternative strategies would be proposed and costed out until a satisfactory solution could be reached. This would then become the budget. In most cases, there would be a budget for the full three years of the strategic marketing plan, but there would also be a very detailed budget for the first year of the plan, which would be included in the one-year operational plan.

It will be obvious from all of this that not only does the setting of budgets become much easier but the resulting budgets are more likely to be realistic and related to what the whole company wants to achieve rather than just one functional department.

The problem of designing a dynamic system for budget setting, rather than the 'tablets of stone' approach, which is more common, is a major challenge to the marketing and financial directors of all companies.

The most satisfactory approach would be for a marketing director to justify all marketing expenditure from a zero base each year against the tasks he or she wishes to accomplish. A little thought will confirm that this is exactly the approach recommended in this chapter. If these procedures are followed, a hierarchy of objectives is built up in such a way that every item of budgeted expenditure can be related directly back to the initial corporate financial objectives. For example, if sales promotion is a major means of achieving an objective in a particular market, when sales promotional items appear in the programme each one has a specific purpose that can be related back to a major objective.

Doing it this way ensures not only that every item of expenditure is fully accounted for as part of a rational, objective and task approach, but also that when changes have to be made during the period to which the plan relates these changes can be made in such a way that the least damage is caused to the company's long-term objectives.

The incremental marketing expense can be considered to be all costs that are incurred after the product leaves the factory, other than costs involved in physical distribution, the costs of which usually represent a discrete subset.

There is, of course, no textbook answer to problems relating to questions such as whether packaging should be a marketing or a production expense, and whether some distribution costs could be considered to be marketing costs. For example, insistence on high service levels results in high inventory carrying costs. Only common sense will reveal workable solutions to issues such as these.

Under price, however, any form of discounting that reduces the expected gross income, such as promotional discounts, quantity discounts, royalty rebates and so on, as well as sales commission and unpaid invoices, should be given the most careful attention as incremental marketing expenses.

The most obvious incremental marketing expenses will occur, however, under the heading of promotion, in the form of advertising, sales salaries and expenses, sales promotional expenditure, direct mail costs and so on. The important point about the measurable effects of marketing activity is that anticipated levels should be the result of the most careful analysis of what is required to take the company towards its goals, while the most careful attention should be paid to gathering all items of expenditure under appropriate headings. The healthiest way of treating these issues is a zero-based budgeting approach.

2.4.9 Step 10 First-year detailed implementation programme

In a one-year tactical plan, the general marketing strategies would be developed into specific sub-objectives, each supported by more detailed strategy and action statements. A company organized according to functions might have an advertising plan, a sales promotion plan, a pricing plan and so on. A product-based company might have a product plan, with objectives, strategies and tactics for price, place and promotion as necessary. A market- or geographically-based company might have a market plan, with objectives, strategies and tactics for the four Ps as necessary. Likewise, a company with a few major customers might have customer plans. Any combination of the above might be suitable, depending on circumstances.

2.5 What should appear in a strategic marketing plan?

A written marketing plan is the backdrop against which operational decisions are taken. The following should appear in a strategic marketing plan:

1 Start with a mission statement.

2 Here, include a financial summary that illustrates graphically revenue and profit for the full planning period.

3 Now conduct a market overview including a market map: Has the market declined or grown? How does it break down into segments? What is your share of each? Keep it simple. If you do not have the facts, make estimates. Use life cycles, bar charts and pie charts to make it all crystal clear.

4 Now identify the key segments and do a SWOT analysis for each one: outline the major external influences and their impact on each segment. List the key factors for success. These should be fewer than five. Give an assessment of the company's differential strengths and weaknesses compared with those of its competitors. Score yourself and your competitors out of 10 and then multiply each score by a weighting factor for each critical success factor (eg CSF 1 = 60, CSF 2 = 25, CSF 3 = 10, CSF 4 = 5).

5 Make a brief statement about the key issues that have to be addressed in the planning period.

6 Summarize the SWOTs using a portfolio matrix in order to illustrate the important relationships between your key products and markets.

7 List your assumptions.

8 Set objectives and strategies.

9 Summarize your resource requirements for the planning period in the form of a budget.

Consequently, too much detail should be avoided. The marketing plan's major function is to determine where the company is, where it wants to go and how it can get there. It lies at the heart of a company's revenue-generating activities, such as the timing of the cash flow and the size and character of the labour force. What should actually appear in a written strategic marketing plan is shown in the list above. This strategic marketing plan should be distributed only to those who need it, but it can be only an aid to effective management. It cannot be a substitute for it.

It will be obvious from the list above that not only does budget setting become much easier and more realistic, but the resulting budgets are more likely to reflect what the whole company wants to achieve, rather than just one department.

The problem of designing a dynamic system for setting budgets is a major challenge to the marketing and financial directors of all companies. The most satisfactory approach would be for a marketing director to justify all marketing expenditure from a zero base each year against the tasks to be accomplished. If these procedures are followed, a hierarchy of objectives is built in such a way that every item of budgeted expenditure can be related directly back to the initial financial objectives.

For example, if sales promotion is a major means of achieving an objective, when a sales promotion item appears in the programme it has a specific purpose that can be related back to a major objective. Thus every item of expenditure is fully accounted for.

Marketing expense can be considered to be all costs that are incurred after the product or offer leaves the 'factory', apart from those involved in physical distribution. When it comes to pricing, any form of discounting that reduces the expected gross income – such as promotional or quantity discounts, overrides, sales commission and unpaid invoices – should be given the most careful attention as marketing expenses. The most obvious marketing expenses will occur, however, under the heading of promotion, in the form of advertising, sales salaries and expenses, sales promotion and direct mail costs.

The important point about the measurable effects of marketing activity is that anticipated levels should result from careful analysis of what is required to take the company towards its goals, while the most careful attention should be paid to gathering all items of expenditure under appropriate headings. The healthiest way of treating these issues is through zero-based budgeting.

We have just described the strategic marketing plan and what it should contain. The tactical marketing plan layout and content should be similar, but the detail is much greater, as it is for one year only.

2.6 How the marketing planning process works

As a basic principle, strategic marketing planning should take place as near to the marketplace as possible in the first instance, but such plans should then be reviewed at higher levels within an organization to see what issues may have been overlooked.

It has been suggested that each manager in the organization should complete an audit and SWOT analysis on his or her own area of responsibility. The only way that this can work in practice is by means of a hierarchy of audits. The principle is simply demonstrated in Figure 2.7. This figure illustrates the principle of auditing at different levels within an organization. The marketing audit format will be universally applicable. It is only the detail that varies from level to level and from company to company within the same group.

Figure 2.8 illustrates the total corporate strategic and planning process. This time, however, a time element is added, and the relationship between strategic planning briefings, long-term corporate plans and short-term operational plans is clarified. It is important to note that there are two 'open-loop' points on this figure. These are the key times in the planning process when a subordinate's views and findings should be subjected to the closest examination by his or her superior. It is by taking these opportunities that marketing planning can be transformed into the critical and creative process it ought to be.

Since in anything but the smallest of undiversified companies it is not possible for top management to set detailed objectives for operating units, it is suggested that

FIGURE 2.7   Hierarchy of audits

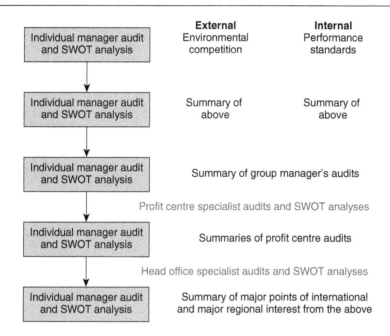

at this stage in the planning process strategic guidelines should be issued. One way of doing this is in the form of a strategic planning letter. Another is by means of a personal briefing by the chief executive at 'kick-off' meetings. As in the case of the audit, these guidelines would proceed from the broad to the specific, and would become more detailed as they progressed through the company towards operating units.

These guidelines would be under the headings of financial, human resources and organization, operations and, of course, marketing.

Under marketing, for example, at the highest level in a large group, top management may ask for particular attention to be paid to issues such as the technical impact of microprocessors on electromechanical component equipment, leadership and innovation strategies, vulnerability to attack from the flood of products from developing economies, and so on. At operating company level, it is possible to be more explicit about target markets, product development and the like.

In concluding this section, we must stress that there can be no such thing as an off-the-peg marketing planning system, and anyone who offers one must be viewed with great suspicion. In the end, strategic marketing planning success comes from an endless willingness to learn and to adapt the system to the people and the circumstances of the firm. It also comes from a deep understanding about the nature of marketing planning, which is something that, in the final analysis, cannot be taught.

FIGURE 2.8 Strategic and operational planning

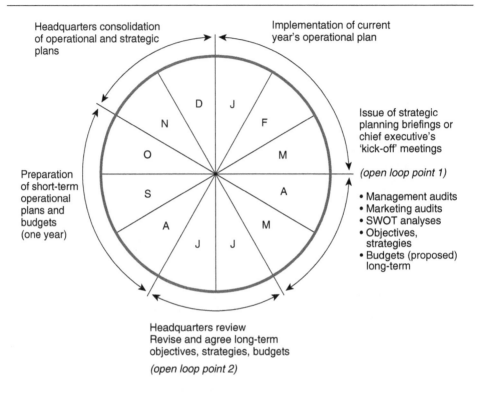

Headquarters consolidation of operational and strategic plans

Implementation of current year's operational plan

Issue of strategic planning briefings or chief executive's 'kick-off' meetings

(open loop point 1)

Preparation of short-term operational plans and budgets (one year)

- Management audits
- Marketing audits
- SWOT analyses
- Objectives, strategies
- Budgets (proposed) long-term

Headquarters review
Revise and agree long-term objectives, strategies, budgets

(open loop point 2)

However, strategic marketing planning demands that the organization recognizes the challenges that face it and their effect on its potential for future success. It must learn to focus on customers and their needs at all times and explore every avenue that may provide it with a differential advantage over its competitors.

The next section looks at some guidelines that lead to effective marketing planning.

2.7 Guidelines for effective marketing planning

Although innovation remains a major ingredient in commercial success, there are nevertheless other challenges that companies must overcome if they wish to become competitive marketers. While their impact may vary from company to company, challenges such as the pace of change, the maturity of markets and the implications of globalization need to be given serious consideration. Some of the more obvious challenges are shown in Table 2.3.

TABLE 2.3   Change and the challenge to marketing

Nature of change	Marketing challenges
Pace of change	
Compressed time horizons	Ability to exploit markets more rapidly
Shorter product life cycles	More effective new product development
Transient customer preferences	Flexibility in approach to markets
Accuracy in demand forecasting	
Ability to optimize price setting	
Process thinking	
Move to flexible manufacturing and control systems	Dealing with micro-segmentation
	Finding ways to shift from single focus to the forging of long-term relationships
Materials substitution	
Developments in microelectronics and robotization	Creating greater customer commitment
Quality focus transaction	
Market maturity	
Overcapacity	
Low margins	
Lack of growth	
Stronger competition	Adding value leading to differentiation
Trading down	New market creation and stimulation
Cost cutting	
Customer's expertise and power: more demanding, higher expectations, more knowledgeable	Finding ways of getting closer to the customer

TABLE 2.3 *continued*

Nature of change	Marketing challenges
Concentration of buying power	Managing the complexities of multiple market channels
More sophisticated buyer behaviour	
Internationalization of business: more competitors, stronger competition, lower margins, more customer choice, larger markets, more disparate customer needs	Restructuring of domestic operations to compete internationally, becoming customer focused in larger and more disparate markets

To overcome these challenges the following guidelines are recommended to help the marketer to focus on effective marketing strategies.

2.8 Twelve guidelines for effective marketing

2.8.1 Understand the sources of competitive advantage

Figure 2.9 shows a universally recognized list of sources of competitive advantage (Porter, 1985). For small firms, these are more likely to be the ones listed on the left. It is clearly possible to focus on highly specialized niches with special skills and to develop very customer-focused relationships not possible for large organizations. Flexibility is also likely to be a potential source of competitive advantage.

FIGURE 2.9   Understand the sources of competitive advantage

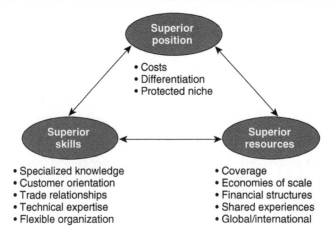

What all firms should seek to avoid wherever possible is competing with an un-differentiated product or service in too broad a market.

This leads on to the second point.

2.8.2 *Understand differentiation*

Guideline 2 takes this point a little further and spells out the main sources of differentiation. In the box below, the fifth item in the list, superior service, in particular is likely to be the main source of competitive advantage, and firms should work relentlessly towards the differential advantage that these sources will bring.

Understanding differentiation covers:

- superior product quality;
- innovative product features;
- unique product or service;
- strong brand name;
- superior service (speed, responsiveness, ability to solve problems);
- wide distribution coverage.

It is essential to be committed to *innovation*. Continuously strive to serve customer needs better.

2.8.3 *Understand the environment*

Guideline 3 spells out what is meant by the word 'environment'.

Although this one will be the least appealing to many organizations, nonetheless there is now an overwhelming body of evidence to show that it is failure to monitor the hostile environmental changes that is the biggest cause of failure in both large and small companies. Had anyone predicted the transformation of IBM over a decade ago, they would have been derided. Yet it was their failure to observe the changes taking place about them that caused a strategic rethink.

Clearly, marketing has a key role to play in the process. This means devoting at least some of the key executives' time and resources to monitoring formally the changes taking place about them. If they do not know how to go about doing this, they should get in a good consultant to start them off and then continue to do it themselves.

Understand the environment (opportunities and threats)

The macro environment:

- political/regulatory;
- economic;
- technological;
- societal.

The market/industry environment:

- market size and potential;
- customer behaviour;
- segmentation;
- suppliers;
- channels;
- industry practices;
- industry profitability.

Carry out a formal marketing audit.

This leads on naturally to the next point.

2.8.4 Understand competitors

Guideline 4 is merely an extension of the marketing audit. Suffice it to say that, if any organization, big or small, doesn't know as much about its close competitors as it knows about itself, it should not be surprised if it fails to stay ahead.

Again, if anyone is unsure how to go about this, use a consultant initially, although our advice is to use a modicum of common sense and sweet reasonableness in this process, stopping short, of course, at industrial espionage!

Closely connected with this is a final piece of information (in the box below) in this process we have referred to as a marketing audit.

Understand competitors

- Direct competitors.
- Potential competitors.
- Substitute products.
- Forward integration by suppliers.
- Backward integration by customers.
- Competitors' profitability.
- Competitors' strengths and weaknesses.

Develop a structured competitor monitoring process. Include the results in the marketing audit.

2.8.5 Understand your own strengths and weaknesses

Guideline 5 sets out potential sources of differentiation for your own organization. It represents a fairly comprehensive audit of the asset bases. Along with the other two sections of the marketing audit (the environment and competitors), it is important to make a written summary of your conclusions from all of this.

If you cannot summarize on a couple of sheets of paper the sources of your own competitive advantage, it has not been done properly. If this is the case, the chances are that you are relying on luck. Alas, luck has a habit of being somewhat fickle!

Strengths and weaknesses

Carry out a formal position audit of your own product/market position in each segment in which you compete. In particular, understand by segment:

- what the qualifying features and benefits are;
- what the differential features and benefits are;
- how relatively important each of these is;
- how well your product or service performs against your competitors' products or services on each of these requirements.

2.8.6 Understand market segmentation

Guideline 6 looks somewhat technical and esoteric, at first sight. Nonetheless, market segmentation is one of the key sources of commercial success and needs to be taken seriously by all organizations, as the days of the easy marketability of products and services have long since disappeared for all but a lucky few.

The secret of success, of course, is to change the offer in accordance with changing needs and not to offer exactly the same product or service to everyone – the most frequent, production-oriented mistake of large organizations.

Closely connected with this is the next point.

Market segmentation

- Not all customers in a broadly defined market have the same needs.

- Positioning is easy. Market segmentation is difficult. Positioning problems stem from poor segmentation.

- Select a segment and serve it. Do not straddle segments and sit between them:
  - Understand how your market works (market structure).
  - List what is bought (including where, when, how, applications).
  - List who buys (demographics, psychographics).
  - List why they buy (needs, benefits sought).
  - Search for groups with similar needs.

2.8.7 Understand the dynamics of product/market evolution

While at first sight Guideline 7 looks as if it applies principally to large companies, few will need reminding of the short-lived nature of many retailing concepts, such as the boutiques of the late 1980s. Those who clung doggedly on to a concept that had had its day lived to regret it.

2.8.8 Understand your portfolio of products and markets

Guideline 8 suggests plotting either products/services or markets (or, in some cases, customers) on a vertical axis in order of the potential of each for you to achieve your personal and commercial objectives as, clearly, they can't all be equal. Organizations will obviously have greater or lesser strengths in serving each of these 'markets'. For each location on the four-box matrix in Figure 2.10, put a circle, the size of which represents current sales. This will give a reasonably accurate 'picture' of your business at a glance and will indicate whether or not it is a well-balanced portfolio. Too much in any one box is dangerous.

Understand your portfolio of products and markets

You cannot be all things to all people. A deep understanding of portfolio analysis will enable you to set appropriate objectives and allocate resources effectively. Portfolio logic arrays competitive position against market attractiveness in a matrix form (Figure 2.10):

FIGURE 2.10   The McDonald Portfolio Matrix

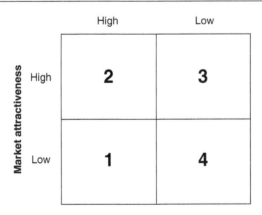

- *Box 1:* Maintain and manage for sustained earnings.
- *Box 2:* Invest and build for growth.
- *Box 3:* Selectively invest.
- *Box 4:* Manage for cash.

Follow the guidelines given and there is no reason why any firm should not have a healthy and growing business.

2.8.9 Set clear strategic priorities and stick to them

Guideline 9 suggests writing down the results of your earlier endeavours in summary form (a marketing/business plan).

Set clear strategic priorities

- Focus your best resources on the best opportunities for achieving continuous growth in sales and profits.

- This means having a written strategic marketing plan for three years containing:
  - a mission statement;
  - a financial summary;
  - a market overview;
  - SWOT analyses on key segments;
  - a portfolio summary;
  - assumptions;
  - marketing objectives and strategies;
  - a budget.

- This strategic plan can then be converted into a detailed one-year plan.

- To do this, an agreed marketing planning process will be necessary.

- Focus on key performance indicators with an unrelenting discipline.

While it is not our intention to stifle creativity by suggesting that any firm should get into a bureaucratic form of planning, it remains a fact that those individuals and organizations that can make explicit their intended sources of revenue and profits tend to thrive and prosper in the long term. This implies something more sophisticated than forecasts and budgets. This implies setting clear strategic priorities and sticking to them.

2.8.10 Understand customer orientation

Guideline 10 will be familiar to all successful firms. BS 5750, ISO 9001 and the like, while useful for those with operations such as production processes, have little to do with real quality, which, of course, can be seen only through the eyes of the customer. It is obvious that making anything perfectly that no one buys is somewhat of a pointless exercise.

Understand customer orientation

- Develop customer orientation in all functions. Ensure that every function understands that it is there to serve the customer and not its own narrow functional interests.

- This must be driven from the board downwards.

- Where possible, organize in cross-functional teams around customer groups and core processes.

- Make customers the arbiter of quality.

While it is, perhaps, easier for small companies than for large companies to check out customer satisfaction, this should nonetheless be done continuously, for it is clearly the only real arbiter of quality.

2.8.11 Be professional

Guideline 11 sets out some of the marketing skills essential to continuous success. Professional management skills, particularly in marketing, are becoming the hall-mark of commercial success in the new millennium. There are countless professional development skills courses available to all firms. Alas, too many directors consider themselves too busy to attend, which is extremely short-sighted. Entrepreneurial skills, combined with hard-edged management skills, will see any firm through in the new world of the 21st century.

Be professional

Particularly in marketing, it is essential to have professional marketing skills, which implies formal training in the underlying concepts, tools and techniques of marketing. In particular, the following are core:

- market research;
- gap analysis;
- market segmentation/positioning;
- product life cycle analysis;
- portfolio management;
- the marketing mix (four or seven Ps):
  - product management;
  - pricing;
  - place (customer service, channel management);
  - promotion (selling, sales force management, advertising, sales promotion);
  - people;
  - process;
  - physical evidence.

2.8.12 Provide leadership

Guideline 12 sets out the final factor for success.

Provide leadership

- Do not let doom and gloom pervade your thinking.
- The hostile environment offers many opportunities for companies with toughness and insight.
- Lead your team strongly.
- Do not accept poor performance in the most critical positions.

Charismatic leadership, however, without the 11 other pillars of success will be to no avail. Few will need reminding of the charisma of Maxwell, Halpern, Saunders and countless others. Charisma, however, without something to sell that the market values, will ultimately be pointless. It is, nonetheless, still an important ingredient in success.

2.9 Conclusions

Lest readers should think that the 12 factors for success are a figment of the imagination, there is much recent research to suggest otherwise. The four ingredients listed in Figure 2.11 are common to all commercially successful organizations, irrespective of their national origin:

1 From this it can be seen that the core product or service on offer has to be excellent.

2 Operations have to be efficient and, preferably, state-of-the-art.

3 The research stresses the need for creativity in leadership and personnel, something frequently discouraged by excessive bureaucracy in large organizations.

4 Excellent companies have professional marketing. This means that the organization continuously monitors the environment, the market, competitors and its own performance against customer-driven standards.

FIGURE 2.11 The four abiding characteristics of successful organizations

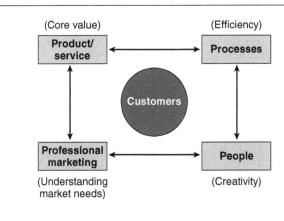

Having taken a quick 'Cook's tour' through strategic and operational marketing planning, it will be made clear later in this book where and how marketing accountability fits in.

References

Ansoff, I (1957) Strategies for Diversification, *Harvard Business Review*, 35 (5), pp 113–24

Booms, B and Bitner, M (1981) Marketing Strategies and Organizational Structures for Service Firms. In Donnelly, J H and George, W R (eds), *Marketing of Services*, Chicago: AMA, pp 47–51

Buzzell, R and Gale, B (1997) *The PIMS Principles: Linking Strategy to Performance*, Free Press, New York

DiMaggio, P J and Powell, W W (1983) The Iron Cage Revisited: Institutional isomorphism and collective rationality in organizational fields, *American Sociological Review*, 48, 147–60

Lubatkin, M and Pitts, M (1985) The PIMS and the Policy Perspective: A rebuttal, *Journal of Business Strategy*, Summer, pp 85–92

Porter, M E (1985) *Competitive Advantage: Creating and sustaining superior performance*, Free Press, New York

Scott, W R (1995) *Institutions and Organizations*, Sage, Thousand Oaks

Smith, B D (2003) 'The effectiveness of strategy making processes in medical markets', PhD thesis, Cranfield University, Cranfield

A three-level marketing accountability framework

03

Summary

This chapter examines marketing investment appraised techniques and then introduces a three-level model for marketing accountability.

The first level spells out how to assess whether marketing strategies create or destroy shareholder value using a technique developed by the Cranfield School of Management Marketing Value Added Research Club. The second-level model – also emanating from the Cranfield Research Club – links all expenditure relating to products, markets and customers to corporate revenue and profit objectives and clearly demonstrates what should be measured, why, when, and how frequently. Finally, the third-level accountability framework relates to promotional expenditure.

3.1 Introduction

The ultimate test of marketing investment, and indeed any investment, is whether it ultimately generates value for shareholders as well as customers. But few marketing investments are evaluated from this perspective, and many would argue that it is almost impossible to link financial results to any specific marketing activity.

But increasingly boards of directors and city analysts the world over are dissatisfied with this lack of accountability for what are, very often, huge budgets. Cranfield School of Management set out to create and test a new framework, which shows how marketing systematically contributes to shareholder value, and how its contribution can be measured in an objective and comparable way.

There is an urgent need for such a framework. Not only does marketing need it, to answer the widespread accusations of poor performance, but corporate and financial strategists need it too, to understand how to link marketing activities to the wider corporate agenda. All too often marketing objectives and strategies are not aligned with the organization's overall plans to increase shareholder value.

The chapter starts with a brief justification of the need for a wholly new approach to measuring the effectiveness of marketing. It then proceeds to the second level in the accountability framework developed in the Cranfield Research Club.

3.2 A three-level marketing accountability framework

3.2.1 What counts as marketing expenditure?

Historically, marketing expenditure has tended to escape rigorous performance appraisal for a number of reasons. Firstly, there has been real confusion as to the true scope and nature of marketing investments. Too often, marketing expenditure has been assumed to be only the budgets put together by the marketing function and, as such, a (major) cost to be controlled rather than a potential driver of value. Secondly, the causal relationship between expenditure and results has been regarded as too difficult to pin down to any useful level of precision.

Because of the demands of increasingly discerning customers and greater competition, marketing investments and marketing processes are under scrutiny as never before. From the process point of view, as a result of insights from management concepts such as the quality movement and re-engineering, marketing is now much more commonly seen as a cross-functional responsibility of the entire organization rather than just the marketing department's problem.

Howard Morganis, past chairman of Procter & Gamble, said, 'There is no such thing as a marketing skill by itself. For a company to be good at marketing, it must be good at everything else from R&D to manufacturing, from quality controls to financial controls.' Hugh Davidson, in *Even More Offensive Marketing* (1997), comments, 'Marketing is an approach to business rather than a specialist discipline. It is no more the exclusive responsibility of the marketing department than profitability is the sole charge of the finance department.'

But there is also a growing awareness that, because of this wider interpretation of marketing, nearly all budgets within the company could be regarded as marketing investments in one way or another. This is especially the case with IT budgets. The exponential increase in computing power has made it possible to track customer perceptions and behaviours on a far greater scale and with far greater precision than previously. When used correctly, these databases and analytical tools can shed a much greater light on what really happens inside the 'black box'. However, the sums involved in acquiring such technologies are forcing even the most slapdash of companies to apply more rigorous appraisal techniques to their investments in this area.

This wider understanding of what 'marketing' is really all about has had a number of consequences. Firstly, the classic textbook treatment of strategic issues in marketing has finally caught up with reality. Topics such as market and customer segmentation, product and brand development, databases and customer service and support are now regularly discussed at board level, instead of being left to operational managers or obscure research specialists.

CEOs and MDs are increasingly accepting that they must take on the role of chief marketing officer if they want to create truly customer-led organizations and because of their 'new' mission-critical status, marketing investments are attracting the serious attention of finance professionals. As part of a wider revolution in thinking about what kind of corporate assets are important in today's business environment, intangibles such as knowledge about customers and markets, or the power of brands, have assumed a new importance. The race is on to find robust methods of quantifying and evaluating such assets for the benefit of corporate managements and the wider investment community.

However, one of the major problems of marketing expenditure is that it takes time for the effects to manifest themselves in the market. This time lag often tran-scends the annual fiscal profit and loss account measurement. The reverse is true, of course, in that, without additional market-based data in the boardroom, directors are often flying blind. When the financials tell them there is a problem, they have already missed the optimal point for taking appropriate corrective action. This can be seen from the data in Table 3.1, from which it would appear that InterTech (a disguised name for confidentiality reasons) is doing extremely well.

A quick glance at Table 3.2, however, shows that most market indicators are negative. It is obvious that, when market conditions are less benign, this company will not last long.

In terms of accountability, this raises the issue of the value of profit and loss accounts in the boardroom. There is often only one line for revenue and dozens of lines for costs. The result frequently is that most of the discussion revolves around variances related to cost ratios. The point here is that there is a case for a more detailed breakdown of revenue, and indeed there is a trend among some leading companies to appoint a 'director of revenue generation' in order to address this problem.

TABLE 3.1   InterTech's five-year performance

Performance (£ million)	Base Year	1	2	3	4	5
Sale Revenue	£254	£293	£318	£387	£431	£454
Cost of goods sold	£135	£152	£167	£201	£224	£236
Gross Contribution	£119	£141	£151	£186	£207	£218
Manufacturing overhead	£48	£58	£63	£82	£90	£95
Marketing & sales	£18	£23	£24	£26	£27	£28
Research & development	£22	£23	£23	£25	£24	£24
Net Profit	£16	£22	£26	£37	£50	£55
Return on Sales (%)	6.3%	7.5%	8.2%	9.6%	11.6%	12.1%
Assets	£141	£162	£167	£194	£205	£206
Assets (% of sales)	53%	55%	53%	50%	48%	45%
Return on Assets (%)	11.3%	13.5%	15.6%	19.1%	24.4%	26.7%

TABLE 3.2   Why market growth rates are important: InterTech's five-year market-based performance

Performance (£ million)	Base Year	1	2	3	4	5
Market Growth	18.3%	23.4%	17.6%	34.4%	24.0%	17.9%
InterTech Sales Growth (%)	12.8%	17.4%	11.2%	27.1%	16.5%	10.9%
Market Share (%)	20.3%	19.1%	18.4%	17.1%	16.3%	14.9%
Customer Retention (%)	88.2%	87.1%	85.0%	82.2%	80.9%	80.0%
New Customers (%)	11.7%	12.9%	14.9%	24.1%	22.5%	29.2%
% Dissatisfied Customers	13.6%	14.3%	16.1%	17.3%	18.9%	19.6%
Relative Product Quality	+10%	+8%	+5%	+3%	+1%	0%
Relative Service Quality	+0%	+0%	−20%	−3%	−5%	−8%
Relative New Product Sales	+8%	+8%	+7%	+5%	+1%	−4%

3.2.2 What does 'value added' really mean?

The term 'value added' has fast become the new mantra for the 21st-century business literature, and is often used quite loosely to indicate a business concept that is intended to exceed either customer or investor expectations, or both. However, from the point of view of this chapter, it is important to realize that the term has its origin in a number of different management ideas, and is used in very specific ways by different sets of authors. Most of the ideas come from the United States, and originated in business school and consultancy research.

3.2.3 Value chain analysis

Firstly, there is Michael Porter's well-known concept of value chain analysis. Porter's concept of value added is an incremental one; he focuses on how successive activities change the value of goods and services as they pass through various stages of a value chain:

> Value chain analysis is used to identify potential sources of economic advantage. The analysis disaggregates a firm into its major activities in order to understand the behaviour of costs and the existing and potential sources of differentiation. It determines how the firm's own value chain interacts with the value chains of suppliers, customers and competitors. Companies gain competitive advantage by performing some or all of these activities at lower cost or with greater differentiation than competitors.
>
> *(Porter, 1985)*

3.2.4 Shareholder value added (SVA)

Secondly, there is Alfred Rappaport's equally well-known research on shareholder value added. Rappaport's concept of value added focuses less on processes than Porter's, and acts more as a final gateway in decision making, although it can be used at multiple levels within a firm. SVA is described as:

> The process of analysing how decisions affect the net present value of cash to shareholders. The analysis measures a company's ability to earn more than its total cost of capital... Within business units, SVA measures the value the unit has created by analysing cash flows over time. At the corporate level, SVA provides a framework for evaluating options for improving shareholder value by determining the tradeoffs between reinvesting in existing businesses, investing in new businesses and returning cash to stockholders.
>
> *(Rappaport, 1986, 1998)*

There are a number of different ways of measuring shareholder value added, one of which, market value added (MVA), needs further explanation. Market value added is a measure which compares the total shareholder capital of a company (including retained earnings) with the current market value of the company (capitalization and debt). When one is deducted from the other, a positive result means value has been added, and a negative result means investors have lost out. Within the literature, there is much discussion of the merits of this measure as against those of another approach – economic value added (EVA).

However, from the point of view of marketing value added, Walters and Halliday (1997) usefully sum up the discussion thus: 'As aggregate measures and as relative performance indicators they have much to offer... [but] how can the manager responsible for developing and/or implementing growth objectives [use them] to identify and select from alternative [strategic] options?'

Market value added is one of a number of tools that analysts and the capital markets use to assess the value of a company. Marketing value added as a research topic focuses more directly on the processes of creating that value through effective marketing investments.

3.2.5 Customer value

A third way of looking at value added is the customer's perception of value. Unfortunately, despite exhaustive research by academics and practitioners around the world, this elusive concept has proved almost impossible to pin down: 'What constitutes [customer] value – even in a single product category – appears to be highly personal and idiosyncratic', concludes Zeithaml (1988), for instance. Nevertheless, the individual customer's perception of the extra value represented by different products and services cannot be easily dismissed: in the guise of measures such as customer satisfaction and customer loyalty, it is known to be the essence of brand success, and the whole basis of 'relationship marketing'.

3.2.6 Accounting value

Finally, there is the accountant's definition of value added: 'value added = sales revenue – purchases and services'. Effectively, this is a snapshot picture from the annual accounts of how the revenue from a sales period has been distributed, and how much is left over for reinvestment after meeting all costs, including shareholder dividends. Although this figure will say something about the past viability of a business, in itself it does not provide a guide to future prospects.

One reason that the term 'value added' has come to be used rather carelessly is that all these concepts of value, although different, are not mutually exclusive. Porter's value chain analysis is one of several extremely useful techniques for identifying potential new competitive market strategies. Rappaport's SVA approach can be seen as a powerful tool that enables managers to cost out the long-term financial implications of pursuing one or other of the competitive strategies that have been identified. Customer perceptions are clearly a major driver (or destroyer) of annual audited accounting value in all companies, whatever strategy is pursued.

However, most companies today accept that value added, as defined by their annual accounts, is really only a record of what they achieved in the past, and that financial targets in themselves are insufficient as business objectives. Many companies are now convinced that focusing on more intangible measures of value added such as brand equity, customer loyalty or customer satisfaction is the new route to achieving financial results.

Unfortunately, research has found that there is no neat, causal link between offering additional customer value and achieving value added on a balance sheet, ie good ratings from customers about perceived value do not necessarily lead to financial success. Nor do financially successful companies necessarily offer products and services that customers perceive as offering better value than competitors.

In order to explain the link that does exist between customer-orientated strategies and financial results, a far more rigorous approach to forecasting costs and revenues is required than is usual in marketing planning, coupled with a longer-term perspective on the payback period than is possible on an annual balance sheet. This cash-driven perspective is the basis of the SVA approach, and can be used in conjunction with any marketing-strategy formulation process.

However, despite the SVA approach's apparent compatibility with existing planning systems, it is important to stress that adherents of the approach believe that, after all the calculations have been made about the impact of different strategic choices, the final decision about which strategy to pursue should be in favour of the one that generates the most value (cash) for shareholders. This point of view adds a further dimension to the strategic debate, and is by no means universally accepted: there is a vigorous and ongoing debate in the literature as to whether increasing shareholder value should be the ultimate objective of a corporation.

Despite these arguments, there is no denying that, during the last 15 years, SVA (or variants on the technique) has become the single most dominating corporate valuation perspective in developed Western economies. Its popularity tends to be limited to the boardroom and the stock exchanges, however. Several surveys (eg CSF Consulting in 2000 and KPMG in 1999) have found that less than 30 per cent of companies were pushing SVA-based management techniques down to an operational level, because of difficulties in translating cash targets into practical, day-to-day management objectives. This is a pity because, apart from its widespread use at corporate level, the SVA approach particularly merits extensive attention of researchers interested in putting a value on marketing, as it allows marketing investments (or indeed any investments) to be valued over a much longer period of time than the usual one-year budget cycle.

Although common sense might argue that developing strong product or service offerings and building up a loyal, satisfied customer base will usually require a series of one- to two-year investment plans in any business, nevertheless such is the universal distrust of marketing strategies and forecasts that it is common practice in most companies to write off marketing as a cost within each year's budget. It is rare for such expenditure to be treated as an investment that will deliver results over a number of years, but research shows that companies that are able to do this create a lasting competitive edge.

Meanwhile, as stated earlier, research into marketing accountability continued apace at Cranfield; a three-level model having been developed and tested, and it is to this model that we now turn.

3.3 Three distinct levels for measuring marketing effectiveness

Marketing managers have long understood the value, indeed necessity, of measuring the effectiveness of the very large expenditures typically under their control. There is a sophisticated industry that has grown up supporting the big budget marketing companies. Traditionally, this was exclusively the B2C sector particularly packaged goods (CPG)/fast moving consumer goods (FMCG); Unilever, P&G, L'Oreal, Diageo and car companies. However, big spenders now include technology firms, financial services, holiday firms, government and some of the largest B2B companies too. Nonetheless, we maintain that best practice initially grew in FMCG because of the number of advertised brands the sheer amount of money spent. The major advertisers have developed very sophisticated means of assessing the value of their advertising and promotion spend.

The proliferation of promotional methods and channels, combined with an empowered and more sophisticated consumer, make the problems of measuring promotional effectiveness increasingly complex. Consequently, this remains one of the major challenges facing the marketing community today as part of the discussion around 'big data'.

But, at this level, accountability can be measured only in terms of the kinds of effects that promotional expenditure can achieve, such as awareness, or attitude change, both of which can be measured quantitatively.

But to assert that such expenditure can be measured directly in terms of sales or profits is highly contested, when there are so many other variables that affect sales, such as product efficacy, packaging, price, the sales force, competitors and countless other variables that, like advertising, have an intermediate impact on sales and profits. Again, however, there clearly is a cause-and-effect link; otherwise such expenditure would be pointless. This issue is addressed later in this chapter.

So the problem with marketing accountability has never been with how to measure the effectiveness of promotional expenditure, for this we have had for many years. No, the problem occurs because marketing isn't just a promotional activity. As explained in detail in Chapter 2, in world-class organizations where the customer is at the centre of the business model, marketing as a discipline is responsible for defining and understanding markets, for segmenting these markets, for developing value propositions to meet the researched needs of the customers in the segments, for getting buy-in from all those in the organization responsible for delivering this value, for playing their own part in delivering this value, and for monitoring whether the promised value is being delivered.

Indeed, this definition of marketing as a function for strategy development as well as for tactical sales delivery, when represented as a map (see Figure 3.1), can be used to clarify the whole problem of how to measure marketing effectiveness. From this map, it can be seen that there are three levels of measurement, or metrics.

FIGURE 3.1   Map of the marketing domain and the three-level accountability framework

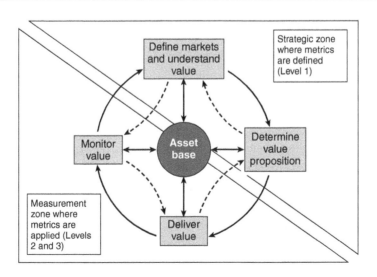

3.3.1 Level 1: shareholder value added

Level 1 is the most vital of all three, because this is what determines whether or not the marketing strategies for the longer term (usually three to five years) destroy or create shareholder value added. It is justified to use the strategic plan for assessing whether shareholder value is being created or destroyed because, as Sean Kelly (2005) agrees: 'The customer is simply the fulcrum of the business and everything from production to supply chain, to finance, risk management, personnel management and product development, all adapt to and converge on the business value proposition that is projected to the customer.'

Thus, corporate assets and their associated competences are relevant only if customer markets value them sufficiently highly for them to lead to sustainable competitive advantage, or shareholder value added. This is our justification for evaluating the strategic plan for what is to be sold, to whom and with what projected effect on profits as a route to establishing whether shareholder value will be created or destroyed.

A company's share price, the shareholder value created and the cost of capital are all heavily influenced by one factor: risk. Investors constantly seek to estimate the likelihood of a business plan delivering its promises, while the boards try to demonstrate the strength of their strategy. Research from Cranfield has focused on what we call Marketing Due Diligence and that study provides insight and tools to do both.

How much is a company really worth? There are innumerable tools that try to estimate the true value of intangibles and goodwill. However, these mostly come from a cost-accounting perspective. They try to estimate the cost of re-creating the brand, intellectual property or whatever is the basis of intangible assets. Our research into companies that succeed and fail suggests that approach is flawed, because what matters is not the assets owned but how they are used. We need to get back to the basics of what determines company value.

We should never be too simplistic about business, but some things are fundamentally simple. We believe that a company's job is to create shareholder value, and the share price reflects how well the investment community thinks that is being done. Whether or not shareholder value is created depends on creating profits greater than investors might get elsewhere at the same level of risk. The business plan makes promises about profits, which investors then discount against their estimate of the chance a company will deliver it. So it all comes down to that. A company says it will achieve $1 billion; investors and analysts think it is more likely to be $0.8 billion. The capital markets revolve around perceptions of risk. What boards and investors both need therefore is a strategic management process that gives a rigorous assessment of risk and uses that to assess and improve shareholder value creation. This is the process we call Marketing Due Diligence (McDonald, Smith and Ward, 2013).

There is a whole chapter dedicated to explaining this process (Chapter 4), so we will provide only a brief summary here.

3.3.1.1 Where does risk come from?

Marketing Due Diligence begins by looking for the risk associated with a company's strategy. Evaluation of thousands of business plans suggests that the many different ways that companies fail to keep their promises can be grouped into three categories:

1 The market wasn't as big as they thought.

2 They didn't get the market share they hoped for.

3 They didn't get the profit they hoped for.

Of course, a business can fail by any of these routes or a combination of them. The risk inherent in a plan is the aggregate of these three categories, which we have called, respectively, market risk, strategy risk and implementation risk. The challenge is to assess accurately these risks and their implications for shareholder value creation.

Our research found that most estimates of business risk were unreliable because they grouped lots of different sources of risk under one heading. Since each source of risk is influenced by many different factors, this high-level approach to assessing business risk is too simplistic and inherently inaccurate. A better approach is to subdivide business risk into as many sources as practically possible, estimate those separately and then recombine them. This has two advantages. Firstly, each risk factor is 'cleaner', in that its causes can be assessed more accurately. Secondly, minor errors in each of the estimations cancel each other out. The result is a much better estimate of overall risk.

3.3.1.2 How risky is a business?

Marketing Due Diligence makes an initial improvement over high-level risk estimates by assessing market, strategy and implementation risk separately. However, even those three categories are not sufficiently detailed. We need to understand the components of each, which have to be teased out by careful comparison of successful and unsuccessful strategies. Our research indicated that each of the three risk sources could be subdivided further into five risk factors, making 15 in all. These are summarized in Table 3.3.

Armed with this understanding of the components and sub-components of business risk, we are now halfway to a genuine assessment of our value creation potential. The next step is to assess accurately our own business against each of the 15 criteria and use them to evaluate the probability that our plan will deliver its promises.

This gradation of risk level is not straightforward. It is too simplistic to reduce risk assessment to a tick-box exercise. However, a comparison of a strategy against

TABLE 3.3   Factors contributing to risk

Overall risk associated with the business plan		
Market risk	**Strategy risk**	**Implementation risk**
Product category risk, which is lower if the product category is well established and higher for a new product category.	Target market risk, which is lower if the target market is defined in terms of homogeneous segments and higher if it is not.	Profit pool risk, which is lower if the targeted profit pool is high and growing and higher if it is static or shrinking.
Segment existence risk, which is lower if the target segment is well established and higher if it is a new segment.	Proposition risk, which is lower if the proposition delivered to each segment is segment specific and higher if all segments are offered the same thing.	Competitor impact risk, which is lower if the profit impact on competitors is small and distributed and higher if it threatens a competitor's survival.
Sales volumes risk, which is lower if the sales volumes are well supported by evidence and higher if they are guessed.	SWOT risk, which is lower if the strengths and weaknesses of the organization are correctly assessed and leveraged by the strategy and higher if the strategy ignores the firm's strengths and weaknesses.	Internal gross margin risk, which is lower if the internal gross margin assumptions are conservative relative to current products and higher if they are optimistic.
Forecast risk, which is lower if the forecast growth is in line with historical trends and higher if it exceeds them significantly.	Uniqueness risk, which is lower if the target segments and propositions are different from those of the major competitors and higher if the strategy goes 'head on'.	Profit sources risk, which is lower if the source profit is growth in the existing profit pool and higher if the profit is planned to come from the market leader.
Pricing risk, which is lower if the pricing assumptions are conservative relative to current pricing levels and higher if they are optimistic.	Future risk, which is lower if the strategy allows for any trends in the market and higher if it fails to address them.	Other costs risk, which is lower if assumptions regarding other costs, including marketing support, are higher than existing costs and higher if they are lower than current costs.

a large sample of a company's other strategies does provide a relative scale. By comparing, for instance, the evidence of market size, or the homogeneity of target markets, or the intended sources of profit, against this scale, a valid, objective assessment of the risk associated with a business plan can be made.

3.3.1.3 What use is this knowledge?

Marketing Due Diligence involves the careful assessment of a business plan and the supporting information behind it. In this assessment, it discounts subjective opinions and sidesteps the spin of investor relations. At the end of the process the output is a number, a tangible measure of the risk associated with a chosen strategy. This number is then applied in the tried-and-trusted calculations that are used to work out shareholder value. Now, in place of a subjective guess, we have a research-based and objective answer to the all-important question: does this plan create shareholder value?

Too often, the answer is no. When risk is allowed for, many business plans fail to return that which is necessary to cover their risk adjusted cost of capital. That means that shareholders are receiving insufficient return for the level of systematic risk they take and will, if rationale, remove their funds from that organization, contributing to its shrinking. An accurate assessment of value creation would make a huge difference to the valuation of the company. The result of carrying out Marketing Due Diligence is, therefore, of great interest and value to both sides of the capital market.

For the investment community, Marketing Due Diligence allows a much more informed and substantiated investment decision. Portfolio management is made more rational and more transparent. Marketing Due Diligence provides a standard by which to judge potential investments and a means to see through the vagaries of business plans.

For those seeking to satisfy investors, the value of Marketing Due Diligence lies in two areas. Firstly, it allows a rigorous assessment of the business plan in terms of its potential to create shareholder value. A positive assessment then becomes a substantive piece of evidence in negotiations with investors and other sources of finance. If, on the other hand, a strategy is shown to have weaknesses, the process not only pinpoints them but also indicates what corrective action is needed.

For both sides, the growth potential of a company is made more explicit, easier to measure and harder to disguise.

For anyone involved in running a company or investing in one, Marketing Due Diligence has three messages. Firstly, business needs a process that assesses shareholder value creation, and hence the value of a company, in terms of risk rather than the cost of replacing intangible assets. Secondly, business risk can be dissected, measured and aggregated in a way that is much more accurate than a high-level judgement. Finally, Marketing Due Diligence is a necessary process for both investors and companies.

Eventually, we anticipate that a process of Marketing Due Diligence will become as de rigueur for assessing intangible value as financial due diligence is for its tangible counterpart. Until then, early adopters will be able to use it as a source of competitive advantage in the capital market.

This high-level process for marketing accountability, however, still does not resolve the dilemma of finding an approach that is better than the plethora of metrics with which today's marketing directors are bombarded, so Cranfield's Research Club took this issue on board in an attempt to answer the following questions:

- What needs to be measured?
- Why does it need to be measured?
- How frequently does it need to be measured?
- To whom should it be reported?
- What is the relative importance of each?

The approach we took to answering these questions was to drive metrics from a company's strategy, and the model shown as Figure 3.2 was developed. This clearly shows the link between lead indicators and lag indicators.

FIGURE 3.2   Overall Marketing Metrics model

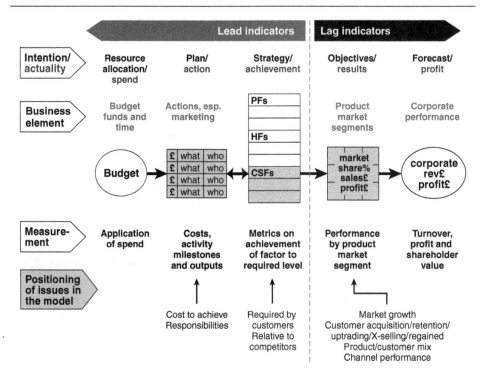

Again, this process model is explained in much greater detail in Chapter 5, so here we will provide a brief summary only.

3.4 Level 2: linking activities and attitudes to outcomes

Few academics or practitioners have addressed this second level to date, which links marketing actions to outcomes in a more holistic way. We shall describe it briefly here, although it must be stressed that it is central to the issue of marketing metrics and marketing effectiveness.

How do we set about linking our marketing activities to our overall objectives? We will start with the Ansoff Matrix (1957) shown in Figure 3.3. We return to this in Chapter 6.

Each of the cells in each box (cells will consist of products for segments) is a planning unit, in the sense that objectives will be set for each for volume, value and profit for the first year of the strategic plan. For each of the product-for-segment cells, having set objectives, the task is then to determine strategies for achieving them. The starting point for these strategies is critical success factors (CSFs), the factors critical to success in each product/service for each segment, which will be weighted according to their relative importance to the customers in the segment. See Figure 3.4.

In these terms, a strategy will involve improving one or more CSF scores in one or more product-for-segment cells. It is unlikely, though, that the marketing function will be directly responsible for what needs to be done to improve a CSF. For example, issues like product/service efficacy, after-sales service, channel management and sometimes even price and the sales force are often controlled by other functions, so marketing needs to get buy-in from these functions to the need to improve the CSF scores.

It is very rare for this information to be perfectly available to the marketer. While models such as price sensitivity, advertising response or even marketing mix or econometric approaches may help to populate the CSF form, there are generally several other factors where information is less easy to gather. Nevertheless, a CSF analysis indicates where metrics are most needed, which can steer the organization towards measuring the right things. We return to this in Chapter 7.

Figure 3.5 shows another level of detail, ie the actions that have to be taken, by whom and at what cost.

FIGURE 3.3   Ansoff Matrix

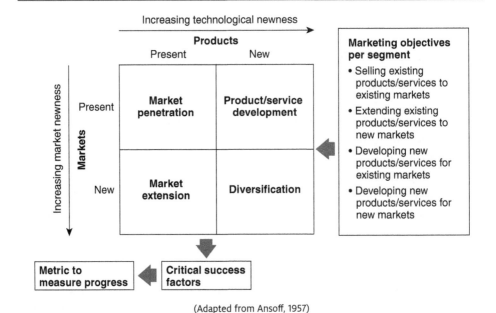

(Adapted from Ansoff, 1957)

FIGURE 3.4   Critical success factors: in each segment, defined by the segment

Critical success factors	Weighting factor	Your organization	Competitor A	Competitor B	Competitor C
CSF 1					
CSF 2					
CSF 3					
CSF 4					
Total weighted score (score × weight)	100				

• Strategies to improve competitive position/achieve objectives over time (4Ps)
• Metrics (each CSF) to measure performance over time in achieving goals

FIGURE 3.5   Actions, responsibilities and costs

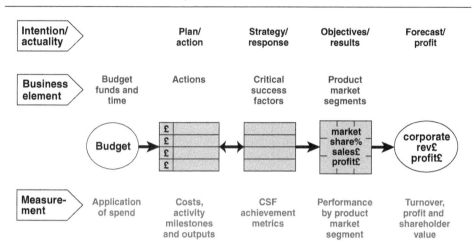

Figure 3.6 shows how these actions multiply for each box of the Ansoff Matrix.

FIGURE 3.6   Expanded model based on the Ansoff Matrix

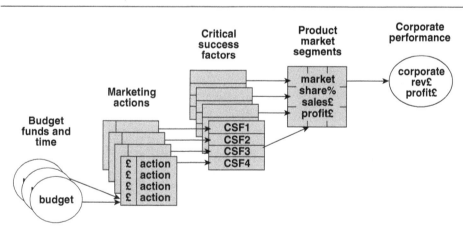

There are other factors, of course, that influence what is sold and to whom. These may be referred to as 'hygiene factors' (HFs), ie those standards that must be achieved by any competitor in the market. Other factors may be referred to as 'productivity factors' (PFs), ie those issues that may impact on an organization's performance unless the required productivity is achieved in its relevant activities.

Thus, it can be seen how the expenditure on marketing and other functional actions to improve CSFs can be linked to marketing objectives and, ultimately, to profitability, and it becomes clear exactly what must be measured and why. It also obviates the contestable assumption that every individual marketing action can be linked to profitability directly. It can be linked only to other weighted CSFs, which, if improved, should lead to the achievement of volumes, value and, ultimately, profits.

Figure 3.2 is repeated here (as Figure 3.7), as it summarizes all of this in one flow chart, which clearly spells out the difference between 'lag indicators' and 'lead indicators'. Lead indicators are the actions taken and the associated expenditure that is incurred. These include, of course, promotional expenditure. Lag indicators are the outcomes of these actions and expenditures and need to be carefully monitored and measured. Thus, retention by segment, loss by segment, new customers, new product sales, channel performance and the like are outcomes, but these need to be linked back to the appropriate inputs.

There is one other crucial implication to be drawn from this model. Most operating boards, on scrutinizing profit and loss accounts, typically see only one line for revenue, while costs are covered in considerable detail, and it is around costs that

FIGURE 3.7   Overall Marketing Value Metrics model

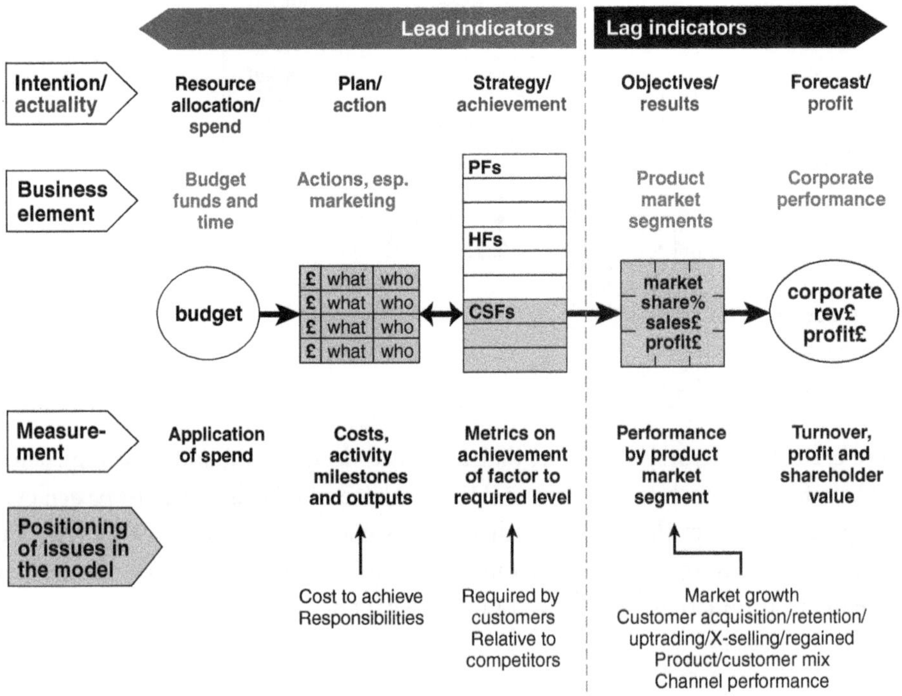

most of the discussion takes place. In the view of the authors, there should be at least two sets of figures – one to detail where the sales revenue has come from, as outlined above, and another to detail costs. A key task of marketers, rarely carried out, is to link the two documents together. Figure 3.7 goes some way towards this.

We stress, however, that the corporate revenue and profits shown at the right of Figures 3.2, 3.5, 3.6 and 3.7 are not the same as shareholder value added, which takes account of the risks involved in the strategies, the time value of money and the cost of capital. This brings us to Level 3.

3.5 Level 3: micro measurement

Level 3 is the fundamental and crucial level of micro promotional measurement we have described above and that was referred to earlier in this chapter. Measurement techniques for measuring the effectiveness of promotional expenditure have been developing over the past 50 years and are relatively sophisticated. This level of marketing measurement is not the sole focus of marketing accountability in our view, although from Figure 3.7 it should be possible to understand how these micro measurements fit in with the other two levels of measurement described in this chapter.

A more detailed exploration of these micro measures is given in Chapters 11 and 12.

Acknowledgement

The authors are indebted to Professor Shaw of Cass Business School, who worked closely with Professor Malcolm McDonald in setting up and running the first Cranfield Marketing Value Added Research Club and for providing some of the domain review material in the early part of this chapter.

References

Ansoff, I (1957) Strategies for Diversification, *Harvard Business Review*, **35** (5), pp 113–24

Davidson, H (1997) *Even More Offensive Marketing*, Penguin Books, London

Kelly, S (2005) *The Customer Information Wars*, Wiley, Chichester

McDonald, M, Smith, B and Ward, K (2013) *Marketing Due Diligence: Marketing and finance: creating shareholder value*, Wiley, Chichester

McGovern, G and Quelch, J A (2004) Marketing Performance Measurement, *Harvard Business Review*, November

Porter, M E (1985) *Competitive Advantage: Creating and sustaining superior performance*, Free Press, New York

Rappaport, A ([1986] 1998) *Creating Shareholder Value*, rev edn, Free Press, New York

Walters, D and Halliday, M (1997) *Marketing and Finance: Working the interface*, Allen & Unwin, St Leonards, New South Wales

Zeithaml, V A (1988) Consumer Conceptions of Price, Quality and Value, *Journal of Marketing*, 52, pp 2–22

A process of Marketing Due Diligence

04

Summary

The purpose of this chapter is to expand on the introduction given to Marketing Due Diligence in Chapter 3.

Despite what many non-marketers think, marketing is much more than just promotion. It is much more, even, than designing and delivering the 'marketing mix' of promotion, product, pricing, place (distribution), people, process and physical evidence. As discussed in Chapter 3, methods for measuring the effectiveness of these more visible marketing activities have been in place for years. While these tactical measures have their place, they tell us little about the effectiveness of the marketing strategy, that part of the marketing process that concerns itself with understanding the market and deciding what parts of it to focus upon and with what value propositions. It is with this aspect of marketing that the Marketing Due Diligence process concerns itself.

Marketing, in this broad strategic sense, is closely correlated to shareholder value. It is the choice of which customer segments to focus upon and what to offer them that lies at the root of sustainable competitive advantage. Good choices create customer preference, which in turn creates better return on investment. Looked at through the lens of business risk, as investors do, strong strategy reduces the risk associated with a promised return. To investors, it is the risk-adjusted rate of return that matters, and managing risk is as important as managing returns, sometimes more so.

The Marketing Due Diligence process involves both diagnostic and therapeutic stages. The first evaluates business risk and assesses whether the plan creates or destroys shareholder value. The second, building on the outcomes of the first, adapts the business plan to improve its risk profile and enhance shareholder value creation. Marketing Due Diligence begins with explicating the strategy, which is often implicit and unclear even to those who need to implement it. This explication results in a clear definition of which customers are to be served and what products, services and overall value proposition are to be offered to them. This explicit strategy is then assessed for market risk, share risk and profit risk.

As explained in Chapter 3, market risk arises from the possibility that the market may not be as large as hoped for in the business plan. It is, to a large degree, a function of the novelty of the business plan. Strategies involving new customers and/or new products are more likely to have higher market risk than those involving existing products and customers. Share risk arises from the possibility that the plan may not deliver the hoped-for market share. It is the corollary of the competitive strength of the strategy. Share risk is reduced when homogeneous segments are targeted with specifically tailored value propositions that leverage strengths, negate weaknesses, avoid direct competition and anticipate future trends.

Profit risk arises from the possibility that the plan may not deliver the intended profits. It is a function of the competitor reaction engendered by the plan and of the aggressiveness of cost assumptions.

Significant levels of market, share or profit risk, or some combination of the three, suggest that the returns delivered by the plan are likely to be less than promised. The final stage of shareholder value creation is therefore to calculate whether this risk-moderated return represents the creation or destruction of shareholder value. This involves calculating the full value of the assets put at risk, including intangibles. Only if the likely return is greater than the cost of this capital is shareholder value created. In addition to shareholder value creation or destruction, a third possible outcome of this diagnostic phase is that the plan is insufficiently thought out to enable a judgement to be made about its value-creating potential.

The Marketing Due Diligence therapeutic process uses the tools of strategic marketing management to manage and reduce the risk associated with the strategy. Using the results of the diagnostic stage to direct efforts suggests improvements to the marketing strategy. Hence the implications of using Marketing Due Diligence are to improve the marketing strategy in terms of its ability to create shareholder value.

4.1 What is the connection between marketing and shareholder value?

As Chapter 3 describes, both boards and investors need a better method of assessing the probability of business plans creating shareholder value. The financial due diligence process, for all its rigour and detail, only really considers the tangible aspects of a company's valuation.

Some methods of valuing intangibles, such as brands, are fundamentally flawed. For example, some value brands by assessing the value of the intangible in terms of what it might cost to replace, or against a hypothetical parallel company without that asset.[1] However, such approaches do not allow for a fundamental truth in asset valuation: value flows from how the asset is utilized, not simply what it costs to make or replace. As a result, valuing intangibles is necessary but not sufficient. What is really needed, to complement financial due diligence and to give boards and investors what they need, is a way of assessing the effectiveness with which assets and resources are applied to the market. Such a process could be accurately described as a process of Marketing Due Diligence. Executed correctly, with rigour and using well-founded methods, such a process will predict accurately the likelihood of a business plan delivering the shareholder value it promises.

For some, giving a process for evaluating business plans and shareholder value creation the name 'Marketing Due Diligence' might seem incongruous. To many, the term 'marketing' is synonymous with its highly visible aspects of advertising, sales promotion and other activities that are more accurately termed 'marketing operations'. If one holds this limited view of what marketing is, one can be forgiven for thinking that 'Marketing Due Diligence assesses the probability of creating shareholder value' is exaggerating the importance of marketing.

However, the wider and more accurate definition of marketing is that marketing has both strategic activities (understanding the markets, defining the target segments and the value propositions) and operational activities (delivering and monitoring value). These activities form a continuous process of marketing that draws on and contributes to the company's asset base. This continuous cycle of activity is the management process known correctly as 'marketing'. It is the assessment of this process and its connection with shareholder value that is properly and accurately called 'Marketing Due Diligence'.

At the risk of being simplistic, the connection between marketing (in the broad strategic and not just marketing operations sense) and shareholder value is straightforward. In most commercial organizations, shareholders or other providers of funds (banks, venture capitalists, etc) provide money with which to create assets. These assets, whether plant and buildings, patents, brands or something else, are then utilized in the market to create goods and services for a group of potential customers. The sale of these goods and services creates revenues, which, once costs are subtracted, become profits or returns on the shareholders' original investment. The shareholders hope that this return is greater than that which might have been obtained by investing the same money in another investment of similar risk. If the investor suspects that the return will not be superior to the alternatives of similar risk, he or she is, within some practical constraints, at liberty to invest elsewhere. The aggregate decision of many investors determines the price of the company's shares. In this simplified world of capital economics, therefore, shareholder value, the combination of share price and dividends, is directly linked to the risk-adjusted rate of return achieved by the company. In the simple, and hypothetical, case of there being one company in each market and one type of customer in each market, shareholder value is simply a function of the operational efficiency with which the company uses its shareholders' funds.

In the real world, however, there are competitors and not all customers are the same. In real markets, being efficient is not enough. As Michael Porter (1985) said, operational efficiency is usually a necessary but insufficient condition for creating shareholder value, and so strategic effectiveness becomes important. The importance of marketing strategy arises from the fact that, in anything but the most embryonic or regulated of markets, there are competitors and different types of customers. Together, the activity of competitors and the heterogeneity of the market mean that companies have to make decisions about how to focus their (that is, their shareholders') resources. Even the biggest and richest company does not have the resources to meet the needs of all customer types perfectly and profitably.

If they attempt to do so, competitors that have focused on one part of the market have a local superiority of resources that allows them to create a stronger, more compelling and more attractive value offer to the customer. In a free market, customers choose whichever supplier provides the best value to them. For some customers, 'best value' might mean superior technical performance, for others high service levels, and for others low cost. Whatever the customers' definition of value, it takes resources to create superior value to that being offered by the competition.

So the critical implication of competitor activity and market heterogeneity is that companies must choose which customers to focus on. Think, for example, of the way in which business-type hotels, motel chains and small country hotels not only offer different value propositions but also target different types of customer. Nor is marketing strategy simply a case of picking the most attractive market segment. Different companies have different distinctive capabilities, which may determine the best choice of segment. Consider, for instance, the different capabilities of Mercedes, Toyota and Ferrari, and what that implies for their choice of target customers and what value proposition to provide.

In most cases, the choice of which segments to target and what to offer them is a difficult one, requiring an understanding of the market opportunities and threats as well as the company's strengths and weaknesses. A poor choice leads to an inferior or merely adequate proposition to the customer and the concomitant lack of customer preference. Alternatively, making and implementing the right choice of target segments and value propositions result in customer preference and sustainable competitive advantage. Higher returns (from higher share, higher margin or both) follow from this customer preference and lead to superior shareholder value. As companies like Diageo, Apple, Tata and BMW have found, it is marketing strategy that drives shareholder value, even as operational efficiency and technical ability underpin it. This is the logic summarized in Figure 4.1.

FIGURE 4.1   From marketing strategy to shareholder value

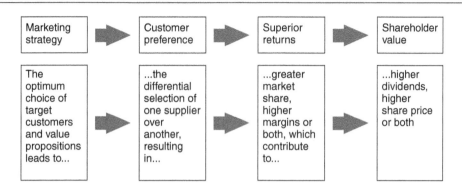

In Chapter 2 we outlined a process of marketing planning for doing this, and in Chapter 6 we explain in more detail the importance of market segmentation.

This strong and direct connection between marketing strategy decisions and shareholder value lies at the root of Marketing Due Diligence. Half a century of research reveals a remarkably clear correlation between certain characteristics of a marketing strategy and the shareholder value that flows from it.

4.2 What is the Marketing Due Diligence diagnostic process?

Before we consider what Marketing Due Diligence is, it is worthwhile considering at what level in the organization it is applied. Strategy (that is, resource allocation) decisions are made at all levels. At corporate level, these decisions involve which businesses to be in. At lower levels, smaller-scale decisions are made about, for instance, single products in a certain country. Between these two extremes lies the strategic business unit (SBU), a unit of the firm that is usually defined as having three distinct characteristics:

1 It is fairly independent in its activities, which do not interact much with those of the rest of the firm.

2 It deals with a relatively self-contained market.

3 It is able to address the market on its own, without much direct support from the rest of the company.

Typical examples of an SBU include the therapy area of a pharmaceutical company, the PC division of an IT hardware company, or the business-to-business (B2B) division of a telecoms company. SBUs should not be confused with the functional division of a firm, such as manufacturing or R&D, which could not meet the three criteria listed above. It is at this SBU level that Marketing Due Diligence is applied. At organizational levels higher than the SBU (for instance, with the board of a multiple SBU business), Marketing Due Diligence can assess shareholder value creation by aggregating the results of each SBU.

Below SBU level, the strategy decisions at product, channel or country level aggregate to determine the Marketing Due Diligence of the SBU. For the rest of this chapter, the descriptions of Marketing Due Diligence therefore refer to processes and analysis carried out at SBU level, rather than corporate or functional levels. Marketing Due Diligence is a sophisticated process. It is not easily reduced to simple mnemonics and acronyms, a fact that reflects the complexity of the strategy–shareholder value linkage. However, the process can be understood by considering each layer of this complexity one step at a time. The first of these layers is to consider Marketing Due Diligence as consisting of a three-stage process, as shown in Figure 4.2. Stage One makes the marketing strategy explicit and so provides the input into Stage Two. In this second stage, the risks associated with the marketing strategy are thoroughly examined. In Stage Three, the risk evaluation is used to calculate whether or not the marketing strategy will create shareholder value.

FIGURE 4.2   The outline process of Marketing Due Diligence

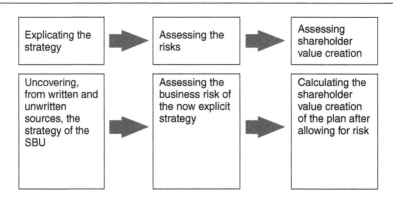

4.2.1 *Explicating the strategy*

The first step of Marketing Due Diligence may seem superfluous. It is a reasonable, if ultimately false, assumption that the strategy of an SBU is laid out in its business plan. Certainly, the length and complexity of the typical annual planning cycle, together with the size of the resultant document, suggest that all that is needed here is to read the plan. In practice, this is not the case. Although all business plans contain the basic outline of the strategy, use of Marketing Due Diligence reveals that, in practice, most plans do not provide a full picture of the strategy, as described in Chapter 2.

The important detail of the strategy, which reveals its inherent risk, is more often held in a labyrinth of unwritten or informal forms. Sometimes these are easily accessible, such as supporting marketing research reports or product design documents. Often, however, they are held in the heads of the executives as implicit and unspoken strategy decisions that have important ramifications for the probability of the plan working. Obviously, to avoid a superficial and incorrect assessment, it is necessary to surface all of the strategy before assessing the risk. In doing so, however, we also realize one of the very important benefits of the Marketing Due Diligence process, which is additional to assessing shareholder value creation. In the act of explicating the strategy, the management team identifies the gaps, inconsistencies and errors that can result from even the most rigorous strategic planning process. This is a very valuable outcome of the process that occurs even before the risk assessment is begun.

Uncovering the unwritten, often implicit, elements of the strategy requires that a structured set of questions are answered. In simple terms, these are:

- What is the business of this SBU?
- Where will its growth come from?
- How will it achieve that growth?

Usually, only a partial answer to these questions will emerge from a careful consideration of the written plan. To uncover the implicit strategy, a detailed set of questions, derived from the three basic questions, are needed. These are summarized in Figure 4.3, although an effective explication of the strategy may require some detailed and intelligent variations and extensions around these questions.

These questions, in addition to being a useful tool for explicating the strategy, reveal a fundamental aspect of the Marketing Due Diligence process. That is, the process looks especially hard at the growth elements of the strategy. Experienced managers will see in the questions their basis in the Ansoff (1957) matrix to which we have referred previously in this book. The focus on growth reflects the essential truth that it is in the growth parts of the strategy – for example, new products or new markets – that most risk lies. This discovery was the foremost lesson of Ansoff's work and is appropriately included in the Marketing Due Diligence process. The fact that, in business plans, 'new' is almost synonymous with 'risky' also means that many companies are habitual and unconscious risk takers. The expectations of shareholders constantly to outgrow the market and the competition means that, for many companies, submitting a low- or zero-growth plan is not an option, and taking risks is inadvertently demanded by investors. Let us be clear that this is not a criticism of growth-oriented plans, or a recommendation in favour of low-growth,

FIGURE 4.3   Questions to explicate the strategy

Explicating the strategy

1. What is the business of this SBU?

1.1 What is the market that it serves?

1.2 What are the adjacent areas of the market, if any, that are not under consideration?

1.3 What are the products/services offered?

1.4 Who are the direct competitors for this business unit's target customers?

1.5 What are the channels to market?

2. Where will its growth come from?

2.1 What is the recent (eg past five years) sales and profit history of the business unit?

2.2 What are the sales revenue and profit growth objectives of the business unit in the next five years?

2.3 What is the expected growth in the addressable market during this period?

2.4 How much of the business unit's growth is expected from increased market penetration (that is, existing product types to existing customers)?

2.5 How much growth is expected from market development (that is, existing product types to new customers)?

2.6 How much growth is expected from new product development (that is, new product types to existing customers)?

2.7 How much growth is expected from diversification (that is, new product types to new customers)?

2.8 How much profit growth is expected to come from cost reduction?

2.9 How much growth is expected to come from acquisition?

3. How will growth be achieved?

3.1 What, if any, are the segments in this market?

3.2 What is the emphasis of resource allocation between these segments?

3.3 What is the value proposition to each segment?

3.3.1 This to include a description of products, pricing (levels and structure), channels and promotion (including branding).

3.3.2 It is particularly important to elucidate the differences between each segment and their respective value propositions, if any.

non-innovative strategies. However, the correlation between growth and risk and between risk and shareholder value does mean that shareholders are making an implicit but insistent demand on companies and their boards: we want you to grow, but at the lowest risk possible. Such a demand requires that managers do all they can to ensure that their strategies minimize risk. Before that can be done, however, the risks inherent in the current strategy must be uncovered and understood.

4.2.2 Assessing the risks

Having explicated the strategy and made clear what the SBU is about, where it is looking for growth and how it intends to realize it, we have to assess objectively the business risk inherent in the strategy. Only then can we make a rigorous assessment of the shareholder value created by the plan.

At first sight, assessing the risks associated with any SBU's business plan seems an impossible task. If we think for a moment what could go wrong, then an endless list of frightening possibilities opens up. There are innumerable things that could go wrong and all of them look unquantifiable and, therefore, practically useless. However, a more detached look at why some plans work and others fail enables a more practicable understanding of business risk, based on the fundamental assertions made in all business plans.

In essence, and at the highest level of detail, all business plans say the same thing. They make three basic assertions, which can be summed up as:

1 The market is this big.

2 We're going to take this share of the market.

3 That share will make this much profit.

Each of these assertions carries a level of risk that it may be wrong. The market may not be as big as asserted, the plan may not deliver the share anticipated and the share may not deliver the profit. Each of the three assertions may fall short of its promise. Business risk is the combined risk of these three things, which can therefore be said to have three components:

1 *market risk* – the risk that the market may not be as big as promised in the plan;

2 *share risk* – the risk that the strategy may not deliver the share promised in the plan;

3 *profit risk* – the risk that the strategy may not deliver the margins promised in the plan.

It is worthwhile here to reflect for a moment on this three-part structure of business risk, because it is fundamental to the concept of Marketing Due Diligence.

As simplistic as it appears, this structure captures all of the hundreds of possible reasons a business plan can fail to deliver its promises. Fickle customers, aggressive competition and flawed forecasts are all addressed within the three components of business risk. Thinking of risk assessment in these terms shifts the problem from one of complexity (have we counted all the risks?) to one of rigour (have we accurately assessed each of the three risks?). This problem of rigour is all the more challenging owing to one of the practical requirements for Marketing Due Diligence. It is not enough simply to assess with rigour; it must be done using information that is practically accessible to the organization rather than requiring lots of new and difficult-to-access data. It is this challenge that is addressed in turn, in the following paragraphs, for each of the components of business risk.

We will repeat the contents of the three columns of Table 3.3, given in Chapter 3's overview of Marketing Due Diligence, but this time with a more detailed explanation.

4.2.2.1 Assessing market risk

If market risk is the probability that the market will not be as large as the business plan promises it to be, assessment of it depends on asking questions that inform an objective judgement of that probability. The research that underpins this chapter revealed that market risk was accurately quantified if five sub-components were assessed and combined into an aggregate value for market risk. These five sub-component risks are described in Table 4.1.

The five sub-components shown in Table 4.1 describe the contributing factors to market risk. It is sufficient to understand what each of the sub-component risks represents and why they are an effective diagnostic for market risk. Each of the sub-components represents a set of assumptions that are built, implicitly or explicitly, into any strategy and business plan. Assumptions, to the extent that they are not completely tested, are sources of risk because they may prove ill-founded and erroneous. Together, the five sub-components represent all of the significant assumptions made and risks taken regarding market size. There will be, in some cases, overlap between the categories. This means not only that the five sub-components cannot simply be added, but also that no important assumptions or risks will be missed. Equally, the risk impact of each sub-assumption is not equally weighted and varies from case to case. These complicating factors mean, on one hand, that some qualitative judgement is needed but, on the other hand, that the assessment is comprehensive.

Assessing market risk accurately, therefore, requires careful questioning of the written and unwritten business plan, using the five-sub-component framework in Table 4.1 with rigorous graduated scales. However, as a general rule of thumb, we can observe that new products and new markets, poorly researched and aggressively forecast on price and volume, constitute high market risk. Existing products and

TABLE 4.1   Sub-components of market risk

Sub-component	Explanation of market risk
Product category risk	This is the risk that the entire product category may be smaller than planned. It is higher if the product category is novel and lower if the product category is well established.
Market existence risk	This is the risk that the target segment may be smaller than planned. It is higher if it is a new segment and lower if the segment is well established.
Sales volumes risk	This is the risk that sales volumes will be lower than planned. It is higher if sales volumes are 'guessed' with little supporting evidence and lower if the sales volumes are well supported by evidence such as market research.
Forecast risk	This is the risk that the market will grow less quickly than planned. It is higher if forecast market growth exceeds historical trends and lower if it is in line with or below historical trends.
Pricing risk	This is the risk that the price levels in the market will be lower than planned. It is higher if pricing assumptions are optimistic and lower if they are conservative.

mature markets, with extensive market research and conservative forecasts, have inherently less market risk. As discussed later in this chapter, our market risk assessment can be used to moderate the market size assertions in the business plan. The next task is to consider how great a share of that moderated market the strategy might win.

4.2.2.2 Assessing share risk

While market risk is a function of both market choice and strategy design, share risk flows solely from the strategic decisions on which the plan is based. In short, share risk is the corollary of strategy strength. A strong strategy has a high probability of delivering the planned share, while a weak strategy has a high probability of failing to meet its promises.

The challenge, therefore, is to understand what constitutes a strong strategy compared to a weak one. More particularly, a useful process must be able to make an objective judgement of strategy strength (and therefore share risk) independent of the SBU's market context.

As with market risk, this appears initially to be an impossible task. How can one judge the strength of a strategy without a mountain of market-specific detail and without making lots of error-prone value judgements?

As with market risk, the research foundations of this chapter considered the issue of strategy strength and share risk. Again, a pattern of consistent factors emerged that clearly differentiated strong strategies from weak, risky strategies. This pattern revealed that the choice of target markets and value propositions can be objectively assessed against five criteria, again representing five sub-components of share risk. These are summarized in Table 4.2.

TABLE 4.2   Sub-components of share risk

Sub-component	Explanation of share risk
Target market risk	This is the risk that the strategy will work only in a part, not all, of its target market. It is higher if the target market is defined in terms of heterogeneous customer classifications and is lower if it is defined in terms of homogeneous needs-based segments.
Proposition risk	This is the risk that the offer to the market will fail to appeal to some or all of the target market. It is higher if all the market is offered the same thing and lower if the proposition delivered to each segment is segment specific.
SWOT (strengths, weaknesses, opportunities, threats) risk	This is the risk that the strategy will fail because it does not leverage the company's strengths to market opportunities or guard its weaknesses against environmental threats. It is higher if the strategy ignores the firm's competitive strengths and weaknesses and lower if the strengths and weaknesses of the organization are correctly assessed and leveraged by the strategy.
Uniqueness risk	This is the risk that the strategy will fail because it goes 'head on' with the competition. It is higher if the target market and value proposition chosen are very similar to those of the competition and lower if they are very different.
Future risk	This is the risk that the strategy will fail because the market's needs have changed or will change in the time from strategy conception to execution. It is higher if the strategy ignores market trends and lower if it assesses and allows for them.

It is important at this stage to grasp what these different risks represent. Instead of assumptions leading to risk, as with market risk, these five factors represent error or wastage in allocation of resources, so that the plan has an increased chance of failure. In short, a plan that targets a tightly defined segment, all of whom want the same thing, is more effective than one in which the target is a broader and necessarily heterogeneous group (eg ABC1 males or 'blue-chip' companies). Chapter 6 spells out market segmentation in more detail. Similarly, plans work when the customer is offered a tailored value proposition and fail with a 'one size fits all' approach. The rare exception to this rule is a situation in which one supplier has a quasi-monopolistic position, in which customers have little choice.

In the situations we more commonly face, then, the best plans understand and use strengths and weaknesses relative to competitors, and align them to opportunities and threats that exist in the environment. The worst plans ignore or neglect such 'SWOT alignment'. Low-risk strategies sidestep the competition and anticipate market changes. High-risk strategies go head on and plan for yesterday's market. Although, as described later, there are other, minor factors contributing to share risk, these five factors are a functionally complete tool by which to assess whether or not the strategy will deliver the promised share.

As with assessing market risk, the sub-components of share risk overlap to some degree and vary in relative weighting between cases. Hence some judgement is still necessary in the assessment. However, the graduated scales for each sub-component and cancelling out effects of multiple errors mean that share risk can be judged accurately and comprehensively.

An objectively moderated view of the probable share can then be combined with the expected market size to calculate the likely future revenue of the SBU. The next task is to see if that revenue will deliver the planned profit.

4.2.2.3 Assessing profit risk

Market risk flows from the strategic decision to allocate resources to a market and assumptions about that market. Share risk flows from strategic decisions about which customers within that market to target and what to offer them. Profit risk, however, arises from assumptions about the implementation of the strategy in the chosen market. In particular, profit risk arises from assumptions about competitor response and from planned versus actual costs and prices. Again, it initially presents a seemingly insuperable task. How can we possibly predict, with any accuracy, what will happen during implementation, how the market will move and what the competition will do? Again, however, this seemingly impossible task is simplified and made practical by considering the implementation failures and successes of good and bad plans. By looking at the detail of why some strategies deliver their promised margins and others do not, we can discern five sub-components of profit risk. These can form the basis of a comprehensive and rigorous assessment of profit risk and are summarized in Table 4.3.

As with market risk, the sub-components of profit risk represent the risks that flow from the various assumptions built into the plan. Profit is threatened when assumptions about costs prove too optimistic, ignoring experience with other similar products, or those about prices prove naive, assuming benign and passive competitors.

TABLE 4.3   Sub-components of profit risk

Sub-component	Explanation of profit risk
Profit pool risk	This is the risk that profit will be less than planned because of competitors' reaction to the strategy caused by a combination of the strategy and the market conditions. It is higher if the profit pool is static or shrinking and lower if the targeted profit pool is high and growing.
Profit sources risk	This is the risk that profit will be less than planned because of competitors' reaction to the strategy. It is higher if the profit growth comes at the expense of competitors, and lower if the profit growth comes only from growth in the profit pool.
Competitor impact risk	This is the risk that profit will be less than planned because of a single competitor reacting to the strategy. It is higher if the profit impact on competitors is concentrated on one powerful competitor and that impact threatens the competitor's survival. It is lower if the profit impact is relatively small, distributed across a number of competitors and has a non-survival threatening impact on each.
Internal gross margin risk	This is the risk that the internal gross margins will be lower than planned because the core costs of manufacturing the product or providing the service are higher than anticipated. It is higher if the internal gross margin assumptions are optimistic relative to current similar products and lower if they are relatively conservative.
Other costs risk	This is the risk that net margins will be lower than planned because other costs are higher than anticipated. It is higher if assumptions regarding other costs, including marketing support, are less than current costs and lower if those assumptions are more than current costs.

As before, the five sub-components do overlap to some extent, and their relative contribution to overall profit risk is different in different cases. However, the deconstruction of profit risk into the five sources allows a much better judgement of risk than if profit risk were assessed as a single entity. As a rule of thumb, implementation risk is lower when the profit pool in the market is large and growing quickly, when the strategy has little impact on competitors, and when assumptions about costs are realistic and supported by other similar activity. The risk of not delivering the promised margins is high when the total profit available in the market is small and shrinking, the strategy impacts heavily on a single powerful competitor and assumptions about costs are overly optimistic.

The assessment of business risk inherent in the strategy, as described above, is a complex and sophisticated part of the overall Marketing Due Diligence process. This is entirely appropriate, and any simple approach to a subject as complex as the business risk of an SBU will inevitably be naive and misleading. In the Marketing Due Diligence risk assessment stage, a single, monolithic judgement about the chances of the plan succeeding is broken down into three separate judgements that are much more amenable to objective evaluation. These three are then further broken down into five sub-component risks, each of which can be measured on a graduated scale using objective and accessible data. Once market, share and profit risk assessments are completed, the result is a quantitative assessment, albeit based on careful, semi-qualitative judgements of each risk. It is these quantified judgements that form a well-founded basis for the third and final stage of the Marketing Due Diligence process, that of assessing shareholder value creation.

4.2.2.4 Assessing shareholder value creation

The notional SBU we have addressed so far has, in the course of its business plan, promised a certain turnover and a certain return on sales. Those returns imply a certain level of shareholder value created, dependent on the capital employed to create those sales. In the traditional capital market model, investors discount this value according to the probability of the promises being delivered. The investors' judgements are based on a number of factors, such as the macroeconomic environment, the health of the sector and historical performance. Each of these factors suffers from being both a lag indicator (that is, it indicates past, not necessarily future, performance) and a general indicator (that is, not being specific to the strategy of the SBU in question). The over- or undervaluation of many, if not most, companies is an indicator of the imperfect nature of this traditional approach to risk assessment. Such an imperfect, judgemental and weakly based method of valuing companies is unsatisfactory for both sides of the capital market. Boards complain that investors fail to appreciate the strategy and consequently undervalue the company. Investors accuse boards of over-promising and imperfect disclosure of key indicators and therefore discount share price valuations to protect themselves.

The Marketing Due Diligence process addresses both the lag indicator and generalization criticisms of traditional methods. It is fundamentally different from the traditional model, in that it considers the specifics of the company's strategy (not sector or macroeconomic effects) and the implications of that strategy for the creation of shareholder value in the future, rather than extrapolating from the past.

The assessment of shareholder value creation in Marketing Due Diligence begins by allowing for sensitivity of the plan to business risk. Some strategies are more sensitive to risk than others, and sensitivity to the three different components of business risk varies according to the internal and external context.

Strategies are sensitive to market risk (that is, they are vulnerable to poor assumptions about market size) if they involve fast growth and high market share. When the SBU's objectives have a large growth component (that is, a lot of the planned-for return is new business) and they already have a large market share, a smaller-than-predicted market will have a large impact on returns. Conversely, a business plan with a low growth component and that involves going from a very small share to only a slightly larger one is less sensitive to misjudgement about the size of the market. Simply put, a company trying to move from $2 million to $2.2 million in a multibillion-dollar market is little affected by even a significant error in its estimate of market size. A company trying to move from $40 million to $50 million in an $80 million market is much more sensitive to market risk. This sensitivity to market risk is illustrated in Figure 4.4.

Strategies are sensitive to share risk (that is, they are vulnerable to weaknesses in their strategy) if they involve fast growth in the face of strong competition. As with market risk sensitivity, when the SBU's objectives have a large growth component in

FIGURE 4.4   Sensitivity to market risk varies with growth intent and share position

	Low market share	High market share
High growth intent	Moderately sensitive to market risk	Highly sensitive to market risk
Low growth intent	Low sensitivity to market risk	Moderately sensitive to market risk

FIGURE 4.5 Sensitivity to share risk varies with growth intent and competitive intensity

	Low competitive intensity	High competitive intensity
High growth intent	Moderately sensitive to share risk	Highly sensitive to share risk
Low growth intent	Low sensitivity to share risk	Moderately sensitive to share risk

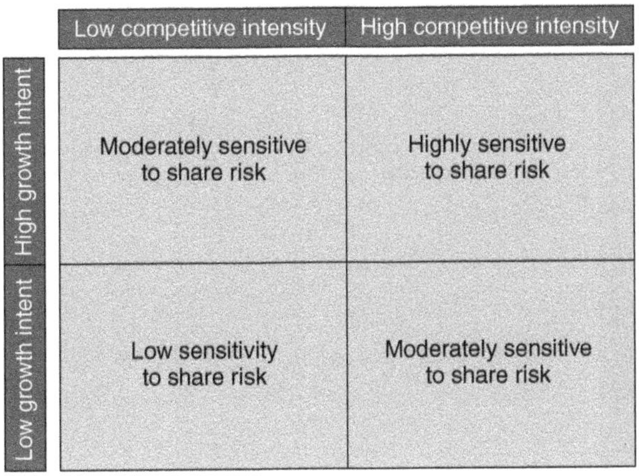

the face of large and effective competitors, a weak strategy will have a large impact on returns. Conversely, a business plan with a low growth component and that involves competing with small or weak competitors is less sensitive to a weak strategy. Simply put, a company trying to take a little share from much smaller and weaker competitors is less sensitive to weaknesses in its strategy. By contrast, a small, new entrant trying to make significant inroads into a market dominated by a strong incumbent is highly vulnerable to share risk. This sensitivity to share risk is shown in Figure 4.5.

Strategies are sensitive to profit risk (that is, they are vulnerable to poor assumptions about price and cost) if they involve fast growth and operate on low margins. When the SBU's objectives have a large growth component and planned margins are low, a lower-than-planned margin will have a large impact on returns. Conversely, a business plan with a low growth component and that involves very high margins is less sensitive to a weak strategy. Simply put, an SBU trying to grow slowly and with 80 per cent margins is less sensitive to a small fluctuation in its costs or prices. By contrast, an SBU planning to grow quickly with margins of less than 10 per cent is very susceptible to even small fluctuations in costs, prices or both. This sensitivity to profit risk is shown in Figure 4.6.

Using these differing sensitivities to the various components of business risk, the Marketing Due Diligence process then considers the market size, market share and profit assertions in the plan and moderates them in the light of the assessed risk and sensitivity. Hence market size is adjusted or confirmed depending on the level of market risk, share for share risk and profit for profit risk. This adjustment is not a simplistic, linear change in line with the value of the risk assessment and the

FIGURE 4.6   Sensitivity to profit risk varies with growth intent and margin

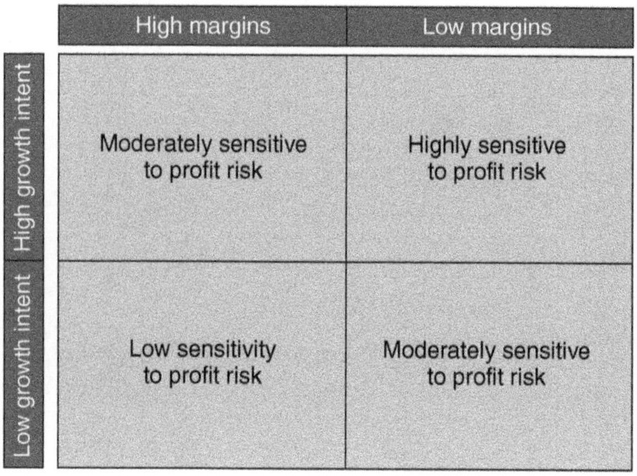

	High margins	Low margins
High growth intent	Moderately sensitive to profit risk	Highly sensitive to profit risk
Low growth intent	Low sensitivity to profit risk	Moderately sensitive to profit risk

sensitivity. Typically, small levels of risk result in little or no adjustment. At the other extreme, very large levels of risk mean that the strategy is so unsound that, frankly, the probability of achieving the growth component of the plan is unknowable, rather than simply low. More usually, moderate levels of risk imply significant changes in the growth assertions. In any case, the non-growth, historical trend of the business is largely unaffected by the risk.

Obviously, the adjustments are cumulative. An adjusted profit assertion is built on an adjusted share, which is built on an adjusted market size. Taken together, the end result is a revised profit figure for the returns reasonably expected from the plan. This figure represents the original assertion reduced, confirmed or, rarely, increased after allowing for the risk associated with the plan.

The next step in assessing whether or not the SBU's strategy delivers shareholder value is to compare the revised or confirmed profit figure with that which would represent the cost of capital. Marketing Due Diligence does not attempt to suggest an appropriate cost of capital. This is usually dictated to the SBU by either its headquarters or its financiers. The critical issue is whether the profit figure represents a return on the capital employed greater than the cost of capital. In assessing this, it is necessary to be realistic about the capital employed to realize the profits. In particular, it is important to count both tangible and intangible assets employed. It is easy, for instance, to make a high return on capital employed if valuable intangibles such as brands or intellectual property are ignored and only tangible assets are counted. This is typically the case when an SBU uses an umbrella branding approach. In doing so, it 'uses' the asset of the brand that has been created by many years of investment. If the strategy fails, that brand value, or part of it, is at risk. Accurate assessment of return on investment should count all assets employed, tangible or otherwise, as they are all 'at risk' in the investment.

So the final stage of this diagnostic phase of Marketing Due Diligence is a relatively simple calculation. The profit figure, adjusted or confirmed in the light of risk levels and sensitivity, is compared to what is necessary to create shareholder value. That comparison figure uses the SBU's cost of capital and counts all the assets used, or put at risk, tangible and otherwise. This simple comparison results in one of two conclusions: 1) The profit generated by the SBU's business plan, when assessed for and adjusted for all three areas of business risk, exceeds the cost of capital. The strategy is likely to create shareholder value. 2) The profit generated by the SBU's business plan, when assessed for and adjusted for all three areas of business risk, falls short of the cost of capital. The strategy is unlikely to create shareholder value. Whichever of these statements is appropriate is the output of the diagnostic phase of the Marketing Due Diligence process.

There is a third outcome of the process that is actually more common than either the positive or negative results. This is the result when one or more of the 15 tests applied during Marketing Due Diligence cannot be answered. It is not uncommon for SBUs not to know (that is, not to have considered) issues such as the existence of segments, SWOT alignment or the impact on competitors. In those circumstances, the only possible statement is that, on the basis of what is known from the written and unwritten strategy, the shareholder value creation of the SBU cannot be verified. To a large degree, this common result is worse than a negative result, in that it demands not just improvements in the strategy but a more thorough understanding of the SBU's strategic position.

4.3 Implications of the Marketing Due Diligence process

At a fundamental level, Marketing Due Diligence is very simple. While it will never be possible to eliminate business risk entirely, it is possible to reduce it to a practical minimum.

In the process, what risk remains is identified, located and, most importantly, understood. To achieve this, the process does not take a naive, simplistic approach. Instead, it uses the results of many years of research in which business successes and failures were examined. This allows us first to group the reasons for failure and then to suggest ways to avoid it. In that sense, Marketing Due Diligence can be considered as analogous to pre-flight checks, with the same implications for the reliability and success of the business plan.

When, in time, Marketing Due Diligence becomes a routine process for assessing the strategic decisions of company directors, the flaws it detects and the challenges it throws up may be fewer and more routine. In the meantime, however, application of Marketing Due Diligence will have many important implications for the board.

4.4 The linkage of strategy risk to shareholder value

The most common financial objective of modern commercial corporations is the sustainable creation of shareholder value. This can be achieved only by providing shareholders with a total return, from capital growth and dividend yield, that exceeds their risk-adjusted required rate of return for this particular investment.

However, for most companies, the current share price already reflects some expected future growth in profits. Thus, these current investors and, even more particularly, potential future shareholders, are trying to assess whether the proposed business strategies of the company will produce sufficient growth in sales revenues and profits, both to support the current share price and existing dividend payments and to drive the capital growth that they want to see in the future. At the same time, these external stakeholders also need a method of assessing the risks associated with these proposed strategies as, obviously, the associated risks have a direct link to their required rate of return.

As already stated, in today's highly competitive environment, the major sources of shareholder value creation are the intangible marketing assets of the business, such as brands, customer relationships and channels of distribution (the 80 per cent of the company's value that does not appear on the traditional balance sheet). Consequently, the critical future marketing strategies of a company, which indicate how these assets are to be developed, maintained and exploited, should be subjected to a rigorous review process. Unfortunately, not only is such focused forward-looking information still normally absent from the externally available data produced by companies, but also, even more worryingly, there is often not even a rigorous internal evaluation of the shareholder value impact of such proposed marketing strategies. Yet these same companies would undoubtedly have formally constituted, board-level audit committees that are responsible for reviewing all the major business risks that they face. Also, they would all conduct comprehensive financial due diligence processes on any major acquisitions or strategic investments.

Indeed, in recent years, the financial appraisal processes applied to major strategic investments have become increasingly sophisticated. The normal discounted cash flow techniques are now supplemented by the use of probability assessments, simulation techniques and even real option analysis. The one major area that has most commonly been excluded from this approach has been the marketing strategy of the business. Obviously, the objective of the Marketing Due Diligence process is to address this significant deficiency, but there are several significant implications of applying such a rigorous evaluation process to most existing marketing strategies.

4.5 The risk and return relationship

As set out earlier in this chapter, the Marketing Due Diligence process subjects any proposed marketing strategy to a structured, sequential process that will indicate the probability of such a marketing strategy leading to increased shareholder value. The whole basis of shareholder value is the direct linking of the level of risk to the level of financial return that is required. Indeed, as shown in Figure 4.7, the causality relationship is that the perceived risk profile of the investment drives the level of return required by investors in this particular investment.

The two axes are deliberately labelled 'perceived risk' and 'required return': the return required by investors is driven by the risks they perceive in the investment. If risk perceptions are so important to the creation of shareholder value, by delivering total returns that exceed this risk-adjusted required rate of return, there is clearly a need for a definition of risk from the perspective of any investor. Risk is created by volatility in future expected returns. In Figure 4.7, a minimum positive required rate of return is shown where the risk/return line cuts the vertical axis. This minimum required rate of return carries a zero-risk perception, which means guaranteed, certain future returns. For investors in stable economies this normally means government guaranteed borrowings (eg US Treasury bills, UK government gilts, European

FIGURE 4.7   Risk-adjusted required rate of return

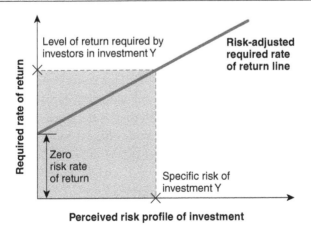

Perceived risk profile of investment

FIGURE 4.8   Risk and return

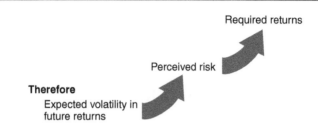

Central Bank debt). At the time of writing, the returns on these investments are low, but they are still seen as risk free owing to their lack of volatility; for example, the interest on a US Treasury bill may be low, but owners are certain of what they will get and when it will arrive.

Logically, therefore, a normal, rational, risk-averse investor requires an increase in the expected future return from any more risky investment in order to compensate for any potential volatility. Thus, the cause-and-effect relationship is as shown diagrammatically in Figure 4.8; any expected volatility in future returns creates an increased perceived risk profile in investors that increases their required rate of return.

Of course, investors know in advance of making their investment in most government-backed debt investments (gilts, Treasury bonds, National Savings certificates, etc) exactly what their return will be (ie the interest rate payable is stated on the debt offering). This is clearly not the case with most equity (ie stocks and shares in companies) investments, and this lack of certainty increases risk perceptions and hence required rates of return. Further, if the historical track record of a company's shares shows significant volatility in share prices and even dividend payments, investors will require much higher returns from the company, as they will extrapolate from this past performance as their best guide to the future performance of the company's shares.

Financial markets use various models to estimate the relative volatility of different industrial sectors and of the companies within each sector. The main formula is derived from the simple risk/return line and is known as the capital asset pricing model CAPM – (Copeland and Weston, 1998). This is shown in Figure 4.9.

The CAPM derives the beta factor for each company by calculating the correlation of the company's historic volatility with that of the stock market as a whole. If the stock market rises or falls by 5 per cent and share A moves by 7.5 per cent but share B moves by only 4 per cent, then share A is relatively more volatile than share B; arithmetically, share A has a beta factor of 1.5 while share B has a beta factor of only 0.8. This means that the required return (K_E) for share A will be significantly higher than for share B. A numerical illustration of this is given in Table 4.4.

FIGURE 4.9   Risk and return – the financial markets formula

The capital asset pricing model (CAPM)

The return demanded by shareholders (often referred to as the cost of equity capital, K_E) increases with the perceived risk of the investment. (Risk is measured in terms of the volatility in the level of return over time.)

Mathematically, this can be represented as:

$$K_E = K_F + \beta\,(K_M - K_F)$$

where

K_F = Return on a risk-free investment

K_M = Return on the stock market in total

β = Volatility of a particular share (by definition, the stock market has a β of 1)

$(K_M - K_F)$ = The premium return required for accepting the risk associated with the stock market

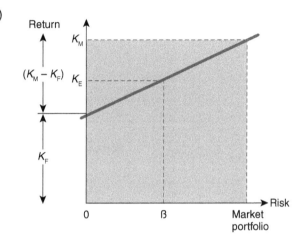

TABLE 4.4   Relative costs of capital (ie required rates of return)

Base assumptions

K_F = Return on a risk-free investment = 4% pa

$(K_M - K_F)$ = Equity market premium = 5% pa

Share A β = 1.5

Share B β = 0.8

Using CAPM, ie $K_E = K_F + \beta(K_M - K_F)$

For share A, K_E = 4% + 1.5(5%) = 11.5%

For share B, K_E = 4% + 0.8(5%) = 8%

4.6 A focus on absolute returns rather than risk

Table 4.4 indicates how much more challenging life is for a highly volatile company, caused by shareholders' natural dislike for risk. However, what is even more important is that the upward-sloping 'risk-adjusted required rate of return' line of

FIGURE 4.10   Risk-adjusted required rate of return as shareholders'
indifference

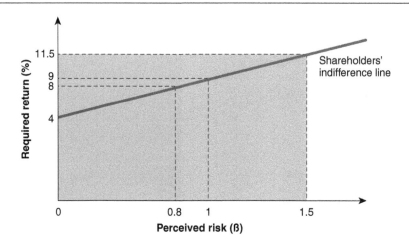

Figures 4.7 and 4.9 is, in reality, the shareholders' indifference line. In other words, moving from any point on the line to any other point on the line merely compensates investors for a change in their risk perception; it does not, of itself, create shareholder value. Thus, using the numerical illustration of Table 4.4, investors who require a 4 per cent per annum return for a risk-free investment will require a 9 per cent per annum return for taking on the overall stock market risk. Similarly, they regard an 11.5 per cent per annum return from share A as equivalent to (ie neither better than nor worse than) an 8 per cent per annum return from share B, owing to their differing risk profiles. This is shown diagrammatically in Figure 4.10.

In financial terms, if shareholders receive, or expect to receive, exactly the level of return that they require from any investment, they have simply swapped a present capital sum (the purchase price of the investment) for a future set of cash flows (the future dividend streams from the company plus any expected ultimate sale proceeds from the investment) that have an equal present value. Shareholder value is created only when total returns are greater than the risk-adjusted required rate of return. Thus, a company can achieve growing profits over time without creating shareholder value if the associated risk profile is also increasing.

Hence we prefer the term 'super-profits' to describe shareholder value-enhancing levels of profit. A super-profit represents the excess rate of return over the required rate of return. Unfortunately, the normal focus of marketing strategies and plans is on predicting absolute financial outcomes, rather than placing these expected outcomes in the context of the required rate of return. There is an implicit assumption in most marketing plans that the risk profile will be unchanged owing to the implementation

FIGURE 4.11 Shareholder value-adding strategies

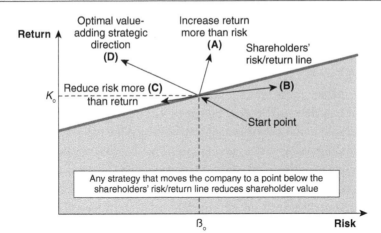

of new strategies, such as launching new products or entering new market segments. One of the key objectives of the Marketing Due Diligence process is to make these critical assumptions about the risk associated with proposed marketing strategies explicit, so that they can be analysed rigorously.

Alternative new strategies can have significantly different impacts on risk, which will change their potential for creating shareholder value. This is shown diagrammatically in Figure 4.11.

Most marketing strategies are aimed at generating growth in sales revenues and profits but, for many mature products and markets, such strategies increase the risk profile of the business; indeed, the word 'growth' can normally be taken to indicate a risk-increasing strategy. This does not automatically mean that these strategies cannot be shareholder value-enhancing, but it does mean, as can be seen from directions A and B in Figure 4.11, that the return from the more risky strategy must increase proportionately more than does the risk profile of the company. (Remember that merely moving along the shareholders' indifference line does not create shareholder value; this is achieved only by moving to a position above the line.)

More interestingly, direction C in Figure 4.11 highlights another type of shareholder value-enhancing strategy that is often ignored in marketing plans. A reduction from the current risk profile of the business (diagrammatically shown as a move to the left) means that shareholder value can be created even if the rate of return is reduced slightly. This time, the reduction in return must be proportionately less than the reduction in the risk profile. Since risk is associated with volatility in returns, this means that marketing strategies that make the future returns more stable and predictable can be shareholder value-enhancing, even if these less volatile future returns are slightly reduced. Thus, marketing strategies designed to increase customer loyalty through long-term discounts and so on can, if properly designed, be shareholder value-enhancing, even though the discounts given actually reduce profit levels.

Obviously, the optimal marketing strategy seeks to increase returns while reducing the associated risk levels (ie the volatility of these increased returns), direction D of Figure 4.11.

Any such strategy must leverage some already established, sustainable competitive advantages, or first seek to develop a new sustainable competitive advantage, as the overall purpose and focus of strategic marketing is the identification and creation of such sustainable competitive advantages. This is why the detailed analysis of marketing strategies is the focus of the Marketing Due Diligence process.

However, as well as needing to put the predicted absolute financial outcomes of marketing strategies into an appropriate relative framework, there are other problems with the current methods of financially appraising marketing plans. Most financial outcomes of marketing strategies are presented as single values, for example the expected profits and cash flows for the next three or five years. These single-value outcomes are self-evidently calculated as some expected value from the wide range of potential outcomes that could be achieved if the plan is implemented. Different planning processes and organizational cultures mean that these single-point financial results can be more or less aggressive or optimistic; this is considered in depth later in this chapter. The potential range of outcomes is, of course, a good indicator of the volatility of the proposed marketing strategies and therefore of its associated risk profile. Therefore, the inputs to the Marketing Due Diligence analysis should incorporate the range of potential outcomes before they have been subjected to any averaging or best-estimate process.

Gaining an understanding of the distribution of potential financial outcomes (ie their range and relative probabilities) is critical to really appreciating the risk profile of the marketing strategy and the key drivers of that risk profile (ie market size risk, market share risk and/or profit risk). Where risk is considered in the appraisal of marketing strategies, this is normally done in an overall way by changing the discount rate that is applied to the predicted future cash flows. Thus, 'higher-risk' strategies have a higher discount rate applied to all their expected future cash flows. Unfortunately, this turns the highly sophisticated financial analysis technique of discounted cash flow into a very blunt instrument that cannot differentiate among the vast array of risks that can impact on the value-creation potential of alternative marketing strategies. The objective of the Marketing Due Diligence process is to assist in the appraisal and control of marketing strategies, by using appropriately tailored analytical tools.

Some companies have trouble with the idea of assessing probabilities of success (ie specific risk profiles) for specific elements of marketing strategies because they 'see the process as subjective'. Yet these same companies see nothing subjective in projecting cash flows many years into the future and then choosing a 'high' discount rate to reflect the overall risk associated with the strategy. The use of specific risk profiling for the key elements of the marketing strategy and using these risk assessments to adjust the expected cash flows directly put the appropriate line managers back in control of the assessment of their strategies. In most companies, the choice of a risk-adjusted discount rate is solely under the control of the finance function. Even more importantly, this is how the external capital markets take account of specific risks. Hence any company that claims to have the objective of creating shareholder value should align its internal processes with those used by its shareholders.

4.7 Alignment with capital markets

As stated earlier in this chapter, investors in financial markets start by assessing the relative risk profile of an industry (its beta factor) and use this to calculate the required rate of return for that sector. This is then translated into a cost of capital for individual companies within this industry. Thus, companies do have different costs of capital, and consequently different rates of discount will be applied to their expected future cash flows. However, these different risk profiles show the degree to which these returns are correlated with the overall capital market, what is technically referred to as systematic risk. Therefore, beta factors only take into account general risk factors that will affect all or most companies. They do not take into account all the specific risks that are faced by a single company with its individual marketing strategy. The financial markets take these into account by adjusting the level of future cash flows that are discounted at the company's cost of capital rate.

4.8 Turning Marketing Due Diligence into a financial value

Given the focus on aligning the Marketing Due Diligence process with the creation of shareholder value, it should come as no surprise that the Marketing Due Diligence diagnostic process adjusts the expected cash flows generated by proposed marketing strategies by using the probabilities assessed through the structured risk analysis process set out earlier in this chapter.

This first stage of the Marketing Due Diligence diagnostic process, therefore, should result in an adjusted set of forecast sales revenues, profits and cash flows from the proposed marketing strategy. We now need to assess these adjusted expected cash flows as to whether they are shareholder value-enhancing. This is done by putting them into the context of the capital employed in implementing the marketing strategy and the resulting required rate of return on this capital employed.

We use the genuine capital that is required in the business in order to assess this marketing strategy. In other words, it includes the value of the relevant intangible assets owned and used by the business and is not limited to the historically based, tangible asset-oriented balance sheets published by most companies.

Clearly, this involves the exercise of judgement in assessing the current value of such intangible assets, but this should be an integral part of the development of the proposed marketing strategy. Marketing expenditure should be split between development and maintenance activities rather than being categorized into the more normal, but much less relevant, categories such as 'above-the-line' media advertising and 'below-the-line' promotions. Development marketing expenditure is aimed at increasing the value of marketing assets such as brands, customer relationships and channels of distribution. These are investments that, if successful, generate financial returns in subsequent years. For most companies it is the return from these successful marketing investments that is the major source of sustainable shareholder value. Thus, a major element in producing a sound marketing strategy is assessing whether and, if so, how existing and/or new marketing assets can be further developed. These marketing investments also represent the main focus of the Marketing Due Diligence process, as they are often quite high-risk expenditures; if they are unsuccessful, the money spent is normally completely irrecoverable.

Maintenance marketing activities are designed to hold existing marketing assets at their current level, as it is very well established that all assets, but particularly intangible marketing assets, decline in value unless they are properly maintained. Therefore, the impact of maintenance marketing expenditure is normally seen in the relatively short term, while the financial return from developmental marketing investments may be several years in the future. Unfortunately, the normal accounting treatment for marketing expenditure does not classify even such long-term marketing activities as true financial investments, with all marketing expenditure being written off in the current year's profit and loss account. This means that it can be possible to improve the short-term financial performance of a business by cutting back on development marketing activities, even though this means that the marketing assets will never achieve their full potential. If development marketing budgets are reduced in an attempt to boost short-term profits, the long-term performance measures used within the business must highlight the risks that are being taken with the sustainability of the business.

It must also be remembered that marketing assets are developed in a competitive environment, and the effectiveness of marketing expenditure is significantly affected by competitors' levels of spending. This is taken into account in the Marketing Due Diligence process.

Where the proposed marketing strategy is primarily aimed at increasing the value of an existing marketing asset or creating a completely new one, there may be little or no increased financial return during the three years or so for which detailed financial outcomes are predicted. The financial returns are expected even further into the future, but can be captured by increasing the value of the particular marketing asset at the end of the projection period. Clearly, the increased time delay between the expenditure of the marketing investment and the anticipated financial return is an indicator of increased risk, as the market may change or competitors may be able to respond effectively. This is again taken into account in the Marketing Due Diligence diagnostic process.

For publicly quoted companies, the assessment of the total value of their intangible assets is relatively easy. The gap between the company's stock market capitalization and the net tangible assets disclosed on the published balance sheet shows their shareholders' estimate of this value. This total value then needs to be analysed across the business so that the major elements are identified, but there are now a number of techniques in use for placing approximate values on marketing assets (eg brand valuation techniques, customer relationship valuations) that can be used as necessary.

Once an estimate of the capital employed in implementing the marketing strategy has been made, we can compute the required return on this investment by applying the appropriate risk-adjusted rate of return to this capital employed. Because the specific risks associated with the marketing strategy have been taken into account by adjusting the projected resulting cash flows, the appropriate rate of return will be close to the company's cost of capital. It may need some adjustment, as this marketing strategy may be relevant to only a part of the total company and discount rates must be appropriate to the risk category of the specific asset or investment being evaluated. Thus, the output of the Marketing Due Diligence diagnostic process is an adjusted cash flow forecast from which is deducted the required return on the investment involved. A resulting positive net cash flow indicates both that shareholder value should be created and the level of this shareholder value that should be created by implementing this marketing strategy.

4.8.1 Allowing for 'capital at risk'

There is still one more adjustment that needs to be made to some marketing strategies. The previous section effectively charged a tax on the return generated by the marketing strategy for the use of the assets employed by the strategy, resulting in what accountants refer to as 'residual income'. This charge represents the opportunity cost of tying up the company's capital, but it assumes that the capital will still exist at the end of the planning period. However, some marketing strategies may make it more likely that part of this capital could be lost if the marketing strategy is not completely successful. In other words, this capital is put 'at risk' by the marketing strategy.

There are many ways in which this can happen, but the most common is in an attempt to reduce the initial costs of implementing a new marketing strategy. This can often be done by leveraging on an existing marketing asset of the business, so that the upfront marketing development investment required is significantly reduced. Focusing initial sales of new products on existing loyal customers can reduce launch selling costs compared with finding completely new customers. However, if these new products do not match either the existing customers' expectations or existing product quality levels, the loyalty of these valuable current customers can be significantly eroded.

Probably the most common example of this leveraging type of strategy is the use of umbrella or corporate branding, where a new product is launched under the umbrella of an existing, well-known, successful brand. Obviously the objective is to create rapid awareness and trial of the new product without the need for massive marketing expenditure. As long as the new product is a very good fit with all the existing brand's attributes and target customers, this can be successful, but there can be a significant risk to the value of the current brand. There are many examples of companies launching brand extensions that had negative impacts on their existing brand franchise; yet, often, this 'capital at risk' is not taken into account in the review of the marketing strategy.

This is clearly unfair, as the financial returns projected from this marketing strategy will include the 'benefit' of the cost savings achieved by placing this capital at risk. It is this anomaly that is addressed by this additional adjustment required in the Marketing Due Diligence process. It is needed only for those marketing strategies that seek to leverage on existing, indirectly associated marketing assets and, by doing so, run the risk of reducing their current value.

The mechanics of making the adjustment require an assessment both of the current value of the marketing asset that is being put at risk and of the potential proportionate reduction in this value that could result from its use in this strategy. In some cases, this could represent a total loss of its current value. The Marketing Due Diligence assessment process is then, as usual, to assign a risk weighting, a probability factor, to this loss in value, and this adjusted loss in value is subtracted from the net expected return from the proposed marketing strategy.

This means that the output from the Marketing Due Diligence diagnostic process should be a numerical value representing the expected shareholder value to be created by any proposed marketing strategy. The computational process has been broken into segments quite deliberately, as some companies may find it difficult initially to do the second and third stages: assessing the return required on the actual capital tied up in the strategy and adjusting for the potential loss from the capital placed at risk by this strategy. Making the Marketing Due Diligence adjustments to the expected financial returns from the proposed marketing strategy enables a much more rigorous review and appraisal to be undertaken, as is discussed in the next section.

The potential shareholder value creation (or destruction, obviously, if the final answer is a negative value) of the proposed marketing strategy should greatly enhance the resource allocation decision process within a company, but the Marketing Due Diligence process can add value even without a final numerical result.

4.9 Highlighting deficiencies and key risks

When we have applied the Marketing Due Diligence process to existing marketing strategies and plans, we find that there are often gaps in the information supporting the resulting financial forecasts. There have also been many instances of self-apparent inconsistencies between the marketing plans and these resulting financial outcomes. In many cases, this lack of information makes it very difficult to conduct a full Marketing Due Diligence appraisal of the marketing strategy. However, the appraisal process has been of value to the company even in these cases, as it clearly highlights the specific deficiencies in the existing marketing plans.

These deficiencies are often readily rectified, as the required knowledge either already exists within the business, but has not been incorporated into the marketing plan explicitly, or data can be easily obtained by management. A logically structured and rigorously applied marketing planning process, which starts by identifying genuine market needs, removes the need for dangerously false implicit assumptions about 'new' opportunities for selling existing products or developing 'new products' for unspecified customers. Perhaps the major non-financial benefit of the Marketing Due Diligence diagnostic process is that it indicates the key risks associated with any proposed marketing strategy. This is achieved by demonstrating the relative impact of the individual risk assessments that are made during a Marketing Due Diligence appraisal. The management team is able to focus its attention on these critical areas of risk and uncertainty and thereby improve the marketing planning process in the future. Consequently, Marketing Due Diligence should be viewed as an ongoing process rather than a one-off review or audit.

By concentrating planning resources and marketing research effort on the identified key areas, the business should be able to make better predictions. This does not mean that future marketing strategies will necessarily be less risky, but that the level of risk that is being undertaken is more fully appreciated and will be better controlled and monitored.

4.10 Implications for business

Hopefully you are convinced that a Marketing Due Diligence process can add value to both internal and external shareholders in a business. For external stakeholders, such as existing and prospective shareholders, the knowledge that all proposed marketing strategies will be subjected to a rigorous and structured review should provide reassurance that the resulting resource allocation decisions are more likely to be shareholder value-enhancing. Indeed, it could be that institutional investors and stock market analysts will require a Marketing Due Diligence process to be put in place as part of any sound corporate governance process. This makes even more sense for the other external financiers involved in non-publicly quoted companies, such as private equity funds and other corporate financiers. Such a process also has significant relevance to debt providers, particularly in highly leveraged companies.

The obvious linkages inside a company should be through the board of directors, who have ultimate responsibility for the corporate governance process operated across their organization. Instigating a Marketing Due Diligence process should seem like a great idea to any non-executive director who wants to be confident that future strategies and plans are being properly reviewed and controlled. With legislation around the world placing more and more emphasis on control procedures and corporate governance, with increasing potential penalties on individual directors, the need for an objective, recognized and well-structured review and approval process is also clear.

The Marketing Due Diligence process should be of interest to external auditors as they seek to validate the effectiveness of their clients' control procedures. However, as their responsibility is still focused on reporting on the actual financial performance of a business, Marketing Due Diligence is even more relevant to the internal audit functions of large, multi-business corporations. Owing to the geographical spread and complexity of most of these modern companies, their boards of directors require reassurance that the information provided to them is as accurate and relevant as possible. This is particularly true for the critical, strategic investment decisions where, by definition, the financial justifications are based on forecasts of future expected outcomes.

Hence the main focus of most internal audit functions is already on business risk identification, assessment and control. Integrating the Marketing Due Diligence process into their existing business risk analysis routines would therefore greatly reinforce their ability to report back to the board-level audit committee on the company's internal control processes.

However, this still casts Marketing Due Diligence in a post-plan preparation review role. Ideally, the Marketing Due Diligence process should be seen as a normal line management responsibility. In other words, no proposed marketing strategy will be considered by the top executive management team unless it has been subjected to a thorough Marketing Due Diligence process review. This is how CEOs can hold their marketing directors to account and ensure that their marketing strategies do deliver shareholder value.

Note

1 A more comprehensive approach to brand valuation has been encapsulated in an international standard for it – ISO 10668

References

Ansoff, I (1957) Strategies for Diversification, *Harvard Business Review*, **35** (5), pp 113–24

Copeland, T and Weston, J (1998) *Financial Theory and Corporate Policy*, Addison-Welsley, Reading, Massachusetts

Porter, M E (1985) *Competitive Advantage: Creating and sustaining superior performance*, Free Press, New York

The Marketing Value Metrics model and process

05

" When marketers do focus on business measures,
they focus on the wrong ones: sales rather than market share,
and volume rather than value.

(BINET AND FIELD, 2007)

Summary

This chapter provides an overview of the Marketing Value Metrics model introduced in Chapter 3. The model was developed to help organizations improve the alignment between marketing activity and its impact on achieving corporate goals. In addition to briefly describing the key steps in the model, the chapter also summarizes the process for practically applying the model. It also identifies why it is important to ensure that other functions within the organization are fully engaged with marketing in the model process to ensure that promises made to the market can be effectively delivered. Also described in this chapter is the process for implementing the model, while Chapters 6–9 provide a detailed description of each key stage within the model.

5.1 Introduction

Identifying the most appropriate metrics for measuring the impact of marketing is obviously fundamental. As Binet and Field (2007) point out, marketers have tended to focus on those that are directly related to their inputs and outputs – advertising-to-sales ratios, share of voice, image and attitudes, for example. These are not usually the measures that demonstrate the value added by marketing in terms of improving the overall performance, profitability, generation of customer or shareholder value of the business. However, this requires rather more than simply replacing one set of metrics for another; it requires a thorough review of the metrics strategy in the context of business goals and the company's position in the market. Answering the key question 'What do I need to spend in order to achieve an x per cent increase in profit?' requires a forensic analysis process to identify whether the current, and planned, direction of marketing activity is aligned with the goals or expectations of the company.

A further issue is that marketing often does not directly control activities essential to enabling goals it sets to be achieved. Often, there is no process in place to identify what these 'other' actions are, who is responsible for them, what impact these actions have on achieving, or not achieving, goals set by marketing, and what measures should be in place to monitor whether these actions are contributing in line with expectations. It is no good if promises made by advertising are not experienced by customers. The customers' experience of the promise is normally generated by production, logistics, sales and customer service processes. An example of this 'inner-connectivity' has been described by Graham Booth, Supply Chain Director of Tesco, shown in Figure 5.1.

FIGURE 5.1   'Inner-connectivity'

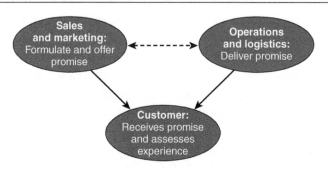

The issue is whether the actions necessary by logistics will match the promise for delivery made by marketing, and achieve the sales targets set by the sales department. 'Inner-connectivity' needs to ensure that all the internal partners in defining and matching the promise are agreed on what is achievable. Maybe an improvement in delivery times is vital to achieving competitive advantage, as perhaps identified through market research conducted to define customer needs and the current perceptions of customer service. For many organizations this will need to involve the external suppliers responsible for delivery to the final customer. These issues will be described in more detail in Chapter 7, on impact factors.

We believe that strategic marketing incorporates sales, customer service and new product development processes. Marketing considers all touch points with the customer, but often the customer experiences generated at these touch points are controlled by functions other than marketing.

A further issue is that, where efficiencies are concerned, marketers are often focused on those solely related to campaigns, and channel management. However, this is only part of the story, and little thought is given by marketers when developing strategy to consider internal efficiencies that could increase the organization's competitive position in the market.

Marketers therefore need to ensure that all necessary resources and functions within the organization are focused on achieving the marketing-related goals within the corporate plan – and that the metric suite covers all the key activities. The challenge implied here is that marketers need to develop and implement a framework that can address the following key questions related to measuring performance:

- What measures are appropriate, and essential, for different audiences within the organization to track the impact of marketing-related activity?

- What key gaps are there in the information currently collected that inhibit or prevent the appropriate measurement of marketing-related activity, and how should filling these gaps be prioritized?

- Which metrics are essential to tracking the performance within core target markets?

- Can the needs of consumers in the market be defined and prioritized, together with the metrics that will be appropriate to tracking performance against competitors in meeting these needs?

- Which key resources are necessary if marketing strategies are to be successful and how should the results of deploying them be measured?

- What are the appropriate actions that should be invested in by the company to achieve marketing goals?

- Where can efficiencies be identified that will contribute towards improving the competitive position of the organization, and how can the impact of these be measured?

- What should be an appropriate budget to achieve the goals set for marketing, and can we measure the 'leverage' from investing in different activities?

- What metrics would be appropriate in measuring the impact of marketing on achieving the business goals of the organization?

There is no doubt that these can be difficult questions to answer. They are also quite sophisticated, and we believe that many organizations would struggle to provide effective answers, if such questions were to be asked, as they should be, by their board. While it is increasingly likely that boards will demand greater accountability from marketing, they may well simplify the above to a more basic list of questions for the marketing director to answer:

- How much are you spending?
- What are you spending it on?
- When will you spend it?
- What return are you forecasting?
- And when can we expect it?

These are essentially financially orientated measures, so the answers need to be developed in association with, and agreed by, finance. Also, these questions do not help the board gain an understanding of what the organization expects to achieve in the market as a result of this spend, for example the expected impact on market share. The task for marketers is to convince the board that, by asking different questions, they will be able to gain a much better understanding of what value marketing is adding to the business. There is the need for a 'meeting of minds' on the most effective measures to use at board level. As Figure 5.2 shows, the terms often used by marketing to measure success are rather different from the finance-based terminology that the board focuses on when determining whether expenditure has been worthwhile.

The model described in this and subsequent chapters provides a solution to these dilemmas.

FIGURE 5.2   Different languages

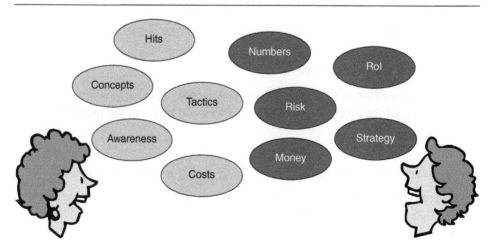

5.2 Overview of the Marketing Value Metrics model

The Marketing Value Metrics model is designed to help organizations answer the questions listed above. At its heart are tried-and-tested business process and strategy analysis tools, but these are applied within an overall framework developed to identify the suite of key metrics that are specific to a particular organization, recognizing that even competing companies within a particular market have set different goals and strategies. The resulting model can be applied within organizations to help prioritize scarce resources, set targets and measure outcomes.

The key objective is therefore to develop an appropriate suite of metrics, customized for the specific organization, which can be used to track the impact of marketing on achieving business goals and identify the resources necessary to achieve objectives within a market. In particular, the aim is to identify the subset of these metrics that should be reported at board level in order to demonstrate the impact that marketing has on building shareholder value. This not only creates greater accountability, but it also helps demystify the role of marketing by linking resource allocation to outcomes – in a language that boards can relate to.

Also implicit within the model are the following critical elements in a measurement strategy:

- *Metric:* what should be measured, including definitions. Some metrics will be direct measurements (eg response and conversion levels for a direct marketing campaign), and others might be derived or modelled (eg customer satisfaction scores).
- *Data:* how the necessary facts will be collected, the format, and who is responsible for this process.
- *Target:* the planned level of future performance in a defined time frame.
- *Result:* the actual level achieved in the defined time frame.

These elements need to be discussed and agreed for each step in the model process.

The Marketing Value Metrics model is shown in Figure 5.3. The model is divided into the following key components, each of which is summarized below and then described in detail in subsequent chapters:

- *corporate performance* – forecasts and actual results;
- *market segments* – objectives for each one, and outcomes achieved as strategy is implemented;
- *impact factors* – necessary in developing an appropriate strategy and as a framework to track response;
- *marketing and other actions* – what the organization plans to do to achieve the strategy;

FIGURE 5.3   Marketing Value Metrics model

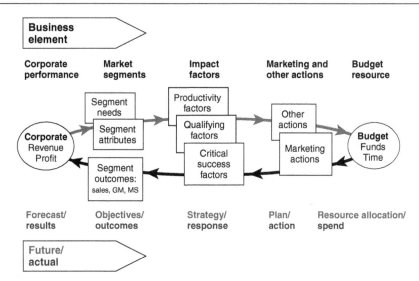

• *budget resources* – what resources and expenditure are necessary to deliver the strategy.

The grey arrows show the flow for identifying what needs to be done in future to achieve corporate goals. The black arrows track what actually happens as the strategy is implemented in order to achieve the defined goals. Both flows identify, and contain, key metrics to measure the overall performance of the organization and changes over time in the market.

The model also provides companies with an audit process, which enables management to track whether there is alignment between marketing plans – comprising strategy and actions – and corporate goals, and ensure that all the appropriate performance and market tracking measures are in place. It also provides management with a checklist to help easily identify whether plans cover all necessary factors.

The key points for each of these stages in the model are as follows.

5.2.1 Corporate performance

This component captures the goals, and associated metrics, at corporate level that relate to marketing activities and the associated measures of marketing's impact on achieving objectives. Some might already be included within a board-level dashboard, balanced scorecard or other key indices reviewed regularly at board level. They cover current targets, results and future forecasts of performance. These may be at corporate, business unit, subsidiary, geographic or divisional level – whatever is most appropriate for the company. In our experience few organizations include all those that are vital in measuring the impact of marketing. While targets and forecasts are not always the same in some organizations, we are assuming that they are the same thing for the purposes of the model. Once targets or forecasts have been agreed, then it is the responsibility of all relevant functions and activities to respond in achieving them. Ambitious targets need an equally ambitious response from marketing. Also, different targets require different responses, for example 'profit improvement' and 'rapid market share growth' targets probably cannot be delivered via the same marketing strategies.

5.2.2 Market segments (Chapter 6)

All markets can, we believe, be divided into segments. Segmentation helps an organization identify target groups to enable appropriate objectives to be set, resources to be effectively deployed where the value added, for the consumer and the business, can be maximized, and outcomes defined. The metrics here cover segment profiles, needs, trends, sales forecasts, revenues, margins and so on. However, there are many definitions of what constitutes segmentation. The definition used in the Marketing Metrics model is as follows:

> Groups of individuals, or organizations, who have the same or similar needs which will be satisfied by the same or similar offers. Segments are:
>
> - Identifiable and recognizable (by the members of a segment)
> - Independently existing (if your organization did not exist, the segment would still be there)
> - Measurable (even if difficult to do so)
> - Substantial (big enough to be worth investing in)
> - Externally accessible and actionable (eg can they be promoted to through channels).
>
> (McDonald, 2012)

The metrics for measuring segments are divided into two groups: 1) *Those that define and track the segment over time*, for example segment members' needs and wants; attitudes/opinions; demographic, geographic, geodemographic and psychographic profiles; media consumption; purchase occasions/channels; etc. These are the factors that exist in the market, independent of organizations selling to members in the segment. 2) *Those that measure the performance of your business within a segment in terms of the organization's goals*. Metrics might include market share, sales volumes, gross margin, brand image, customer value, etc. The metrics will also need to include those that benchmark your organization against the needs and attitudes of customers, and against the performance of key competitors operating in this segment.

5.2.3 Impact factors (Chapter 7)

Marketing needs to develop strategies as a response to the analysis of each segment of interest to the organization. The tool used in the model, and described in the chapter, is an impact factor analysis. Three types of impact factors are considered within the model:

1 *Qualifying factors* are those factors, and associated levels of performance, that all organizations operating in a market are expected to deliver from a consumer's perspective. Unless a company can provide these at the expected level it is unlikely to prosper in the market.

2 *Critical success factors* are the factors that really matter to consumers in a market – they focus on important customer needs. They attract attention in the market and help you win, and retain customers. Focusing on improving performance against these creates positive and powerful advantage over competitors. Improving performance against these factors should lead to increased market share.

3 *Productivity factors* are essentially about reducing costs. Productivity factors are actions that the organization needs to take internally to become more efficient and focused in delivering the overall strategy for each segment. This can include increasing output, by leveraging economies of scale.

Extended definitions for each of these, and how they are applied within the model, are described in Chapter 7. Impact factors help identify the appropriate strategies for each market segment, and the anticipated response from consumers. Metrics can be set for each set of impact factors.

5.2.4 Identifying actions, setting budgets and establishing linkages (Chapter 8)

The impact factors analysis enables the overall strategy for each segment to be defined. The next step is therefore to agree the actions that will enable the strategy to be successfully delivered for each segment to help achieve the overall goals. As illustrated in Figure 5.1, these actions may include ones currently outside the control of marketing but essential to achieving the goals that marketing is responsible for. A tool to help identify the most appropriate actions is described within Chapter 8.

Actions are likely to consume resources, either internally or externally. There might be the need to argue for a reallocation of internal resources already allocated to other plans, or an investment in an increase in resources if this makes financial sense in terms of achieving the overall goals of the organization. External actions might be additional expenditure on market research or advertising. This analysis enables an appropriate budget, or spending plan over a longer time frame, to be derived. This spending plan should also include the 'gearing', or return, expected from allocating these resources in terms of increased market share, increases in sales revenues, improved gross margin, etc.

This process enables a detailed plan to be constructed for each segment. These can then be developed into a plan for the market as a whole and the identification of the appropriate metrics to track progress and changes over time in the market.

5.2.5 Finalizing the metrics strategy (Chapter 9)

The final step in the model is to draw together the metrics from the earlier stages and finalize the overall measurement strategy. This step includes identifying any metrics that are not currently in place, and deciding how to address these gaps. The strategy also needs to finalize issues such as who will be responsible for each measure, who will be responsible for taking action if the measure indicates that agreed progress is not being achieved, and who will see each metric.

5.3 Implementing the Marketing Value Metrics model

The model described above needs an appropriate process to enable each component to be thoroughly considered if the final strategy is to be both actionable and corporately acceptable. The method for implementing the model has been developed by working through the full process with a small number of organizations operating in different market sectors. The key objective of the process is to identify the metrics appropriate for the organization to track:

- the impact of marketing strategy;
- performance against forecast;
- that agreed actions are on target;
- changes in the market and activities of competitors.

It is also important to establish in the context of the model what the term 'marketing' covers and the planning 'time frame'. The definitions of these are as follows:

- *Marketing:* as mentioned earlier, the definition of 'marketing' covered in the process needs to include all market or customer-facing activities – marketing, sales, customer service, new product development, websites, etc. However, as also mentioned earlier in this chapter, delivering against the promises made by marketing is almost always reliant on collaboration with other parts of the company, which will need to be responsible for implementing actions outside the direct control of marketing. Therefore the discussions need to be wide-ranging, and some of the metrics identified in the strategy will be measuring the performance of other business areas.

- *Time frame:* the focus is on those metrics that will measure performance against goals in the strategic plan's three- to five-year time frame. The metrics strategy therefore has a medium-term focus. This means that, although tactical, or operational-marketing, measures may be included in the overall framework, the model is concerned with measuring the cumulative impact of shorter-term strategy, such as that resulting from marketing communications campaigns, in terms of impact on achieving the medium-term goals for each segment (eg performance in the market, such as an increase in market share) and any consequential effect on corporate goals (eg increases in the value of intangible assets such as brand or customer equity). Tracking of short-term strategy, such as the effect of an advertising campaign, is often restricted to the period of activity, whereas the impact may be felt for longer and in other areas of the business. An example of this covering General Motors is described in Chapter 11. Measurement strategies need to reflect the whole time frame over which any impact can be expected to occur and take into account the wider consequences. Another example is that a direct mail campaign to sell a book through that channel may increase sales through other outlets, such as bookshops.

Overall, the positioning of the model process is illustrated in Figure 5.4 by the right-hand triangle, the model zone, covering the market positioning and the value proposition that has been identified as the most appropriate for the particular segment in that market. Once the metrics strategy has been identified through the model, the subsequent step is to apply the measures in the left-hand triangle, the measurement zone, to track performance.

The process for applying the model, summarized in this chapter, and explained in more detail over subsequent chapters describing each stage, will also help organizations:

- identify which metrics are already used or available;
- develop a framework for using currently available data to develop new metrics;
- identify gaps in data collection that prevent key metrics being implemented;
- identify any other issues with data collection or developing necessary metrics.

These issues are also discussed in more detail in Chapter 9, covering the finalizing of the overall measurement strategy.

FIGURE 5.4   Map of the marketing domain

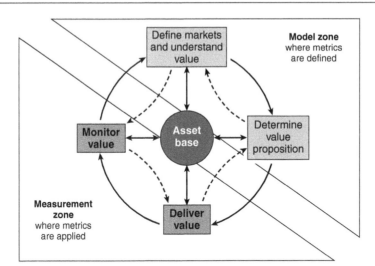

The implementation process used to identify the appropriate metrics strategy for the organization is shown in Figure 5.5. It is based around a series of four workshops conducted within the organization; this process was originally developed and tested at Cranfield with industry partners.

The workshop process is described in detail in the following sections, including a discussion on the appropriate participants in section 5.4.

5.3.1 Workshop 1

This workshop has two objectives. The first is to identify those current corporate-level metrics that might be expected to be influenced by marketing activity, and the second is to develop a set of metrics for the key segments in the organization's market.

5.3.1.1 Corporate metrics

Those likely to be influenced by marketing activity might include measures such as gross sales, market share, gross margin, loyalty, customer satisfaction, brand equity/image, etc. The reporting might be by total market or by key market segments. The metrics might be those included within the 'Customer' section of a standard four-business-perspective balanced scorecard model. The discussion should also lead to possible gaps in the current measures being identified. For example, in one of the pilot studies, a balanced scorecard reported at board level simply contained the monthly spend on advertising against budget, but no outcomes of this expenditure

FIGURE 5.5   Marketing Value Metrics model process

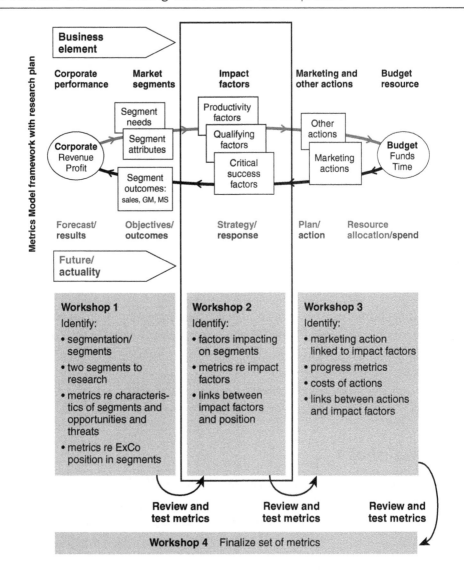

– either as forecasts or as outcomes – were included. As the model is designed to help meet medium-term targets, the corporate-level goals for the current year and each of the measures over the following three years need to be identified. At this stage in the process, the key objective is simply to list the current metrics and the targets set for them over this three-year period. This list needs to be revisited at the end of the process to see if any other metrics should be recommended at board level, and to ascertain whether the application of the model has identified links between the actions proposed and the corporate measures (the black arrows in the model).

5.3.1.2 Market segment metrics

In Chapter 6, we will discuss in more detail how markets can be divided into a number of key, differentiated segments, to enable the organization to focus its resources more effectively. However, to apply the model to all segments in one go would be overly complex. Therefore organizations applying the model are advised to start by focusing on two segments in the initial application in order to gain a detailed, and manageable, understanding of the overall process, and then repeat it for remaining segments over time. In most situations, organizations don't try to cover an entire market. The objective of segmentation is to identify those segments likely to be most attractive when consumer needs/profiles are matched to the capabilities and goals of the organization. This means that once an organization has analysed the market and divided it into segments, using the methodology described in Chapter 6, a few key segments will be the focus of future attention, perhaps at the expense of others that the organization decides are no longer of prime interest. So the second objective of the first workshop is to focus on two market segments and identify the metrics that are critical, firstly, to tracking the segment in the market over time and, secondly, to measuring the performance of the organization against the goals set for each segment. It is recommended that the selected segments for the first application of the model are those likely to be of most value to the future success of the organization. Selected initial segments could be of three types:

- ones that are currently delivering a high level of value, and forecast to continue to do so;
- one that is identified as currently delivering poor returns but is considered as offering high future potential;
- one that the organization considers has potential but an appropriate strategy to deliver value has yet to be identified.

The factors covered in the first workshop are described in detail in Chapter 6.

5.3.2 Workshop 2

Once the segments have been identified and a full analysis of the two selected segments has been undertaken, the next step is to ensure that the strategies for achieving the goals defined in the marketing plan are appropriate, and that the key metrics necessary to track performance towards achieving these goals have been identified. The focus in the second workshop is on how to use an impact factor analysis to help develop effective strategies for each segment, and identify the metrics necessary to track performance of the strategy. This process is described in detail in Chapter 7.

5.3.3 Workshop 3

Once the strategy for each segment has been confirmed, and the necessary metric set identified using the impact factor analysis framework described in Chapter 6, the next steps, covered in the third workshop, are:

- Identify the actions necessary to deliver the strategy. Some of these actions might be under the control of marketing (eg developing and implementing a specific direct marketing campaign), but others may be within the responsibilities of other departments (eg improving customer satisfaction either through changes in the logistics chain or through revised call centre goals).

- Agree the budgets necessary to fund the agreed actions.

- Estimate the likely impact of these actions, in financial terms, and identify those actions that are forecast to give a disproportionately high return on investment – that is, those with a high 'gearing'.

- Identify and agree the appropriate metrics to track the actions, budget funding and impact in achieving goals.

These processes are described in Chapter 8.

5.3.4 Workshop 4

The objective of the final workshop is to finalize the list of metrics and develop an outline plan for implementing the agreed measurement strategy, for example who will be exposed to different metrics, who will be responsible for collecting the data and producing the metrics, and who will be responsible for corrective action if a metric indicates that performance is below target.

This is all discussed in detail in Chapter 9.

5.4 The workshop team

As described in section 5.3, the implementation of the model process within the workshops is through a team of appropriate individuals drawn from relevant functions across the organization. Therefore identifying the key members of this team, and deciding whether or not to have an independent facilitator or to appoint one of the team to lead the discussions, is vitally important to the success of the process. Success is not achieved merely in terms of developing a set of metrics; it is also about agreeing the implementation, which in turn relies on the organization having bought into the process and seeing the value to be gained, particularly important at board level.

Experience gained in the pilot applications suggests that, for the workshops to be effective, this team needs to be kept small – but it is vital that its members are individuals who play key roles in the marketing, financial and business processes within the organization. It is also important that the members are sufficiently empowered by senior management to develop a strategy that stands a fair chance of being implemented. For example, in one of the pilot studies the team presented their recommended strategy to the main board; in another the sponsor reported to the board and was a key, and influential, member of the senior management team.

The workshop team should comprise no more than six to eight members. Based on the pilots, suggested key team members are:

- market research manager;
- corporate planning manager;
- corporate finance manager;
- customer database manager;
- market planning manager;
- finance manager (with responsibility for marketing);
- marketing communications/advertising manager;
- senior marketing manager (to act as champion of the process);
- customer service (or operations) manager;
- brand, product or customer segment manager.

In some companies, a logistics specialist as a key team member might also be appropriate.

Good facilitation will be essential to success. This means that all participants are adequately briefed at the outset; the workshops are run objectively; goals are clearly defined; discussions remain focused on the themes and objectives described for each workshop, all members are treated as equal participants; evidence provided by members is discussed and approved by the whole team; opinions are challenged; the principles of effective brainstorming are adhered to; the conclusions from each stage are clearly summarized; and actions/tasks are clearly identified at the end of each workshop and allocated to the appropriate members of the team.

As will be seen in the subsequent chapters, in addition to developing a marketing metrics strategy appropriate for the organization a further key role of the team is to identify responsibility within the strategy for:

- collecting the data to ensure the metrics can be defined;
- undertaking the measures;
- taking action if the metrics show that performance is not on target.

Figure 5.5 identifies that team members are also responsible for subsequently reviewing and, if possible, testing the agreed metrics identified in each workshop. This includes identifying whether the data necessary to develop the agreed metrics are currently available and, if not, assessing whether this might be possible in the future.

The subsequent chapters (Chapters 6–9) covering the component parts of the model include templates that can be used in undertaking the programme of workshops.

References

Binet, L and Field, L (2007) *Marketing in the Era of Accountability*, WARC/IPA, London

McDonald, M H B (2012) *Market Segmentation: How to do it, how to profit from it*, 4th edn, Wiley, Chichester

Segmentation – the basic building block for markets

06

Summary

This chapter is crucial as segments are the basic building blocks of any marketing accountability model, as shown in Chapter 5. The chapter starts with an introduction to 'market segmentation'. It is followed by a section on whom we sell to, including an explanation of the difference between consumers and customers, and a discussion of why market share is important and why the term 'market' must be carefully defined.

The market segmentation process is outlined. The steps are:

- market definition;
- market mapping;
- listing who buys;
- combining this into lists of who buys what;
- listing why these micro-segments buy what they buy;
- combining the micro-segments into larger segments by means of cluster analysis.

Methodologies are outlined and explained throughout. Three segmentation case studies are provided to illustrate how correct market segmentation turned around loss-making situations. The chapter concludes by relating segments to the metrics model.

6.1 Introduction

This chapter deals with the very heart of successful marketing – market segmentation. No accountability system will be effective unless it is measuring metrics by
segment as a precursor to higher levels of accountability aggregation. It can be seen
from Figure 6.1 that market segments are the central holding point for lower-level

FIGURE 6.1 Information use in marketing

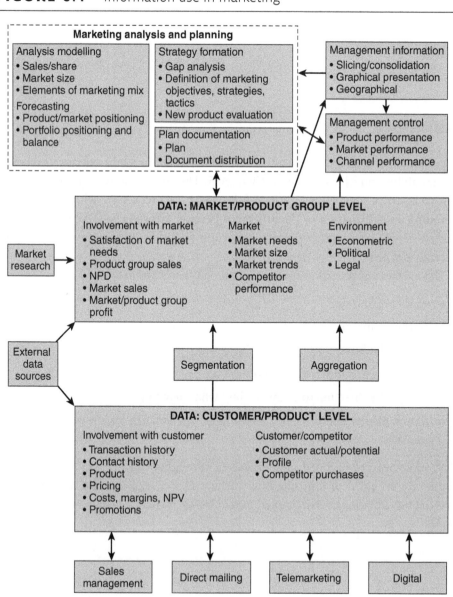

data, which in turn feed into higher-level processes such as strategic marketing planning. Hence, market segmentation is crucial to any understanding of systems for marketing accountability.

The very term 'market segmentation' conjures up images of a whole being divided into smaller parts (segments). Yet market segmentation has become a confusing metaphor, badly explained and poorly implemented. Indeed, a *Harvard Business Review* article (Christensen, Cook and Hall, 2005) reviews 30,000 failed product launches in the United States and puts their failure down principally to inadequate market segmentation.

The construction industry, until the 2008 global recession, was booming in many countries in the world. During the boom times, we were discussing a superb 185 per cent increase in profit growth with a director of a construction firm but he was not sure how much came from market growth, price increases, share improvement or improved productivity. When pushed, he answered that 'we had a mild winter'. There is a grossly mistaken view that, in high-growth markets, marketing and market strategy somehow doesn't matter. But even a cursory glance at the fortunes of US and European companies over the past 20 years reveals how the mightiest firms almost collapse from a position of incredible growth; the market moves or the growth stops.

The defining characteristic of professional marketing strategy has always been *market segmentation*. Mediocre offers are only going to reap mediocre results. Going a stage further, what sort of company would make a commodity out of bread, fertilizer, glass, paper, chlorine, potatoes or mobile phones? Well, just observe consumers buying potatoes in Marks and Spencer in the UK at a premium price. Then ask whether anyone can tell the difference between Castrol GTX, Alfa Laval Steel, SKF bearings, Apple and its their competitors. Yet these great companies are able to charge premium prices and have massive global market shares.

Practitioners and thought leaders concur over the elements of world-class marketing:

1 a profound understanding of the marketplace;

2 proper market segmentation;

3 powerful differentiation, positioning and branding;

4 integrated marketing strategies.

The order is significant. Even now, many companies are trying to manage their brands without really understanding their market, how it is segmented, or where they are positioned.

Excellent strategic marketing is essential for high-performance outcomes (Table 6.1).

TABLE 6.1   Characteristics of successful marketing strategies

Excellent strategies	Weak strategies
Target needs-based segments	Target product categories
Make a specific offer to each segment	Make similar offers to all segments
Leverage their strengths and minimize their weaknesses	Have little understanding of their strengths and weaknesses
Anticipate the future	Plan using historical data

6.2 Markets we sell to

Companies frequently confuse target markets with products – pensions or desktop computers, for example – and this, coupled with a lack of knowledge about the sources of differential advantage against each segment, signals trouble.

Many companies pride themselves on their market segmentation even though these so-called 'segments' are in fact *sectors*, which is a common misconception. A segment is a group of customers with the same or similar needs and that there are many different purchase combinations within and across sectors.

But the gravest mistake of all is *a priori* segmentation. Most books incorrectly state that there are several bases for segmentation, such as socio-economics, demographics, geo-demographics and the like. But this misses the point. For example, Boy George and the Archbishop of Canterbury are both A-listers, but they don't behave the same! Nor do all 18- to 24-year-old women (demographics) behave the same! Nor does everyone in our street (geo-demographics) behave the same!

All goods and services are made, distributed and used, and the purchase combinations that result make up an *actual* market, so the task is to understand market structure, how the market works and what these different purchase combinations (segments) are.

Firstly, let us examine the factors that cause markets to break into smaller groups (see Figure 6.2).

Many years ago, a US sociologist, Everett Rogers (1976) generated profound observations about how innovation diffuses through a population. His work is still widely cited and we are all familiar with terms such as the early adopter and laggard that he coined. Essentially, for Rogers, adapting new ideas is a social phenomenon and people adapt as a function of the number of people that adapt before them. Some are predisposed to being first and willing to suffer all the consequences of the

FIGURE 6.2 Non-cumulative diffusion pattern

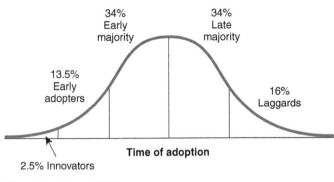

34%
Early
majority

34%
Late
majority

13.5%
Early
adopters

16%
Laggards

Time of adoption

2.5% Innovators

Adapted from Rogers (1976)

solutions not being fully worked out: these are innovators. Next are early adopters, followed by the early majority, then late majority and finally the last 16 per cent of the population are considered laggards. The progress through the adaption curve approximates an S shape with which most readers are familiar.

Although this is not the purpose of this chapter, it is useful to note, before we leave Rogers's diffusion of innovation curve, that when launching a new product or service it is advantageous to know who the opinion leaders are in a market, as these people should be targeted first by the sales force and by other promotional media, as they will be the most likely to respond. For example, certain doctors will be more open-minded about new drugs, whereas other doctors will not risk prescribing a new drug until it has been on the market for a number of years.

The diffusion of innovation curve also explains the phenomenon known as the product life cycle, and why, after the 50 per cent point on the diffusion of innovation curve is reached, the market continues to grow but the rate of growth begins to decline until maturity is reached (see Figure 6.3).

FIGURE 6.3 Market life cycles and managerial phases

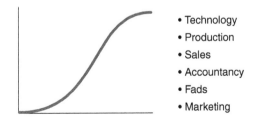

- Technology
- Production
- Sales
- Accountancy
- Fads
- Marketing

At the beginning of any market, *technology* tends to be the driving business force, largely because new products tend to be at the cutting edge. As the new technology begins to take hold, as explained in the earlier references to the research of Everett Rogers, *production* tends to be very important, because at this stage it is not unusual for demand to be greater than supply. However, as the market grows and new entrants begin to introduce competitive products, *sales* as a function becomes increasingly important, as the new competition entails a growing consumer choice. A problem frequently occurs at the next stage of the market life cycle, as there is now more supply than demand, so frequently organizations attempt to cut costs, so *accountancy* tends to come to the fore. Finally, however, all organizations come to the same conclusion, which is that they need to understand their consumers and customers better in order to meet their needs, and this of course is where market segmentation, the subject of this chapter, becomes crucial.

All this has been explained in order to introduce the key concept of market segmentation and why it happens. Clearly, in the early days, markets will tend to be homogeneous. But, as demand grows rapidly with the entry of the early majority, it is common for new entrants to offer variations on the early models, as just explained, and consumers now have a choice. In order to explain this more clearly, let us illustrate the approximate shape of markets. If we were to plot the car market in terms of speed and price (see Figure 6.4), we would see very small, inexpensive cars in the bottom left-hand corner. In the top right, we would see very fast, expensive cars. Most cars, however, would cluster in the middle, what we might call 'the Mr and Mrs Average Market'.

Similarly, the lawnmower market would look very similar (see Figure 6.5). With lawn size on the vertical axis and price on the horizontal axis, at the bottom left

FIGURE 6.4   The natural shape of markets – cars

FIGURE 6.5 The natural shape of markets – lawnmowers

would be small, inexpensive, hand-pushed mowers, with expensive sit-on machines for large estates in the right-hand corner. That leaves the mass of the market with average-sized lawns and average-sized lawnmowers, which is where the mass market is.

We can now redraw this to represent the shape of any market, particularly at the early growth stage (the shape on the left in Figure 6.6). But when rapid growth begins, new entrants join the market and offer variations on standard products in order to attract sales, and it is at this stage that markets begin to break into smaller groups, while still growing overall (this is represented by the shape in the middle).

FIGURE 6.6 The shape of markets from birth to maturity

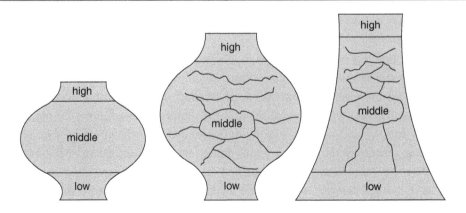

Eventually, when markets mature and there is more supply than demand, any market growth tends to come in the lower price end of the market, while the top end of the market tends to be immune (this is represented by the shape on the right). It is usually the middle market that suffers at this stage, with many competitors vying with each other on price. This, however, is the whole point of market segmentation, for competing only on price is to assume that this is the main requirement of customers, whereas the truth is that this is rarely the case. It is just that a general lack of understanding about market segmentation on the part of suppliers about the real needs of customers in mature markets forces them to trade on price, so encouraging the market to become a commodity market.

The starting point in market segmentation is correct market definition, which is crucial for measuring market size, growth and share, identifying relevant competitors and formulating strategies to deliver differential advantage. Few companies give sufficient attention to correct market definition, and few can draw an accurate market map and therefore have little chance of doing anything remotely resembling correct market segmentation at the key influence points or junctions on the map.

At each if these junctions, segmentation is not only possible but crucial. (McDonald and Dunbar, 2012)

The process will be expanded on later in this chapter, but, before this, let us clarify the terminology about customers and consumers.

6.2.1 *The difference between customers and consumers*

Let us start with the difference between customers and consumers. The term 'consumer' is interpreted by most to mean the final consumer, who is not necessarily the customer. Take the example of parents who are buying breakfast cereals. The chances are that they are intermediate customers, acting as agents on behalf of the eventual consumers (their family) and, in order to market cereals effectively, it is clearly necessary to understand what the end-consumer wants, as well as what the parents want.

It is always necessary to be aware of the needs of eventual consumers down the buying chain.

Consider the case of the industrial purchasing officer buying raw materials such as wool tops for conversion into semi-finished cloths, which are then sold to other companies for incorporation into the final product, say a suit, or a dress, for sale in consumer markets. Here, we can see that the requirements of those various intermediaries and the end-user are eventually translated into the specifications of the purchasing officer to the raw materials manufacturer. Consequently, the market needs that this manufacturing company is attempting to satisfy must in the last analysis be defined in terms of the requirements of the ultimate users – the consumer – even though the direct customer is quite clearly the purchasing officer.

Given that we can appreciate the distinction between customers and consumers and the need constantly to be alert to any changes in the ultimate consumption patterns of the products to which our own contributes, the next question to be faced is: who are our customers?

Direct customers are those people or organizations that actually buy direct from us. They could, therefore, be distributors, retailers and the like. However, there is a tendency for organizations to confine their interest, hence their marketing, to those who actually place orders. This can be a major mistake, as can be seen from the following example.

A fertilizer company that had grown and prospered during the 1970s and 1980s, because of the superior nature of its products, reached its farmer consumers via merchants (wholesalers). However, as other companies copied the technology, the merchants began to stock competitive products and drove prices and margins down. Had the fertilizer company paid more attention to the needs of its different farmer groups and developed products especially for them, based on farmer segmentation, it would have continued to create demand pull-through differentiation.

The segmentation study revealed that there were seven distinct types of farmer, each with a different set of needs. See Figure 6.7. Firstly, there was a segment we called Arthur (the person at the top of the figure), a television character known for his deals. He bought on price alone but represented only 10 per cent of the market, not the 100 per cent put about by everyone in the industry, especially the sales force. Another type of farmer we called Oliver (the figure in the bottom right of the figure). Oliver would drive around his fields on his tractor with an aerial linked to a satellite and an on-board computer. He did this in order to analyse the soil type and would then mix P, N and K, which are the principal ingredients of the fertilizer, solely to get the maximum yield out of his farm. In other words, Oliver was a scientific farmer, but the supply industry believed he was buying on price because he bought his own ingredients as cheaply as possible. He did this, however, only because none of the suppliers bothered to understand his needs. Another type of farmer we called David (the figure in the bottom left of the figure). David was a show-off farmer and liked his crops to look nice and healthy. He also liked his cows to have nice, healthy skins. Clearly, if a sales representative had talked in a technical way to David, he would quickly switch off. Equally, talking about the appearance of crops and livestock would have switched Oliver off, but this is the whole point. Every single supplier in the industry totally ignored the real needs of these farmers, and the only thing anyone ever talked about was price. The result was a market driven by price discounts, accompanied by substantial losses to the suppliers. ICI, as it was then, armed with this new-found information, launched new products and new promotional approaches aimed at these different farmer types, and got immediate results, becoming the only profitable fertilizer company in the country.

FIGURE 6.7   Personalizing segments

Let us now return to market dynamics and what happens to markets at the rapid growth stage. At this stage, new entrants come into the market, attracted by the high sales and high profits enjoyed by the industry. Let us illustrate this with another example.

In the early 1970s, a photocopier company had an 80 per cent market share and massive profit margins. This is represented by the big circle in the middle of Figure 6.8. When a Japanese newcomer entered the market with small photocopiers, the giant ignored it. The Japanese product grew in popularity, however, forcing the giant to reduce its prices. Within three years, the giant's share was down to 10 per cent, and the battle was lost. It had failed to recognize that the market was segmented and tried to compete in all segments with its main product, a mistake made by hundreds of erstwhile market leaders. The main point about this example is that companies should not attempt to compete in all segments with the same product, but should recognize that different segments or need groups develop as the market grows, and that they should develop appropriate products and services, and position and brand them accordingly.

Let us summarize all of this by showing a product life cycle representation with some generalizations about how marketing strategies change over time. Figure 6.9

FIGURE 6.8   Perceptual map of the photocopier market

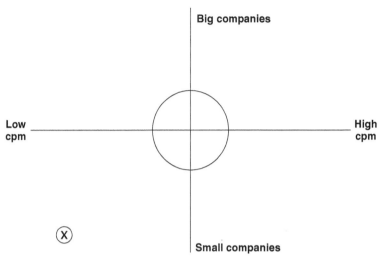

Note: cpm = copies per month

FIGURE 6.9   The product/market life cycle and market characteristics

Key characteristics	Unique	Product differentiation	Service differentiation	'Commodity'
Marketing message	Explain	Competitive	Brand values	Corporate
Sales	Pioneering	Relative benefits Distribution Support	Relationship based	Availability based
Distribution	Direct selling	Exclusive distribution	Mass distribution	80 : 20
Price	Very high	High	Medium	Low (consumer controlled)
Competitive intensity	None	Few	Many	Fewer, bigger international
Costs	Very high	Medium	Medium/low	Very low
Profit	Medium/high	High	Medium/high	Medium/low
Management style	Visionary	Strategic	Operational	Cost management

FIGURE 6.10   A simplified market map

illustrates four major changes that occur over the life cycle. At the top of the far right-hand column, at maturity, most offers end up as commodities. However, this is contestable and good strategic marketing can resegment markets to renew growth as in the fertilizer example. There are other options, of course, including the option to get out of mature markets. Another is to move the goal posts, as it were, somewhat in the manner of First Direct, Direct Line, Dell, Virgin, Amazon.com and countless others. The strategy we want to concentrate on here, however, is market segmentation, which in our view should be the very first consideration as markets begin to mature.

An excellent example of good practice is Procter & Gamble in the United States supplying Wal-Mart, the giant food retailer. As can be seen from the simple diagram in Figure 6.10, P&G create demand pull (hence high turnover and high margins) by paying detailed attention to the needs of consumers. But they also pay detailed attention to the needs of their direct customer, Wal-Mart. Wal-Mart is able to operate on very low margins because, as the bar code goes across the till, this is when P&G invoice Wal-Mart, produce another and activate the distribution chain, all of this being done by means of integrated processes. This way, they have reduced Wal-Mart's costs by hundreds of millions of dollars.

Closely related to the question of the difference between customers and consumers is the question of what the term 'market share' means.

6.2.2 Market share

Most business people already understand that there is a direct relationship between relatively high share of any market and high returns on investment, as shown in Figure 6.11.

Clearly, however, since BMW are not in the same market as Ford, for example, it is important to be most careful about how 'market' is defined. Correct market definition is crucial for: measuring market share and market growth; the specification of target customers; recognition of relevant competitors; and, most importantly of all, the formulation of marketing strategy, for it is this, above all else, that delivers differential advantage.

FIGURE 6.11   The relationship between market share and return on investment

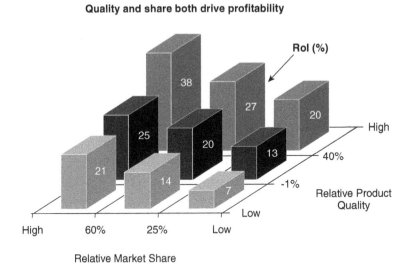

Quality and share both drive profitability

Source: Profit Impact of Market Strategy (PIMS), Strategic Planning Institute **www.pimsonline.com**

The general rule for 'market' definition is that it should be described in terms of a customer need in a way that covers the aggregation of all the products or services that customers regard as being capable of satisfying the same need. For example, we would regard the in-company caterer as only one option when it came to satisfying lunchtime hunger. This particular need could also be satisfied at external restaurants, public houses, fast food specialists and sandwich bars. The emphasis in the definition, therefore, is clearly on the word 'need'.

To summarize, correct market definition is crucial for the purpose of:

● share measurement;
● growth measurement;
● the specification of target customers;
● the recognition of relevant competitors;
● the formulation of marketing objectives and strategies.

6.2.3 *Market segmentation*

We can now begin to concentrate on a methodology for making market segmentation a reality, market segmentation being the means by which any company seeks to gain a differential advantage over its competitors.

Markets usually fall into natural groups, or segments, which contain customers who exhibit a similar level of interest in the same broad requirements. These segments form separate markets in themselves and can often be of considerable size. Taken to its extreme, each individual consumer is a unique market segment, for all people are different in their requirements. While customer relationship management (CRM) systems have made it possible to engage in one-to-one relationships, this is not viable in all organizations. Most firms still produce offers that appeal to groups of customers who share approximately the same needs for reasons of scale, complexity and indeed, customer preference.

There are certain universally accepted criteria concerning what constitutes a viable market segment (McDonald and Dunbar, 2012): segments should be of an adequate size to provide the company with the desired return for its effort; and members of each segment should have a high degree of similarity in their requirements, yet be distinct from the rest of the market. Criteria for describing segments must enable the company to communicate effectively with them.

While many of these criteria are obvious when we consider them, in practice market segmentation is one of the most difficult of marketing concepts to turn into a reality. Yet we must succeed; otherwise we become just another company selling what are called 'me too' products. In other words, what we offer the potential customer is very much the same as what any other company offers and, in such circumstances, it is likely to be the lowest-priced article that is bought. This can be ruinous to our profits, unless we happen to have lower costs, hence higher margins, than our competitors.

There are basically three stages to market segmentation, all of which have to be completed:

- The first establishes the scope of the project by specifying the geographic area to be covered and defining the market that is to be segmented, followed by taking a detailed look at the way this market operates and identifying where decisions are made about the competing products or services. Successful segmentation is based on a detailed understanding of decision makers and their requirements.

- The second is essentially a manifestation of the way customers actually behave in the marketplace and consists of answering the question 'Who is specifying what?'

- The third stage looks at the reasons behind the behaviour of customers in the marketplace, answers the question 'Why?' and then searches for market segments based on this analysis of needs.

The following sections provide an overview of the steps required to complete these three stages and are presented in a format for conducting a segmentation project using internal resources.

6.3 Stage 1 – defining the market

The first step in market segmentation establishes the scope of the segmentation project by specifying the geographic area covered by the project and by clearly understanding from a customer's perspective the market in which your products or services are competing with those of your competitors. Where necessary, the scope is modified to take into account the realistic capabilities of your organization.

A clear geographic boundary enables you to size the market, to identify the localities in which the dynamics of the market have to be understood and, once the segments have been identified, to develop the appropriate marketing objectives and strategies for those localities.

Keeping the project within the borders of a single country is a manageable starting point because the stage of market development, the available routes to market and the pattern of marketing activity will probably be the same throughout the country. Even this, however, may be too broad for some companies, simply because their geographic reach is limited by physical and/or economic considerations, or even because their appeal has a strong local sentiment attached to it.

For companies trading in numerous countries around the world, there is clearly an enormous attraction in finding a single global segmentation model that can be applied to every country. However, the experience of 'globalization' has highlighted for many of these companies that they have to 'act locally' in order to succeed in their market. This doesn't mean that every country is completely unique in respect of the segments found within it. For the international company, a useful guide to predetermining which countries can be included in a single segmentation project is to ensure that in each of these countries the stage of market development, the available routes to market and the pattern of marketing activity are the same, or at least very similar.

All that said, there are some truly global markets emerging due to the prevalence of certain internet platforms: Apple and Google have created global marketplaces for online applications, streaming video services (Netflix, Amazon) are rapidly becoming global standards, computer operator systems, digital SLR cameras, online services (Flickr, Facebook, Twitter, etc) are forcing us to rethink the global-local dynamic.

As a reminder, the general rule for market definition is that it should be described in a way that covers the aggregation of all the alternative products or services that customers regard as being capable of satisfying that same need.

Table 6.2 is an example from financial services, repeated from Chapter 2.

TABLE 6.2   Some market definitions (personal market)

Market	Need
Emergency cash ('rainy day')	Cash to cover an undesired and unexpected event (often the loss of/damage to property)
Future event planning	Schemes to protect and grow money that are for anticipated and unanticipated cash calling events (eg car replacement/ repairs, education, weddings, funerals, health care)
Asset purchase	Cash to buy assets they require (eg car purchase, house purchase, once-in-a-lifetime holiday)
Welfare contingency	The ability to maintain a desired standard of living (for self and/or dependants) in times of unplanned cessation of salary
Retirement income	The ability to maintain a desired standard of living (for self and/or dependants) once the salary cheques have ceased
Wealth care and building	The care and growth of assets (with various risk levels and liquidity levels)
Day-to-day money management	Ability to store and readily access cash for day-to-day requirements
Personal finance protection and security from motor vehicle incidents	Currently known as car insurance

6.3.1 *Market mapping*

A useful way of identifying where decisions are made about competing products and services and, therefore, those who then proceed to the next stages of segmentation is to start by drawing a market map. A market map defines the distribution and value added chain between final users and suppliers of the products or services included within the scope of your segmentation project. This should take into account the various buying mechanisms found in your market, including the part played by influencers. An example of a generic market map is given in Figure 6.12, repeated from Chapter 2.

It is useful to start your market map by plotting the various stages that occur along the distribution and value added chain between the final users and all the

FIGURE 6.12   Generic market map

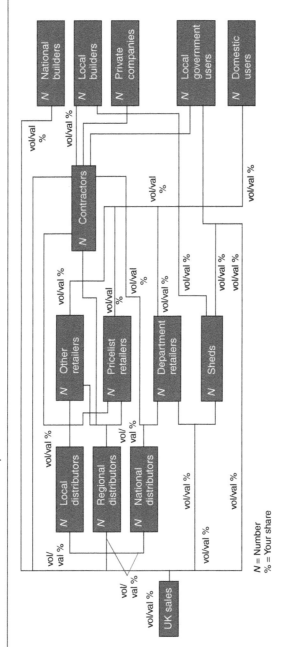

FIGURE 6.13 Market map listing the different junction types

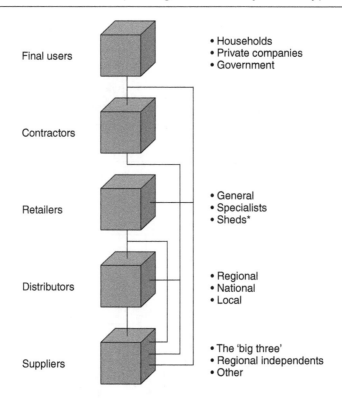

Final users
- Households
- Private companies
- Government

Contractors

Retailers
- General
- Specialists
- Sheds*

Distributors
- Regional
- National
- Local

Suppliers
- The 'big three'
- Regional independents
- Other

Note: * 'Sheds' is the name sometimes used to refer to hardware superstores.

suppliers of products or services competing with each other in the defined market. At the same time, indicate the particular routes to market the products are sourced through, as not all of them will necessarily involve all of these stages.

Note at each junction on your market map, if applicable, all the different types of companies/customers that are found there, as illustrated in Figure 6.13.

It is useful at this point to split the volume or value quantity dealt with by each junction between the junction types. This is shown in Figure 6.14. The easiest junction at which to start this stage of market mapping is at the final users' junction, noting at each junction with leverage the volume/value (or percentage of the total market) that is decided there. Estimate these figures if they are not known and note this as a requirement for any follow-up work generated by this first pass at segmenting your market. This is also illustrated in Figure 6.14, where we see a market in which 30 per cent of annual sales are decided at junctions other than the final user junction.

FIGURE 6.14   Market leverage points on a market map

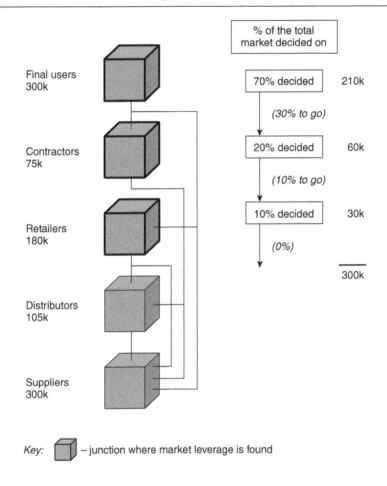

Key: ⬛ – junction where market leverage is found

So far, we have built a market map by tracking the distribution and value added chain found between final users and suppliers, and shown the various routes that are taken through the map to link the two together. We then quantified the map. This was followed by expanding the detail to show the different types of companies/ customers found at each junction on the map, and these were also quantified.

6.4 Stage 2 – who specifies what, where, when and how

In this step we are developing a representative sample of different decision makers that identifies the characteristics and properties of a purchase on which decisions are made along with the customer attributes that will be used to describe the decision makers. Each constituent of this sample is called a micro-segment.

The uniqueness of a micro-segment is that, when determining which of the alternative offers is to be bought, the decision makers it represents demonstrate a similar level of interest in a specific set of features, with the features being the characteristics and properties of what is bought, where it is bought, when it is bought and how it is bought as appropriate to the micro-segment. To this are added the descriptors that describe who the micro-segment represents, along with an estimate of the volume or value they account for in the defined market.

The principle behind this step is that, by observing the purchase behaviour of decision makers and understanding the key constituents of this behaviour, we have a platform for developing a detailed understanding of their motivations. It is, therefore, a critical link with the next step of the segmentation process, which looks at why decision makers select the particular products and services they specify. This, in turn, becomes the basis on which the segments are formed.

The process chart in Figure 6.15 shows a number of steps that will now be described. From this, you will see that the process begins with market mapping, which corresponds to a deep understanding of the market. This has already been discussed above.

FIGURE 6.15   The market segmentation process

Stage 1: Your market and how it operates

> **Step 1 – Market mapping**
> Structure and decision makers

Stage 2: Customers and transactions

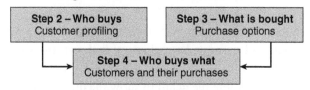

> **Step 2 – Who buys**
> Customer profiling

> **Step 3 – What is bought**
> Purchase options

> **Step 4 – Who buys what**
> Customers and their purchases

Stage 3: Segmenting the market

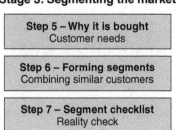

> **Step 5 – Why it is bought**
> Customer needs

> **Step 6 – Forming segments**
> Combining similar customers

> **Step 7 – Segment checklist**
> Reality check

FIGURE 6.16   Micro-segments

Micro-segment	1	2	3	4	5	6	7	8	9	10
What is bought										
Where										
When										
How										
Who										
Why (benefits sought)										

We can now turn to the process again, and move to steps 2, 3, 4 and 5, although it must be pointed out that segmentation can and should be carried out at all major junctions on the market map, not just at the final user junction.

Essentially, these time-consuming steps involve listing all purchase combinations that take place in the market, including different applications for the product or service (see Figure 6.16), principal forms such as size, colour, branded, unbranded, etc, the principal channels used, when (such as once a year, weekly) and how (such as cash or credit). Next it's important to describe who behaves in each particular way, using relevant descriptors such as demographics. For industrial purchases this might be standard industrial classifications, size of firm, whereas for consumer purchases this might be socio-economic groups, such as A, B, C1, C2, D and E, or stage in the life cycle, or age, sex, geography, lifestyles or psychographics. Finally, and most difficult of all, each purchase combination has to have a brief explanation of the reason for this particular type of behaviour. In other words, we need to list the benefits sought, and it is often at this stage that an organization needs to pause and either commission market research or refer to its extant database of previous market research studies. Although in Figure 6.16 there are only 10 micro-segments, it is normal in most markets for companies to identify 30 or so micro-segments. Remember, these micro-segments are actual purchase combinations that take place in a market.

To summarize so far, it is clear that no market is totally homogeneous (see Figure 6.17). The reality is that actual markets consist of a large number of different purchase combinations (see Figure 6.18). However, as it is impracticable to deal with

FIGURE 6.17   An undifferentiated market, but one with many different purchase combinations

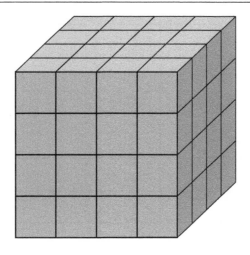

FIGURE 6.18   Different needs in a market

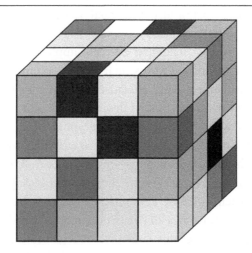

more than between 7 and 10 market segments, a process has to be found to bring together or cluster all those micro-segments that share similar or approximately similar needs (see Figure 6.19).

Once the basic work has been done in describing micro-segments, that is steps 2, 3, 4 and 5, cluster analysis will generate a smaller number of segments. The final step consists of checking whether the resulting segments are big enough to justify separate treatment, whether they are indeed sufficiently different from other segments,

FIGURE 6.19   Segments in a market

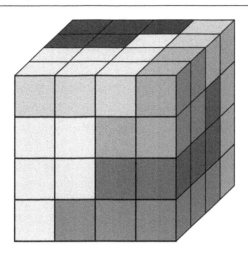

and whether they have been described sufficiently well to enable the customers in them to be reached by means of the organization's communication methods; the company then has to be prepared to make the necessary changes to meet the needs of the identified segments.

Before the process of market segmentation can be summarized, it will by now be clear that market segmentation is fundamental to corporate strategy. It is also clear that, since market segmentation affects every single corporate activity, it should not be just an exercise that takes place within the marketing department, but has to involve other functions. Finally, the most senior levels of management must lead this initiative if their organization is to be truly market or customer need driven.

Table 6.3 is a summary of what we have discussed so far. Once market segmentation has been carried out, positioning products and services to meet the different needs of the different segments is comparatively straightforward, but not easy. The most intellectually challenging task is segmenting markets. It is also vital to focus on serving the needs of the identified segments, while it is dangerous to straddle different segments with the same offer. The photocopier example was only one example of thousands of well-known companies that suffered from this mistake as markets began to break into segments. The computer industry during the 1980s and 1990s was also replete with examples of this mistake.

The process of market segmentation itself consists of five steps: One, understand how your market works. This involves defining the market and drawing a market map. Two, list what is bought, including where, when, how, and the different applications of the product or service. Three, list who buys, using descriptors such as demographics and psychographics. Four, list why they buy, especially the benefits sought. Five, search for groups with similar needs. These will be the final market segments.

TABLE 6.3   Understand market segmentation

- Not all customers in a broadly defined market have the same needs.
- Positioning is easy. Market segmentation is difficult. Positioning problems stem from poor segmentation.
- Select a segment and serve it. Do not straddle segments and sit between them.
  1 Define the market to be segmented and size it (market scope).
  2 Determine how the market works and identify who makes the decisions (market mapping).
  3 Develop a representative sample of decision makers based on differences they see as key (including what, where, when and how); note who they are (demographics) and size them.
  4 Understand their real needs (why they buy, the benefits sought).
  5 Search for groups with similar needs.

Market structure and market segmentation are the heart and soul of marketing. Unless an organization spends time on it, driven from the board downwards, it is virtually impossible for it to be market driven, and in any organization that isn't market driven the marketing function will be ineffective or, at best, will spend its time trying to promote and sell products or services that are inappropriate for the market. Figure 6.20 describes in more detail each of the important steps in the market segmentation process:

- share measurement;
- growth measurement;
- the specification of target customers;
- the recognition of relevant competitors;
- the formulation of marketing objectives and strategies.

To summarize, the objectives of market segmentation are:

- to help determine marketing direction through the analysis and understanding of trends and buyer behaviour;
- to help determine realistic and obtainable marketing and sales objectives;
- to help improve decision making by forcing managers to consider in depth the options ahead.

FIGURE 6.20 The market segmentation process – summary

Market mapping

1. Market definition – 'A customer need that can be satisfied by the products or services seen as alternatives'. It is based around what the customers perceive as distinct activities or needs they have, which different customers could be satisfying by using alternative products or services.

2. The distribution and value added chain that exists for the defined market.

3. The decision makers in that market and the amount of product or service they are responsible for in their decision making.

Who buys

1. Recording information about the decision makers in terms of who they are – customer profiling, demographics, geographics, etc.

2. Testing a current segmentation hypothesis to see if it stacks up – preliminary segments.

What is bought

1. Listing the features customers look for in their purchase – what, where, when and how.

2. Focusing in on those features customers use to select between the alternative offers available – key discriminating features (KDFs).

Who buys what

1. Building a customer 'model' of the market – based on either the different combinations of KDFs customers are known to put together, or derived from the random sample in a research project. Can be constructed by preliminary segment. Each customer in the model (sample) is called a micro-segment.

2. Each micro-segment is profiled using information from the data listed in 'Who buys'.

3. Each micro-segment is sized to reflect the value or volume they represent in the market.

Why

1. As customers only seek out features regarded as key because of the benefit(s) these features are seen to offer them, the benefits delivered by each KDF should be listed. For some customers it is only by combining certain KDFs that they attain the benefit(s) they seek – benefits should also be looked at from this perspective. These benefits are critical purchase influences (CPIs).

2. For thoroughness, benefits can be looked at from the perspective of each preliminary segment.

3. Once the CPIs for the market have been developed their relative importance to each micro-segment is addressed (by distributing 100 points between the CPIs).

Forming segments

1. By attributing a 'score' to all the CPIs for each micro-segment, the similarity between micro-segments can be determined.

2. Micro-segments with similar requirements are brought together to form clusters.

3. Clusters are sized by adding the volumes or values represented by each micro-segment.

Segment checklist

1. Is each cluster big enough to justify a distinct marketing strategy?

2. Is the offer required by each cluster sufficiently different?

3. Is it clear which customers appear in each cluster?
   If all 'yes', clusters = segments.

4. Will the company change and adopt a segment focus?

6.5 Case study

Summary

This case study describes the use of market segmentation to assist in the development of a service product. Customer requirements were captured via qualitative research. The segmentation was completed through the use of quantitative research. The result was a set of segments that enabled the development of a new approach to delivering service while improving customer satisfaction. GlobalTech is the fictitious name of a real company marketing high-tech and service products globally. Customers are counted in hundreds of thousands. The markets are mainly business-to-business, with a very few large customers buying thousands of items. Service is a major revenue stream measured in billions of dollars. The lessons learnt could be of interest to any organization having to care for a large number of customers.

Background

A failed segmentation

An internal GlobalTech team tried to complete a marketing audit early in 2000. This included market definition, market segmentation and quantification. The product divisions conducted their audits separately. They used mainly brainstorming techniques to define their markets and produce the data required.

Lesson 1

Markets transcend your internally defined product divisions. Therefore it is best to understand the markets and monitor your overall performance in those markets. To reshape market information to meet the needs of internal reporting will lead to misinformation.

On completion, the results were compared across the divisions. It rapidly became apparent that each division addressed almost all the markets. However, the market definitions they produced were different, with significant bias towards just the products they offered. Similarly, the segments each division identified were in conflict with the outputs from the other divisions. On reflection, it was agreed that the results were unreliable. They could not be used to help shape future strategies or marketing investments.

GlobalTech was now in the uncomfortable situation of being in a market information vacuum. Any confidence it had had in its understanding of the market had been destroyed. Consequently, the decision was taken that all future market analysis and understanding tasks would be supported by appropriate investments in market research.

First market segmentation

The following year the segmentation was redone, supported by extensive qualitative and quantitative market research. The objective was to understand and group into segments the product buyers in the overall market.

The qualitative study produced a very clear picture and definition of the markets addressed by GlobalTech. It also provided the customers' view of the benefits they sought from the products and the differences in their attitudes towards their suppliers. The questionnaire for the quantitative study was based on the results of the qualitative study. The result was seven clearly defined product buyer segments.

This enhanced understanding of the market assisted with hardware and software product marketing but did not address service products or customer satisfaction and loyalty issues.

The internal need

At the dawn of the 21st century, the market life cycle had matured. All but the more sophisticated products were perceived as commodities. Consequently, the opportunities for effective product differentiation had diminished. GlobalTech, in common with its competitors, was finding that customers were becoming increasingly disloyal.

For many years, product churns and upgrades from existing customers had accounted for some 70 per cent of GlobalTech's product revenues. Service and exhaust revenues almost equalled total product revenues. (Exhaust revenues are those revenues that follow on, almost automatically, from an initial product sale. These would normally include service plus training, consumables, supplies and add-ons, etc.) Service was perceived to be a key influencer of loyalty, but the costs of delivering service were becoming unacceptable to customers. Concurrently, service pricing was coming under increasing competitive pressures.

The challenge was to increase loyalty while achieving a step function improvement in margins. Thus it was decided to invest in a better understanding of the service market as an enabler to delivering cost-effective differentiation and loyalty. This case study covers the project from inception to implementation.

The segmentation project

Buy-in

The GlobalTech main board director responsible for customer service sponsored the project. This was a critical prerequisite, as the outcome would have a significant impact on the organization, its processes and behaviours.

Similarly, the project team included key members of service, marketing and finance to ensure buy-in. However, at that time it was deemed inappropriate to include representatives from all but two of the countries, owing to travel implications, cost, and resource impacts. In retrospect, this was not a good decision.

Lesson 2

Try to anticipate the scale of the organizational change that may result from a major segmentation project. Then ensure that the buy-in planned from the start of the project embraces all those who will have a say in the final implementation.

Business objectives

The project team agreed the overall business objectives as:

- to develop strategies for profitable increase in market share and sustainable competitive advantage in the service markets for GlobalTech's products;

- to identify opportunities for new service products and for improving customer satisfaction within the context of a robust customer needs segmentation that can be readily applied in the marketplace;

- to identify the key drivers of loyalty so that GlobalTech may take actions to increase customer loyalty significantly;

- to provide the information required to help develop a new and innovative set of service products designed and tailored to meet differing customer requirements while significantly reducing internal business process costs.

Results from the qualitative study

The output from the qualitative study was a 93-page report documenting the results, in line with the desired research objectives. Some of the more surprising aspects were supported by verbatims. A key output was the polarization of very different attitudes towards service requirements that some buyers had in comparison with others. For example:

- Some wanted a response within a few hours, whereas many others would be equally happy with the next day.

- Some wanted their staff thoroughly trained to take remedial actions supported by a specialist on the phone, while others did not want to know and would just wait for the service provider to fix the problem.

- Some wanted regular proactive communications and being kept up to date, while others wanted to be left alone.

- Some would willingly pay for a premium service, under a regular contract, while others would prefer to take the risk.

- The attitudes of professional buyers, procuring on behalf of user departments, were consistently different from those of the user departments.

Results of the quantitative study

The output from the quantitative study was extensive. Much of the output was detailed demographic data, opportunities information and competitive positioning comparisons. However, the focus was on a fairly extensive executive summary for internal communications within GlobalTech. What follow are summarized extracts from those outputs.

The segments

Six market segments were identified as a result of iterative computer clusterings. Initially the clustering routines had identified more segments, but by careful analysis these were reduced to what was decided to be the most manageable level. Some previously very small segments were merged with very similar larger segments.

Polarizations in attitude

The computer clustering generated the segments by grouping customers with similar attitudes and requirements. This resulted in some marked differences in attitude between segments. As illustrated in the list below, the Koalas really did not want to know about being trained and having a go, but the Teddies, Yogis and Polars had an almost opposite attitude:

- *Koala Bears:* Preserve their assets (however small) and use, say, an extended warranty to give them cover; won't do anything themselves, but prefer to curl up and wait for someone to come and fix it.
  Small offices (in small and big companies), 28 per cent of market

- *Teddy Bears:* Lots of account management and love required from a single preferred supplier; will pay a premium for training and attention. If multisite, will require the supplier to cover these sites effectively ('Protect me').
  Larger companies, 17 per cent of market

- *Polar Bears:* Like Teddy Bears except colder! Will shop around for the cheapest service supplier, whoever that may be. Full third-party approach. 'Train me but don't expect to be paid.' Will review annually (seriously). If multisite, will require the supplier to cover these sites effectively.
  Larger companies, 29 per cent of market

- *Yogi Bears:* 'Wise' Teddy or Polar Bears working long hours; will use trained staff to fix if possible. Need skilled product specialist at the end of the phone, not a booking clerk. Want different service levels to match the criticality of the product to their business process.
  Large and small companies, 11 per cent of market

- *Grizzly Bears:* Trash them! Cheaper to replace than maintain. Besides, they're so reliable that they are probably obsolete when they break. Expensive items will be fixed on a pay-as-and-when basis – if worth it. Won't pay for training.
  Not small companies, 6 per cent of market

- *Andropov Big Bears:* My business is totally dependent on your products. I know more about your products than you do! You will do as you are told. You will be here now! I will pay for the extra cover but you will...!
  Not small or very large companies, 9 per cent of market

Satisfaction and loyalty

GlobalTech was measuring customer satisfaction for use both locally, as a business process diagnostic tool, and globally, as a management performance metric. These satisfaction metrics were averaged across all customers, both by geographic business unit and by product division to meet internal management reporting requirements.

However, the outputs from the quantitative study clearly showed that these traditionally well-accepted metrics were, in fact, almost meaningless. What delighted customers in one market segment would annoy customers in another, and vice versa. To make the metrics meaningful, they had to be split by key criteria and the market segments. Loyalty was obviously highest where GlobalTech's 'one size fits all' service deliverable coincidently best matched the segment's requirement, as illustrated in Figures 6.21 and 6.22.

FIGURE 6.21 Key criteria for the market segments

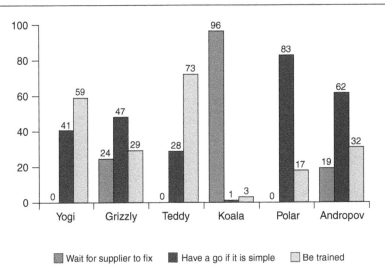

FIGURE 6.22 Likelihood of repeat buying from GlobalTech

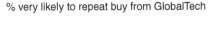
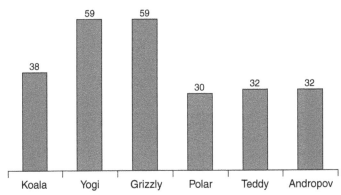

Correlation between loyalty and customer satisfaction

The market life cycle for many of GlobalTech's products was moving into the commodity phase. Therefore, not surprisingly, customers were becoming less loyal.

Each percentage point increase in loyalty translated into almost the same increase in market share. Each percentage point in market share added many millions of dollars of gross revenues. The cost of reselling to a loyal customer was about one-sixth the cost of winning a new customer. Consequently, each percentage point increase in loyalty had a significant impact on the bottom line.

Because of this, the quantitative study included correlating the key drivers of satisfaction and loyalty within each market segment. The qualitative study identified some 28 key customer requirements of their service provider. The quantitative study prioritized these to provide a shorter list of 17 common requirements. The correlation exercise reduced this to only two requirements that drew a significant correlation between satisfaction and loyalty: 1) providing service levels that meet your needs; and 2) providing consistent performance over time. Although GlobalTech was achieving the second, it was delivering the first in only two of the market segments.

Segment attractiveness

As an aid to deciding where best to invest, a chart of segment attractiveness was produced using attractiveness factors determined by GlobalTech (Figure 6.23). Demographic data from the quantitative study were combined with internal GlobalTech financial data. Each factor was weighted to reflect the relative importance to GlobalTech. This highlighted quite

FIGURE 6.23   Market attractiveness factors

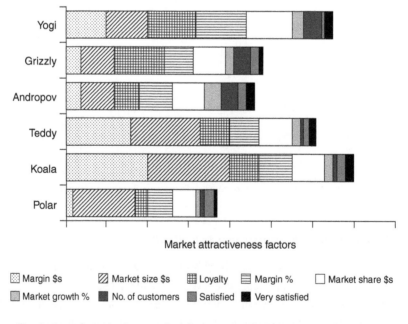

Market attractiveness factors

☷ Margin $s   ▨ Market size $s   ⊞ Loyalty   ☰ Margin %   ☐ Market share $s
▨ Market growth %   ■ No. of customers   ▨ Satisfied   ■ Very satisfied

• The further a factor is shown to the left, the greater its importance to GlobalTech.
• The longer the bar, the more attractive the segment is to GlobalTech.

a few issues and some opportunities. For instance, the highest margins were coming from some of the least loyal segments.

Competitive positioning

Fortunately for GlobalTech, its competitors did not appear to have an appreciation of the market segments of the differing requirements of their customers. They were also mainly delivering a 'one size fits all' service offering. However, there were some noticeable differences in their offerings. These resulted in each major competitor being significantly stronger in just one or two market segments where their deliverable best matched the segment needs.

The quantitative study provided detailed ranking of the DBCs and CSFs for each market segment. These were to prove invaluable during the phase of designing the service products and developing the strategy to achieve competitive advantage.

Decision buying criteria (DBCs) are the needs (benefits) buyers are seeking to have satisfied by their choice of product or service.

Critical success factors (CSFs) are the constituents of the factors required to deliver each DBC.

Reachability

Key to GlobalTech successfully implementing any strategies or communications that were to be market segment based would be being able to identify each customer by segment. As part of the quantitative study, two statistical reachability tasks were completed.

A sampling of internal GlobalTech databases showed that there were sufficient relevant data to achieve better than 70 per cent accuracy, using statistical imputation methods, to code each customer record with its market segment. This was considered to be good enough to enhance marketing communications measurably, but might not be sufficiently accurate to ensure always making the most appropriate offer. Statistical analysis identified four questions that would provide acceptable accuracy in segment identification. These questions could then be used during both inbound and outbound call centre conversations until such time as all customers had been coded.

The recommendation was to use both methods in parallel so that accuracy would improve over time. Also, the coding of larger customers should be given a priority.

> ### Lesson 3
>
> Understanding the different market segments helps in designing the required offers, but do not get too concerned about reachability. It is not essential to code every customer to the right segment from day one. Where you are not really sure, let them see different offers and so position themselves. Similarly, be willing to accept that within a large organization some buyers may fall into different market segments, though the difference will be on only one or perhaps two buying criteria rather than across all the buying criteria.

Strategy development and implementation

Market understanding and strategy development

The challenge now was for the project team to absorb and understand all the findings from the two research studies. The team then had to turn that understanding into realizable strategies. To achieve this, a workshop process covering opportunities, threats and issues (OTIs) was used. Briefly, the process involved an extensive, but controlled, brainstorming session followed by a series of innovative strategy development workshops.

A facilitator took the team systematically through each piece of relevant information available. Using brainstorming, the team tried to identify every conceivable opportunity, threat or internal issue associated with each item of information. The information was also then tested against a predetermined list of business behaviours and processes in an endeavour to entice additional and creative ideas out of the brainstorming. Using the DBCs and CSFs from the market model, strengths and weaknesses were added, thus turning the process into a SWOT. Like ideas were merged and de-duplicated.

Each idea was given two scores in the range of 1–9. The first ranked the probable financial impact; the second ranked the probability of success. The ideas were then grouped by like activity and where they had the same or an overlapping financial impact. This ensured that double-counting was eliminated, and that opportunities and threats were offset as appropriate. Any one group of ideas would take on the highest single financial impact score and a reassessed probability-of-success score. If the resolution of an internal issue was a prerequisite for capturing an opportunity or overcoming a threat, then the issue plus associated costs and resources was included in the same group as the opportunity or threat. The norm was for a single issue to be attached to many groups. The groups were named and then ranked by both financial impact and probability of success. This provided a prioritized shortlist of imperatives that should deliver the maximum realizable benefits to both GlobalTech and its customers. Iterative discussions developed this into an overall strategy with a number of prioritized sub-strategies. Each sub-strategy was supported by a documented description of the opportunity. At this stage, encouragement was given to creating innovative, yet simple, implementation options that would maximize the chances of success. Each implementation option was supported by market, revenue and organizational impact data, associated issues, resources, costs, and required control metrics. Board members were involved in an option selections and investment approvals process. Finally, the implementation programmes and project plans were created.

The strategy

The overall recommendation was to create a set of service deliverables tailored to the individual needs of each segment. These would be complemented by a set of premium add-ons that could be offered to the appropriate segments. By focusing on business process simplification during the design of the offering for each segment, redundancy was eliminated.

The objective of each offering was to increase customer satisfaction significantly, with an emphasis on those items that would most positively impact on loyalty. Some offerings were quite different from others, in terms both of the deliverable and of the internal processes that made it possible. This differentiation was also intended to create a measurable competitive advantage in a number of market segments.

A key to the implementation of the project was a recommended change to the customer satisfaction metrics, so that they became an effective diagnostic tool for tuning the ongoing deliverables for each market segment.

Implementation

Throughout the project, the same core team had been intimately involved with each stage of the project. They guided the work and took on board the results. They delved deeply into the analysis and did their best to understand the markets, their customer requirements and likely competitive impacts. Finally, they worked hard at developing the proposed strategies. They thought buy-in had been achieved by the project being sponsored by a main board director.

The implementation roll-out across country boundaries became difficult. Each country wanted its say. Each country had different views of its customer needs and how things should be done in the country. The countries did not easily understand or even accept the findings of the research and the meaning of the outputs.

The majority of these internal barriers were eventually overcome. Inevitably, there were compromises. These led the project team into believing that not all the market segments would be fully satisfied with the new offerings in all countries.

6.6 Segmentation and the Metrics model

6.6.1 Summary

The purpose of this section of the chapter is to describe briefly how the necessary segmentation data should be captured in the Metrics model. The stage in the overall model process is shown in Figure 6.24.

FIGURE 6.24   Marketing Value Metrics model process: market segments

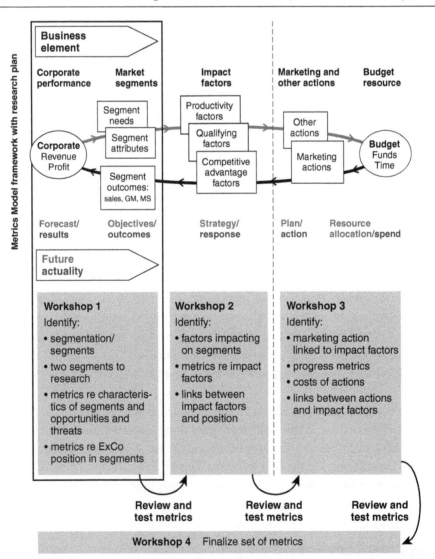

6.6.2 *The Ansoff Matrix*

The Ansoff Matrix (Ansoff, 1957) also provides a useful framework for identifying the products/services that might be most appropriate for each selected segment (Figure 6.25). This is a two-dimensional matrix mapping what is sold (products/services) and to whom (segments), divided into four possible strategies:

1 Sell existing products/services to existing segments.

2 Sell existing products/services to new segments.

3 Develop new products/services to sell to existing segments.

4 Develop new products/services to sell to new segments.

FIGURE 6.25 Ansoff Matrix

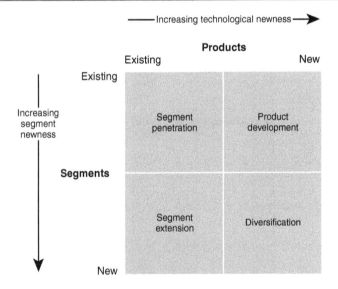

'Existing' segments can also be interpreted as those segments in a market that the company is already serving, while 'new' segments can also mean segments existing in a market that the company has not served in the past.

6.6.3 *Applying the Metrics model*

As shown in Figure 6.25, some strategies will be about increasing penetration within an existing segment, whereas others might be about entering new markets, requiring the company to diversify beyond its historical 'comfort zone' and take a higher risk.

The data that need to be captured for each selected market segment have two main components (Figure 6.26): 1) data that describe the type of people or organizations within the segment (what they are like, their aspirations, behaviour and attitudes, what their needs and wants are, etc); and 2) what the organization's aspiration is within that segment. In addition there is the need to identify the key metrics that will measure the current situation and the changes over time, and how the measuring will be undertaken – the sources of the data and who is responsible for the measurement process.

FIGURE 6.26   Segment metrics

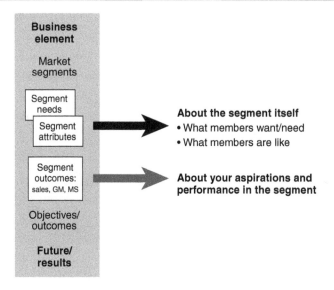

Remember to ensure that the golden rule of segmentation is kept in mind – a segment exists independently of the organizations providing it with products and services. Apply the acid test: if my organization no longer existed, would the segment still be there? If so, then this is a true segment.

The first template captures the profile for each segment, as illustrated in Table 6.4 for two segments in the financial services investment products market.

In the next template, Table 6.5, the metrics and sources of the metrics are captured for each key factor for the segment. In the example shown, there are two needs/wants of those in the affluent greys segment, plus two attributes.

The final template, Table 6.6, captures what the organization ('us') is hoping to achieve by marketing to a particular segment, and how the performance compares with that of our key competitors.

TABLE 6.4   Segment profiles

Example: investment products market

Important drivers	Segment 1	Segment 2
Segment need	Generate income	Generate wealth
Who buys?	Empty-nesters, married, aged over 55, AB social class	Age: 25–45, families, AB social class
What do they buy?	Income generation products	Education fees plans; pension plans
Why do they buy and when (time/occasion)	Retirement	Presence of young children
How do they buy?	Buy through intermediaries	Buy direct (internet/press advertisements)
How do they use?	Passive	Active portfolio management
Total value/volume	£ No. in the segment	£ No. in the segment
Segment as proportion of total market	20%	30%
Segment title	Affluent greys	Aspiring families

TABLE 6.5   Segment metrics: needs/wants/attributes template

Segment title: Affluent greys

Need/want	Metric	Measurement method
Generate income	Income generated by products in sector	Market research (perceptions); analysis of product field
Queries answered at first enquiry	% of queries	Benchmark customer satisfaction research; mystery shopping
Attributes		
What do they buy	Types of products	Market research/ industry stats
Frequency of purchase	No. of purchases per year	Market research

TABLE 6.6   Segment performance metrics: 'us' versus key competitor(s) template

Segment title ....

Performance	Metric	Measurement method	Us	Competitor 1	Competitor 2
Market share	%	Market research			
Share of wallet	£ & %	Market research			
Sales revenue					
Value of customer	£ (margin?)	Modelled from market research; market intelligence			
Gross margin					
Awareness					
Share of voice					
Retention	Score	Market research; internal stats			
Take-up of new products					

6.6.4 Segmentation ground rules

Members of the Measurement and Marketing Accountability Forum at Cranfield University identified a set of ground rules that they considered assisted the development of a segmentation strategy. These were divided into two parts: firstly, those that will help gain commitment to the concept of segmentation; secondly, points that will help the development and implementation process.

6.6.4.1 Gaining and maintaining commitment

- Gaining the commitment of top management is crucial, for example to provide reasons why a seemingly profitable business opportunity is not being pursued.
- Ensure that those expected to work with the segmentation fully understand what it is and what implementation entails.

- Does it match existing business rules, or will new ones be needed?
- Ensure that the implications for resources are fully considered.
- Start with a simple model, perhaps based on estimated data, to gain experience and commitment.
- Cost and revenue profiles can provide a starting point in gaining commitment to the principles.
- Don't underestimate the feasibility, or how long the process might take.
- Manage expectations, especially the payback period.
- Developing personality profiles for the segments helps bring them alive and helps the communication of the key differences.

6.6.4.2 Development and implementation

- Ensure there is a clear rationale and objectives (that are SMART[1]).
- Different segmentation models may be needed to achieve different goals.
- Use can dictate methodology/criteria. For example, segmenting the market with an emphasis on billing requirements may be different from a segmentation aimed at identifying the best new prospective customers.
- Behaviour and attitudes can produce different outcomes in terms of segmenting customers.
- Take into account the maturity of the overall market.
- Strategies based on a segmentation may lead to future behaviour that moves customers from one segment to another.
- The ability to deal with complexity may lead to competitive advantage.
- Ensure that the segmentation strategy doesn't create conflict with other, high-performing strategies.
- Data availability is a vital consideration.
- Ensure that the organization has the flexibility to face the market in a different way from that of pre-segmentation.

Note

1 SMART: Specific, Measurable, Achievable, Results-orientated, Time-bound

References

Ansoff, H I (1957) Strategies for Diversification, *Harvard Business Review*, September–October, pp 113–24

Christensen, C, Cook, S and Hall, T (2005) Marketing Malpractice: The cause and the cure, *Harvard Business Review*, December, pp 74–83

McDonald, M and Dunbar, I (2012) *Market Segmentation: How to do it, how to profit from it*, 4th edn, Wiley, Chichester

Rogers, E M (1976) New Product Conception and Diffusion, *Journal of Consumer Research*, 2 March, pp 220–30

How to become the first choice for the customers you want

07

Summary

Once key segments in the market have been identified and profiled, objectives agreed, and the metrics identified as described in Chapter 6, the next step is to develop strategies that will enable goals to be achieved and appropriate measures of performance identified. This chapter describes how to identify what an organization must focus on in order to provide consumers with what they want profitably. The framework we recommend and describe in this chapter is called an 'impact factor analysis'. The position of this stage of the overall model is shown in Figure 7.1. This is a critically important step in the process described in this book, so it requires quite a lot of discussion and explanation. Metrics identified here are at the heart of the overall measurement strategy. The results from this analysis help address the view expressed at the start of this chapter, as it proves the rationale for allocating resources to marketing.

7.1 What are impact factors?

As briefly described in Chapter 5, impact factors are divided into three types:

1 qualifying factors;
2 critical success factors;
3 productivity factors.

FIGURE 7.1   Marketing Value Metrics model process: impact factors

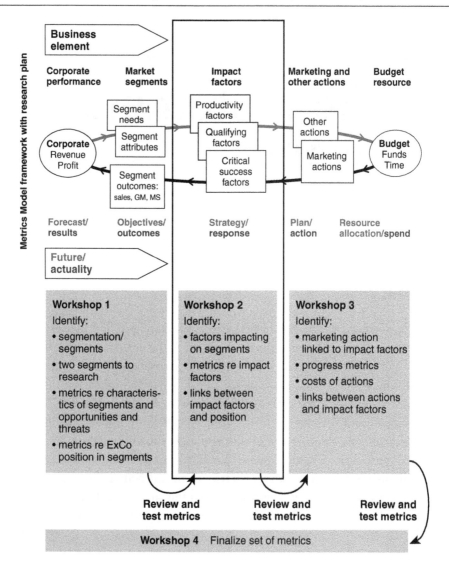

These are described in detail in the following sections of this chapter. The templates needed to undertake an analysis for each set of factors are shown, including examples.

As shown in Figure 7.2, the objective of the analysis described in this chapter is to identify the impact factors for each market segment that the organization wants to focus on.

FIGURE 7.2   Impact factors

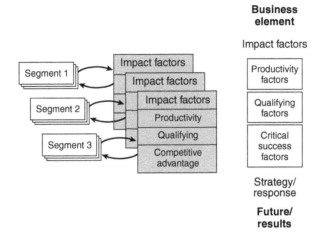

7.2 Qualifying factors

Qualifying factors are those factors, and associated levels of performance, that all organizations operating in a market are expected to deliver from a customer's perspective. Unless a company can provide these at the level expected by customers it is unlikely to prosper in the market.

The key characteristics of qualifying factors are:

- They need to be at a minimum level.
- They only differentiate negatively.
- Improving performance for these factors does not create competitive advantage.

Qualifying factors are all about not losing out to competitors or being disadvantaged in a market. They are essential to maintaining the current position relative to other players in a market. As such they do not provide any differentiation from others operating in a market or confer any competitive advantage.

A simple example of a qualifying factor might be the logistics requirement specified by a supermarket for suppliers delivering to a central distribution depot. The supermarket specifies next-day delivery following receipt of an order to its five regional warehouses. The key account manager for this customer at Supplier A established that with some additional investment it would become possible for them to make same-day deliveries to the customer for any order placed up to 5 pm. The account manager believed that their competitors would not be easily able to match this level of service. However, discussions with the customer identified the reason for specifying a next-day service. This requirement was based on the need to plan each evening for the flow of deliveries scheduled for the following day in order to maximize the unloading capacity of the warehouse, ensure that delivery truck queuing time was kept to a minimum and balance incoming delivery capacity with the need to have sufficient outgoing slots for vehicles delivering to its stores. Therefore, being able to offer a faster service was ascertained as being of no value to the customer. However, the conversation clearly underlined that being unable to guarantee a next-day delivery service would rule a supplier out of contention – this was the qualifying service level required for all suppliers to this customer.

7.2.1 Qualifying factors template

The template shown in Table 7.1 is for listing the qualifying factors for each segment in the market and the information needed to identify the appropriate metrics strategy for each one. The necessary content comprises:

- the list of all the qualifying factors that are essential to operating effectively in this segment of the market;
- the metrics that will be necessary to measuring whether or not the organization is meeting the requirements of the market;
- the methods that will be used to derive or obtain the measures, for example the source of the metric, or the data from which it will be derived;
- the importance of each factor relative to the others, to help assess priorities for actions, which is based on a percentage applied to each factor, adding up to 100 per cent;
- an assessment of current performance – what the organization is achieving at present against the performance expected in the market;
- the performance level necessary, if the organization is currently under- or over-performing, against market expectations;
- the current performance expected by those in this segment of the market.

The template (Table 7.1) includes an example for a catalogue clothing company to illustrate how the cells might be completed. The market segment shown for the clothing company in Table 7.1 is described as 'stylish urbanites'. Market research and competitive intelligence have identified three key factors that are required to meet customers' basic expectations: customer orders are accurately recorded, phones are quickly answered, and prices are in line with those of competitors. The company

TABLE 7.1 Qualifying factors template

Segment title: 'Stylish urbanites'

Qualifying factor	Metric	Measurement method	Importance weighting %	Our current position	Our target position	Benchmark
Accurate recording of customer order	Number of returns from customers	Customer database: returns per order	60	20%	5%	3–6%
Accessible by phone	Calls answered within six rings	Call centre performance stats	30	60%	80% (in two yrs)	80%
Price	Parity with good competitors	Market research consumer panel	10	Parity	Parity	Average for five key competitors
Total			100			

has therefore set targets for all three to bring its performance into line with the performance of other companies serving this sector. For example, the company has decided that the metric for measuring the accuracy of order taking is the number of products returned where the customer states as the reason that the goods were not what was ordered. The current level of returns for this reason is 20 per cent, compared to 3–6 per cent for competitors. The target is set at 5 per cent, as this is in line with the performance of others and the expectation of customers.

How do qualifying factors become established in a market? At the beginning of this chapter a brief example was described for a key account customer covering deliveries to a supermarket. A further example, from the financial services sector, provides an illustration for consumer markets. Some years ago a leading UK high street bank advertised that customer service calls would be answered in six rings. By promoting this through imaginative television commercials, in addition to establishing an initial advantage over competitors, they established in consumers' minds an expectation for all these types of calls, to any organization. In addition, consumer research also established that consumers did not want phone calls to be answered in a shorter time, as they needed a breathing space between dialling and connecting to an agent to prepare themselves mentally for the conversation to come. Therefore there was no incentive for organizations to invest in additional resources in order to answer calls any faster. Six rings became at that time the qualifying factor for customer service calls. The metric is obvious, and the measurement process would be found in the elapsed time between a call arriving in the centre and being answered, or through mystery shopping. As described in Chapter 10, organizations can be tempted to manipulate their data, perhaps by measuring only calls put through to agents and ignoring those that callers terminated before being connected, introducing complicated menus and measuring only wait time once callers had navigated their way to an appropriate section of the call centre, or deciding to include only calls made for particular purposes. Obviously, while such practices may enable budgets to be met in terms of agent resources and productivity targets, consumers will eventually recognize that this organization does not meet their expectations and, if this is an important factor for them, they will transfer their business to a competitor.

Organizations would be ill advised to invest resources in improving performance above the qualifying level if customers do not care, or do not want improved performance, as illustrated by the supermarket example described earlier in the chapter.

Examples where organizations fail to attain qualifying levels include those with customer service websites that provide no other method to contact the organization, and contact centres being unable to deal immediately with common enquires at the time of a call or not having up-to-date information about the customer available to support the conversation.

7.3 Critical success factors (CSFs)

These are the factors that really matter to consumers in a market, or segment. They focus on important customer needs: hence the alternative name 'competitive success factors'. These are the factors that attract attention in the market and help an organization win, and retain, customers. Focusing on improving performance against these creates positive, and powerful, advantage over competitors. Improving performance against these factors should lead to increased market share. However, there is likely to be a lag effect between improving performance and a noticeable impact on market share, and this needs to be allowed for in plans, cash flow forecasts and metrics. To be successful, in addition to understanding the needs of consumers, a company must also monitor the activities and performance of key competitors, and be tuned into changing circumstances. The important point to bear in mind when identifying CSFs and performance levels is that the perspective must be that of consumers and their needs and expectations – not what an organization might want to offer or think might be acceptable and not based on what competitors are doing.

Undertaking a SWOT analysis, as described in Chapter 2, helps identify how the organization stands up against the needs of consumers and competitors. Market research is obviously another vital source of consumer understanding, and inspiration for developing innovative solutions to meet needs. For example, market research conducted on a regular basis among customers that are new to a company may identify issues of importance to consumers that are not being adequately met by competitors.

Issues to consider in identifying CSFs are:

- *Demand from consumers, or needs (fulfilled and unfulfilled):* Sometimes market research establishes a common need across a market, but by breaking the analysis down by segment, one can identify differences that can be exploited to make your offer appeal more versus competitors to a target segment. An illustration of this is from the car breakdown service market. Research identified that drivers who were competent mechanics wanted a service that delivered their broken-down vehicle to their home so they could repair it for themselves, rather than being towed to the nearest garage. This led to the thought that there might be a demand for a more flexible service from other types of car owners. Further research proved this to be the case, leading to the very successful development of an optional service that took the car to a destination of the driver's choice (eg the driver's home, local dealer or garage) and provided a replacement car either for the completion of the journey or until the driver could make other arrangements if the repair was going to take time.

- *Importance to the customer:* Organizations need to ensure that they can prioritize the needs of consumers in order to ensure they focus on those that matter most. The opportunities for differentiation can then be identified by analysing the performance of competitors against their own for each need. This might also identify where a competitor is over-achieving against the requirements of customers, and therefore squandering its scarce resources. Undertaking a critical success factor analysis is one way to identify what really matters to consumers and whether there are any opportunities that can be exploited to deliver competitive advantage. This is also a tool that could be used in market research focus groups. As Jeremy Bullmore comments in his book *Apples, Insights and Mad Inventors* (2006): 'We all have invisible maps in our heads, on which we plot the position of competing brands. Every brand is allocated to its own, unique space. There may or may not be such things as parity products; there are certainly no parity brands.'

- *Level required by consumers, and how a company matches these expectations:* This is a further extension of the critical success factor analysis. For example, if customers require a quicker delivery service, what precisely does this mean and what degree of latitude is the customer prepared to tolerate? Are consumers wanting a faster service, and are they prepared to pay extra for it (eg the different delivery options offered by Amazon)?

- *The company's performance relative to that of key competitors:* The important issue here is to see competitors through the eyes of consumers. Do not rely on the perspective taken of competitors by the organization itself.

- *Perceptions of consumers:* Consumers do not necessarily interpret the messages from organizations in the way intended. Often they do not read the small print. They also have their own individual prejudices and see what they want to see. So-called 'irrational' cognitive processes are the focus of the popular field of Behavioural Economics but can be said to really be underpinned by the Nobel prize winners Kahneman and Tversky (1972, 2012). New messages do not necessarily replace, or erase, experiences from the past. Take brand image as an example. Organizations claim to own brands but, turning again to Jeremy Bullmore (2006), he reminds us: 'But for a company to feel it owns its brands is to tempt it to believe that it has total control over them: and it does not.' Bullmore continues: 'Forget the marketing-speak. The image of a brand is no more nor less than the result of its fame: its reputation. And like a reputation, it can be found in only one place: in the minds of people.' When the Automobile Association introduced its Relay service in the UK to recover members' cars (and occupants) to their home or local garage, the name was deliberately chosen, as on a recovery journey of any length the car and occupants might be transferred at operational area boundaries to other vehicles, just as a baton is passed from one runner to another in a relay race. However, some members missed this connotation, or didn't read how the service operated, and were therefore surprised to find that their journey was not completed in one stage. Their perception was that this would always be the case. Organizations have to decide how to deal with consumers' perceptions – but the key point is to know they exist, and how they are developed, if effective action to try to correct them is to be taken.

- *Identifying opportunities where excellence has potential leverage with customers:* In some cases it may be possible to make changes to a product formulation, or how a service is delivered, that provides customers with a level of benefit out of all proportion to the investment. The added advantage here is that this drives word-of-mouth marketing – the impact of customers speaking so positively about an organization that it persuades their friends and relatives to try out the brand. The level of customer service provided by First Direct in the financial services sector and the level provided by Zen Internet Ltd in the broadband market are prime examples where excellence has driven advocacy.

CSFs are all about winning through differentiation against key competitors. The winning strategies are born out of an in-depth understanding of consumers and their needs – and the creative ability to turn this knowledge into innovatory solutions.

Taking the call centre example described earlier in the chapter, how could customer service centres create competitive advantage if answering calls faster wasn't a worth-while solution? The answer lay in the quality of the conversations with customers, which in turn relates to the training of the agents, the processes that support them, the attitude of management, and the objectives and metrics set for the call centre by senior management. Market research was used to identify what consumers defined as excellent customer service over the phone, collecting examples from con-sumers covering a wide range of organizations operating in different market sectors. Elements of best practice that consumers wanted included:

- quickly answered (the qualifying factor level);
- 24/7 service;
- a pleasant greeting;
- professional service;
- confidence in the process;

- providing a name and reference number;
- customer details and history to hand.

The research also indicated that the benchmark organizations were First Direct (banking services) and Direct Line (car, home and contents insurance), both of which at the time had business models based on providing their services via the phone.

If the core metrics for the call centre focused on the productivity of the agents, then it was unlikely that the service could be differentiated from that of competitors. (In fact, a focus on productivity can lead to customers being ill served, for example by paying agents a bonus based simply on the number of calls answered in a defined time period. This was the strategy adopted by the directory enquiry service 118 118 when it was initially launched, with callers sometimes being given incorrect numbers simply to enable the call to be quickly ended so that the targets of calls handled could be achieved.)

The solution was to develop a scorecard of metrics that include measures reflecting the needs and expectations of customers, the conversational skills of agents, and their ability to handle a range of queries and offer appropriate additional products and services, in addition to metrics measuring productivity. The main measurement processes might include 'mystery shopping' surveys to measure responses by agents against defined criteria, and customer satisfaction market research, together with call centre system statistics such as the level of abandoned calls.

Over time, the competitive advantage factors of today may become the qualifying factors of the future. As in the call centre example, any initial market advantage gained from telling consumers that 'Our phones are answered in six rings' as a competitive advantage factor could in fact be readily matched over time by competitors as they saw that this was creating an expectation among key customers. This does not mean that the factor has diminished in importance; it has simply become the expected norm in the market, and other factors need to be identified if an organization is to gain competitive advantage.

7.3.1 Critical success factors template

Table 7.2 shows the template for recording the CSFs analysis, illustrated by an example for the telecommunications industry for a segment based on small to medium-sized enterprises (SMEs) with an annual turnover (TO) less than £500,000. The analysis shows that a key factor creating differentiation would be a new service aimed at meeting the specific needs of companies in this segment, rather than continuing to provide services tailored to market sectors. As the template shows, there is a benchmark competitor (Competitor X) identified as offering a similar product to that planned, but with a lower performance than the market requires (measured through

TABLE 7.2 Critical success factors template

Segment title: SMEs with TO under £500,000

Competitive advantage factor	Metric	Measurement method	Importance weighting %	Our current position	Our target position	Benchmark (Co. X)
Fastest available	Delivered in four days from specification	Production and logistics reports	40	8 days	6 days (yr 1) 4 days (yr 2)	6 days
Understanding me/my needs	Customer perception	Customer satisfaction survey	20	50% (Agree/ Agree strongly)	65% (yr 1) 80% (yr 2)	70%
New, do-it-all-for-you service	Defect-free on delivery (100%)	Returns and complaints stats	20	Nil	100% (yr 3)	90%
	Awareness of customers	Market research (industry panel)	10	Nil	70% (yr 3)	50%
	Uptake by customers	Sales data Market share	10	Nil	3,000 units & 10% share (yr 1)	15%
Total			100			

market research), which will need to be constantly monitored. The information needed to complete this template for the first CSF in Table 7.2 includes:

- a description of each CSF (eg fastest available service);
- the metric that can measure performance (eg meeting a four-day service delivery target);
- where this performance is measured (eg production and logistics reports);
- the importance to customers relative to other factors (eg a weighting of 40);
- what the current level of performance is (eg eight days);
- what the realistic target might be, and when this can be achieved by (eg the four-day target will take two years to achieve fully);
- what the current benchmark is (eg the best performer in the market provides service in six days).

7.4 Productivity factors

While qualifying and competitive advantage factors are primarily about increasing market share, sales volumes and, in the case of CSFs, protecting or improving margins, productivity factors are about finding ways to create efficiencies and thereby improve profitability. Productivity factors enable the organization to become more efficient and focused in delivering the strategy for each segment. This can include increasing output, leveraging economies of scale and reducing the cost to serve each customer. Factors to consider when identifying productivity factors opportunities include:

- *reducing inefficiencies, or eliminating wasteful activities:* restructuring the sales force to focus on key accounts with a call centre or website to serve the needs of lower-value customers;
- *process improvement and alignment:* decreasing the time from order placing to when the product reaches the customer by using web-based technology and restructuring the logistics operation;
- *restructuring:* replacing product-based teams with account teams;
- *matching channel to segment preference:* ensuring that a range of channels is available to meet the needs of different customer types and provide service capabilities outside normal working hours cost-effectively;
- *pipeline, or value chain, effectiveness:* using tools such as Porter's value chain analysis, as described below, to identify strengths and weaknesses in the organization's overall capability to serve customers as efficiently as possible.

● *Customer service effectiveness:* Customer management processes and systems, particularly online channels, allow companies to reduce the cost to serve while improving customer experience in some instances.

The following case study illustrates how a leading UK engineering company has added value and reduced costs by developing a new web-based facility for customers. The measures used to assess the outcomes are also described.

CASE STUDY 7.1 Adding value through the internet within engineering

To facilitate online product ordering, a leading global engineering company developed an online offer that allowed customers to specify detailed sub-assemblies and customize fitting for components, submit the resulting specification, which CAD technology on the supplier's server turns into a three-dimensional engineering drawing for the customer to view. The customer can then submit any amendments to the specification and input the final order into the system.

This process provided an added value, highly flexible service to the customer, saving time and the necessity of producing individual drawings of what is required. For the company, the automated CAD created a significant cost saving of £5 per drawing, or £2,500 per week based on the average weekly demand for 500 drawings. The site is supported by a 24/7 centralized multilingual customer service contact centre handling queries from phone calls or the website. Overall, the site attracted 24,000 visitors per week and generated 11 per cent of UK turnover for the company.

While the initial web store development was not subject to a detailed justification, the subsequent business cases were primarily based on reducing the average cost of order processing, plus measuring:

● overall levels of system usage (measured as 'traffic');

● the number of downloads;

● sales generated;

● the number of registrations.

A further important measure is provided through a monthly report comparing benefits with costs.

(Mouncey, McDonald and Ryals, 2004)

A key future development will be to expand the functionality of the site and develop strategies to maximize the opportunities for additional business from site visitors, especially from the large proportion who visit only the home/news or technical information pages. Of course, we can speculate that additive printing can take this co-creation process even further and allow the firm to sell the file that enables the production of sub-assemblies.

One mistake by marketers that Binet and Field (2007) highlight is that they can forget that the profit margin on incremental sales is normally higher than the average profit margin. Marketers, in building the case for investment, would be wrong to calculate margin at the increment if the activity requires more assets to meet additional demand. For example, filling empty seats on a scheduled airline incurs only a small additional cost and all incremental ticket sales go straight to the bottom line. Incremental production in a factory that has spare capacity enjoys high margin as there is no need to incur further overheads. However, a major increment in, for example, car sales that requires new plant and equipment, will enjoy 'average' margins for that firm rather than the higher marginal rate.

7.4.1 Using a value chain analysis to identify productivity factors

As mentioned above, one proven method that can help identify possible areas where efficiencies or improvements might be found is to undertake an analysis of the organization's value chain, using a tool such as Porter's (1980), as shown in Figure 7.3.

FIGURE 7.3   Internal value chain: looking for strengths and weaknesses from the inside out

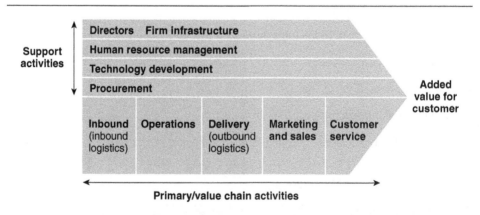

Adapted from Professor Michael Porter, Harvard Business School

FIGURE 7.4   Identifying the strengths and weaknesses in the primary activities within a value chain

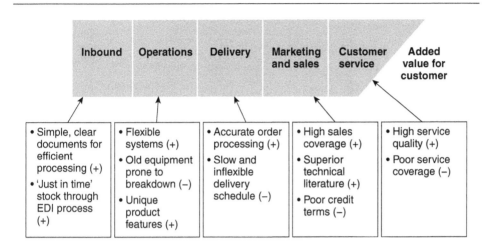

(+) Strengths   (−) Weaknesses

Adapted from Professor Malcolm McDonald, Cranfield School of Management

The objective of this commonly applied tool is to identify the strengths and weaknesses within the primary and support activities that contribute to delivering value to the market. The primary factors are the essence of what the organization does to serve customers and generate profits. Figure 7.4 illustrates an analysis of the primary value part of the chain for a manufacturer. As in all cases, the picture shown is a mixture of things the organization does well and some that are less good. The importance of these factors will depend on how they impact on meeting customer needs in different segments. It is vital that the analysis identifies the implications of each strength and weakness ('This means that...'). For example, if the customers in a key segment set tight deadlines for orders being delivered, reliable production facilities are important, but of less importance in serving a group of customers who are less demanding in this respect. Similarly, the analysis suggests that once a customer gets through to speak to the call centre, the staff will quickly resolve the problem – unfortunately, this facility is often available only during a normal working day (UK time), and is closed at weekends. Again, this might be fine for UK customers, but not those in other time zones or those who are operating 24/7. It is also possible to compare an organization's primary chain with known facts about those of key competitors.

Figure 7.5 continues the value chain analysis for this manufacturer, for support activities. As with the primary activities, some strengths are shown, together with weaknesses. This is an organization that has invested heavily in technology, which should be delivering benefits, especially in terms of efficient procurement and e-auctions

FIGURE 7.5 Identifying the strengths and weaknesses in the support activities within a value chain

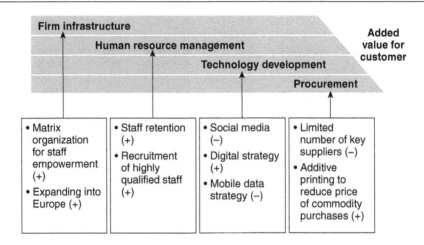

(+) Strengths   (−) Weaknesses

for commodities. The matrix structure should facilitate efficient decision making, especially as the organization appears to be able to recruit and retain professional staff. The reliance on a limited number of key suppliers could make the company vulnerable to price rises and shortages. Analysing the support activities also provides an understanding of the organization's culture and its focus. Again, this profile can be compared with that of competitors.

The focus in identifying productivity factors should be on those areas of the value chain where performance is significantly below that of competitors, or where internal factors are inhibiting the ability to meet consumer expectations. An example from an organization that one of the authors has worked with concerned the performance of the 250-strong sales team. A benchmark study revealed a high level of under-performance compared with the sales teams of rival organizations. A small budget for training quickly transformed the performance in terms of the number and quality of sales calls, which made a significant improvement in productivity. While this didn't result in competitive advantage, it definitely avoided disadvantage in a very competitive market.

7.4.2 Productivity factors template

Table 7.3 shows the template for analysing the productivity factors. In this case a manufacturer is left with a high level of obsolete stock in its dealings with a segment defined as specialist retailers, mainly because the call centre is missing calls from customers in this segment. In addition, profitability is hit by an inefficient invoicing and payments process. The information needed to complete this template includes:

TABLE 7.3 Productivity factors template

Segment title: 'Specialist retailers'

Productivity factor	Metric	Measurement method	Importance weighting %	Our current position	Our target position	Benchmark
Reduce level of missed calls	Missed calls	Call centre stats	40	15%	5% (yr 1)	10%
Minimize obsolete stock	Dumped stock £ & %	Stock stats	40	10%	2%	–
Lower average time to payment collection	Invoice to payment days	Accounts receivable stats	20	60 days	30 days	–
Total			100			

- a description of each productivity factor (eg reduce the level of missed calls);
- the metric that will measure performance (eg the volume of missed calls from customers);
- where the metric will be sourced (eg call centre statistics);
- the importance of each factor, relative to other factors (eg a weighting of 40);
- the current performance (eg 15 per cent of calls are missed);
- the target level of performance and when it can be achieved (eg 5 per cent achieved by the end of one year);
- the benchmark performance achieved by the best competitor (eg 10 per cent of calls missed).

Looking further at the call centre example shows that relevant solutions might be to look at less costly ways to deliver customer service, such as via a website that would also provide 24/7 service at lower cost than a call centre operation outside normal business hours, or outsourcing the call centre operation either to regions of the world where operating costs would be lower or to call centre outsource specialists. However, here we are starting to discuss the topic covered in the next chapter, Chapter 8, which is about deciding appropriate actions. This latter example also underlines the point made in Chapter 5 – marketers need to ensure that their strategies engage with other areas of the business.

7.5   Analysing impact factors: a strategy-based alternative

In some applications of the model, organizations found it easier to apply an impact factor analysis for a particular strategy for a segment rather than across all the strategies identified for that segment. Using the call centre example described in this chapter, researching the needs of consumers identified the need to improve significantly the level of service provided to callers. The first step was therefore to establish the *qualifying factors* for delivering a telephone-based customer service by studying the needs of consumers and the service provided by competitors (using mystery shopping methods) – what the norm was that was expected in the market. The second step was to identify what would deliver a service level that would clearly create additional benefits in the minds of consumers – the *critical success factors*. The final step was to define the *productivity factors* to ensure that the improved service would be delivered as efficiently as possible. This process would be repeated for each strategy, identifying any common factors that apply across strategies, and across key segments of customers. The revised template to capture the required information and identify the metrics is shown in Table 7.4.

TABLE 7.4 Impact factors: analysis by strategy

Segment: Wealthy empty-nesters. Strategy: Improving call centre customer service

Type of factor/level	Criteria	Current	Target	Metric	How measured	Who measures
Qualifying level	• All calls answered in six rings	50%	95%	Abandoned calls	Call stats	Customer services
	• Available 8.00 am–8.00 pm, 6 days	8.00 am–6.00 pm, 5 days	Parity	Availability	Management reports	Customer services
	• Agent friendly and professional	70%	100%	Customer satisfaction	Market research	Market research
	• Able to deal with queries related to core product – other queries resolved by calling customer within 24 hours	40%	80%	Mystery shop	Mystery shop/ market research	Market research
Competitive advantage level	• All calls answered in six rings, 24/7	24/7 not offered	95% (1 yr)	Call stats	Management report	Customer services
	• Able to deal with queries related to all products held by customer – resolved during call	Not offered	100% (yr 2)	Customer satisfaction	Market research	Market research
	• Able to answer queries about other products available	Not offered	60% (yr 2)	Mystery shop/ customer stats	Market research	Market research
	• Third-party partners meet required standard	Variable level	5 main partners (yr 2)	Audit/customer satisfaction/ mystery shop	Operations reports	Operations dept
Productivity	• Use of CRM system	50% of calls	80%	CRM stats	CRM system	CRM team
	• Average length of call	10 mins	5 mins	Call stats	Telephony stats	Customer services
	• Data collected/amended	Ad hoc	All possible calls	Database audit	Data quality report	Database team
	• Additional products sold	3% of calls	6% of calls	Sales stats	Sales reports	Sales

The template records the criteria required for each type of impact factor. These show that the organization does not currently meet the qualifying factors expected by customers in the particular segment 'Wealthy empty-nesters'. However, as shown for the competitive advantage factors, customers would like to see service levels above those currently provided by competitors. Finally, the organization has also identified opportunities to provide service more efficiently, use the opportunity of contacts with customers to update information held about them on the customer database, and increase cross-selling additional products by the call centre. The current position, the target levels (and by when in the plan), the metrics that will track performance, how the performance will be measured, and who will be responsible are recorded.

7.6 Impact factors: using 'gap' analysis for creating organizational alignment

A further tool helpful in identifying whether the organization is in tune with the needs of the consumer is a form of gap analysis, such as can be found within the SERVQUAL (Parasuraman, Berry and Zeithaml, 1988, 1991) model for measuring customers' perceptions of service quality. The full model was developed in the 1980s and based on a questionnaire covering 22 criteria most commonly found in the initial qualitative research conducted among consumers to identify the factors that participants used in assessing service quality. These were divided into five initial dimensions, with a further one added a few years later:

- *tangibles:* the physical aspects or service, such as the equipment used, the appearance of the service personnel, etc;
- *reliability:* the ability to deliver the promised service dependably and accurately;
- *responsiveness:* the willingness to help customers and provide service promptly;
- *assurance:* the attitude of employees, their knowledge and the extent to which they inspire trust and confidence;
- *empathy:* the ability to deliver a caring, individualized service;
- *recovery:* the ability of the organization to rectify problems (added in the late 1980s by a further researcher).

From this initial research, the authors developed a service quality gap model. In this model, service quality was defined as a function of the gap between customers' expectations of a service and their perceptions of the actual service delivered. This is the part of the overall SERVQUAL model that is useful in identifying whether an organization is aligned with the needs of customers, and is shown in Figure 7.6.

While SERVQUAL is widely used, it is not without its critics who argue that it focuses too much on particular customer service episodes rather than the customer's experience over time and across multiple channels. One of the authors has proposed EXQ (Experience Quality) to address some of these limitations (Klaus and Maklan, 2012). Lemke, Clark and Wilson (2011) also extend SERVQUAL to capture a more holistic conceptualization of customer experience.

The customer/organization interface is where the expectations, and perceptions, of the consumer – based on needs, past experience, the views of others and the claims made by the organization in its marketing and public relations activity – meet the reality of what the company is actually delivering. Obviously, market research can play a major role in understanding consumers, their needs and expectations, and what influences their attitudes and behaviour. As important is to ensure that all of those responsible within the organization (or those responsible for external, third-party providers) for ensuring that a defined level of service is delivered are committed to meeting the defined level of service that will create competitive advantage. Each of the 'gaps' shown in Figure 7.6 can lead to the service provision failing to match market needs. In essence, this is the customer service subset within Porter's

FIGURE 7.6   'Gap' analysis for the customer service value chain

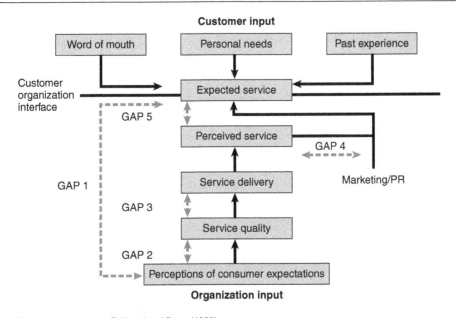

Source: Parasuraman, Zeithaml and Berry (1990)

value chain described earlier in this chapter. The point is that marketers need to ensure that there is alignment at the customer/organization interface. However, traditionally, marketing may be responsible only for the marketing activity that informs consumers or makes the promises, but this must be aligned with perceived, or expected, levels of service – Gap 4 in Figure 7.6. Therefore, marketers need to take responsibility for ensuring this alignment is in place and committed to by all others involved in service delivery, and that the appropriate internal and external metrics are in place to measure performance over time.

A 'gap' analysis can also be helpful in identifying actions, covered in Chapter 8.

7.7 Helpful pointers

Common mistakes when undertaking an impact factor analysis are:

- Thinking that improving performance for qualifying factors beyond that of competitors will confer competitive advantage. This will only lead to wasting scarce resources that could be more effectively employed in addressing needs identified in the competitive advantage analysis.

- Not being objective when comparing the performance of their own organization against that of key competitors, or not considering the actions competitors might take in response to their own moves in the market.

- Not taking the consumer's perspective when assessing what will create competitive advantage in the market.

- Not undertaking a thorough enough analysis of their supply chain to identify areas where efficiencies or improvements might be possible in order to reduce costs or improve profitability.

- Not monitoring the impact of productivity factors to ensure that these do not compromise achieving necessary performance against qualifying and competitive advantage factors, for example forcing customers to use a particular channel when contacting the organization in order to create maximum cost savings.

Finally, think of the following points when analysing impact factors and how the appropriate metrics can be identified:

- There are some offers and levels of performance that are now expected by this segment. What do you have to do just to stay in the market alongside good competitors?
  - Identify the qualifying factors that are the least you must do.
  - What metrics enable you to track them?

- What would make consumers want to buy from you, rather than from a competitor?
  - Which critical success factors would really make a difference to this segment?
  - What would you measure to establish whether this competitive advantage, or a strategy/value proposition based on it, was achieving your goals?
- You want to optimize your return from the segment while making sure that any efficiency measures do not impact negatively.
  - Identify the productivity factors that are relevant.
  - What metrics will help you monitor them?
- While the analysis is segment specific, some impact factors may span other, or all, segments.
  - This could apply, for example, to customer service. One leading financial services organization when introducing a website to reduce the load on the call centre, and thereby reducing costs, promoted this development to high-value customers as providing the benefit of 24/7 access.
- In the Marketing Metrics model, strategies are derived from the impact factors, which in turn determine the responses to the needs of the segment.
- There are three kinds of impact factors:
  - qualifying: maintain position, potential business losers;
  - critical success: differentiators, business winners (to provide competitive advantage);
  - productivity: internal efficiency/cost improvements.
- Identifying impact factors will often require external market research, which will require external spend. However, the cost should be balanced against the danger of not having the information. Opportunities exist to consolidate research and keep costs to manageable levels. Do not ignore the knowledge and experience that are available within most established organizations which can be harnessed in developing a full picture of the market and filling gaps in information – just ensure that the final agreed view is objective.
- Addressing the issues raised in the factor analysis will often require the marketing team to liaise with other key teams within the company in order to develop effective business cases, or arguments, to stimulate commitment and change.

Do not forget that, regardless of who has to take action to address any of the impact factors, the responsibility for monitoring their impact rests with marketing.

References

Binet, L and Field, P (2007) *Marketing in the Era of Accountability*, WARC/IPA, London

Bullmore, J (2006) *Apples, Insights and Mad Inventors*, Wiley, Chichester

Kahneman, D (2012) *Thinking, Fast and Slow*, Penguin, London

Kahneman, D and Tversky, A (1972) Subjective Probability: A judgment of representativeness, *Cognitive Psychology*, **3** (3), pp 430–54

Klaus, P and Maklan, S (2012) EXQ: A Multi-Item Scale for Assessing Service Experience, *Journal of Service Management*, **23** (1), pp 5–33

Lemke, F, Clark, M and Wilson, H (2011) Customer Experience Quality: An exploration in business and consumer contexts using repertory grid technique, *Journal of the Academy of Marketing Science*, **39** (6), pp 846–69

Mouncey, P, McDonald, M and Ryals, L (2004) *Key Customers: Identifying and implementing IT solutions that add value to key account management strategies*, Cranfield University, Cranfield

Parasuraman, A, Berry, L L and Zeithaml, V A (1991) Refinement and Reassessment of the SERVQUAL Scale, *Journal of Retailing*, **67** (4), pp 420–50

Parasuraman, A, Zeithaml, V and Berry, L (1988) Servqual: A multiple-item scale for measuring consumer perceptions of service quality, *Journal of Retailing*, **64** (1), pp 12–40

Porter, M (1980) *Competitive Strategy*, Free Press, New York

Turning strategy into action, and measuring outcomes

08

> *So how many bacon and egg breakfasts do I have to sell to pay for that?'*
>
> (ATTRIBUTED TO SIR CHARLES FORTE IN RESPONSE TO A MARKETING PROPOSAL)

Summary

The impact factor analysis described in Chapter 7 enables strategies to be identified and developed for each segment. The metrics for measuring the performance of these strategies have also been defined and listed. However, strategies can be delivered only through appropriate *actions*. It is the actions that incur costs, that lead to revenues being generated and that lead to increased efficiency. Pinpointing these actions, and the associated performance measures, are the topics covered in the first section of this chapter. This obviously leads to considering the *budget* implications – the costs of delivering these actions, and the forecast revenue flows or efficiencies that together form the basis for developing a compelling business case for implementing the proposed strategy. As recommended by Binet and Field (2007), this should be task or zero based (developing a new budget based on the cost of the resources required), with budgets being determined by the goals, strategies and actions set for the segment, rather than rolling forward an annual budget for marketing that is then divvied up across various activities, aimed at different audiences. Finally, this chapter covers the linkages that can be expected as a result of implementing a costed strategy – the assumptions made about likely cause and effect. This stage of the model relative to the others is shown in Figure 8.1.

FIGURE 8.1   Marketing Value Metrics model process: actions and budgets

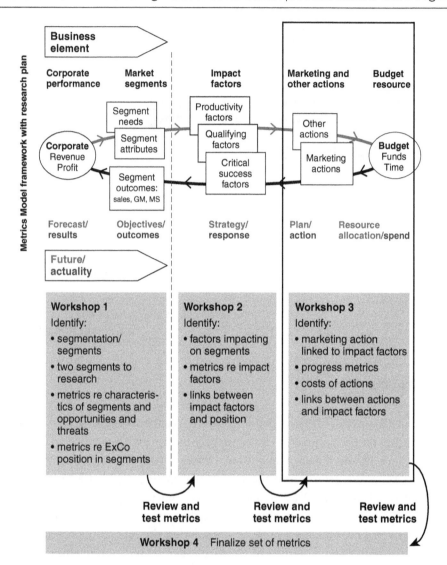

8.1 Developing action plans

As described in earlier chapters, actions necessary to deliver a strategy may be only partially managed by the marketing function. Marketing, however, cannot take responsibility for ensuring that all actions required by other parts of the company to deliver an agreed strategy are implemented and that other teams are measuring performance. The marketing team has to develop a convincing plan that clearly demonstrates to other areas of the company why actions are required, and the benefits that lead to achieving corporate goals, in order to gain cooperation. This is easy to say, but company structure, preoccupation with achieving short-term goals, conflicting priorities, variable levels of commitment from senior management, accounting conventions and so on are all examples of challenges that are likely to be faced in gaining the necessary cooperation from colleagues. For example, if required actions require collaboration with operations and logistics, then there will be the need to influence decisions across all these areas. Porter's value chain model, described in Chapter 7, can be very helpful in identifying where actions might be necessary, who might need to be influenced, and the arguments that might be successfully used to gain cooperation.

The marketing team may be responsible for assessing both the value required by customers and their value to the company, but the whole organization is involved in delivering, and sustaining, that value.

Actions might be linked to individual impact factors by segment or to a particular strategy; they might cover a need identified across several, or all, segments. For example, the need to answer a service call in six rings might be an appropriate strategy for all valued customer segments.

8.1.1 Identifying actions

Some actions are more obvious than others. For example, an FMCG company that regularly introduces new products to the market will have a defined process developed over time that identifies the key actions necessary across the organization. Whatever the process that is used, it must help ensure that all necessary actions, and the dependencies between them, are identified. A tool developed at Cranfield School of Management to provide such a process is the Benefits Dependency Network BDN (Peppard, Ward and Daniel, 2007) shown in Figure 8.2. While this model was initially developed to identify appropriate IT solutions in order that business goals can be achieved, in a modified form it can be used to help identify the actions necessary to achieve marketing strategies, and the metrics necessary to track performance. The example shown in Figure 8.2 is based on an analysis conducted for a leading international packaging company as an input to its key account management strategy.

The process runs from right to left, starting with the *strategy* defined in the impact factor analysis described in Chapter 7. The position relative to the impact factor analysis is shown, as this is where the strategies are identified.

The first step is to brainstorm all the possible *benefits* that might be derived from this strategy – for the organization, customers in the segment(s) and other stakeholders. This also provides a framework for developing any necessary business case for supporting investment.

FIGURE 8.2   Using the Benefits Dependency Network to derive actions (key account management, global packaging manufacturer)

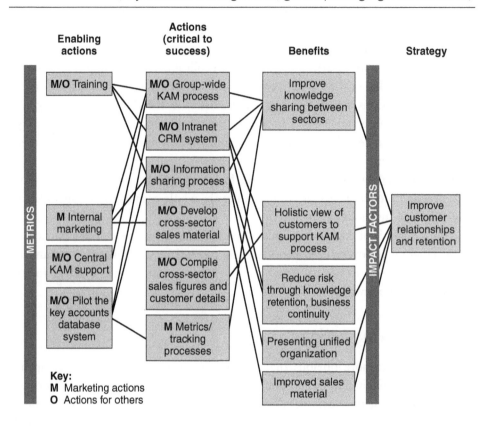

The next step is to identify all the *actions* that are critical to achieving success for the strategy, followed by identifying *enabling actions* – the other actions necessary to ensure that those critical to success can be implemented. The last step is to finalize the *metrics* necessary to track progress.

In this particular example, the strategy was to improve relationships and retention with key customers, based on an analysis of customer needs. The goal was to provide competitive advantage in the market. One of the benefits identified was that the proposed strategy would enable current and potential customers to have a clear understanding of all that the company might have to offer them – and provide this in a consistent way at all touch points. A further key benefit would be improved knowledge management about customers and their needs. Finally, it was felt that the business risks faced by the company would be reduced, owing to improved market knowledge and increased retention of existing customers.

Actions critical to success included a unified process for handling key accounts, compiling holistic data about customers and sales, new sales support literature, and developing a measurement process. A key investment would be in a new intranet system to be developed by IT to a specification developed by marketing plus input from other areas, such as sales. All of these actions would require significant support or collaboration with areas outside of marketing. A metrics process was also identified as a key action for marketing to track progress.

The key actions could be delivered only if a number of enabling actions were also put in place, such as appropriate training programmes (in association with human resources), support to enable the key account process to be embedded across the organization, internal marketing to sell the new strategy to employees, and a pilot to test the proposed intranet system (to be developed by IT).

The process used to apply the BDN process was initially a one-day workshop, including key people from outside marketing, followed up with a detailed plan refined through further discussion across the company.

As a result of using the BDN process, the company realized that the current system was inappropriate for meeting the key account goals. The process identified the need for a more user-friendly intranet-based product, which was subsequently developed and implemented. In addition, by using the BDN process, those responsible for the necessary key actions could be readily identified. Collaboration was enhanced by ensuring that all the key parts of the company were involved in the discussions.

In the organization concerned, the key members of an implementation team were identified as needing to be:

- a sales director representing one of the main market sectors;
- an executive sponsor;
- an IT/data strategist;
- a member of the sales team;
- a project manager.

Organizations within the Cranfield Key Account Management Research Club (Mouncey, McDonald and Ryals, 2004) confirmed that the key benefits of using the BDN model were:

- *economic* – establishing whether, and where, the project will add value;
- *political* – obtaining funds, winning hearts and minds;
- *change management* – early identification of issues (eg feasibility, desirability, resources, ownership, organizational impact);
- *control* – establishing project measurement criteria (eg benefits, costs, resources, etc).

The BDN helped us work through the requirements needed to implement a new system that was more appropriate to our business than the previous one. Looking at the objectives first and working through the benefits and the requirements in detail was very beneficial. Looking at the graphical representation helped to visualize and work through some of the changes required.

(Global manufacturer)

It enabled us to understand better what we were actually trying to achieve.

(Global information company)

8.1.2 Capturing actions, metrics and costs

Table 8.1 shows the template that can be used to capture all the marketing actions necessary to achieve each of the critical success factors identified in the impact analysis. This template captures for each action:

- who is responsible for that action within the marketing team;
- the metric(s) that will be used to track the impact of the action;
- how frequently the action needs to be measured;
- who will be responsible for undertaking the measurement;
- who will see the metric(s);
- the likely cost of each marketing action.

Table 8.2 shows a similar template for capturing the information about the other actions that will be necessary outside the marketing team. The example included is the action on IT to build the website as specified in the brief prepared by marketing shown in Table 8.1. The key issue here is to ensure that the template captures all the necessary actions required from other parts of the company and is therefore completed with input from all concerned.

Templates similar to Tables 8.1 and 8.2 will need to be completed for qualifying and productivity factors.

8.1.3 Analysing actions by strategy

In Chapter 7, an alternative analysis format for impact factors by strategy was described in section 7.5 and illustrated in Table 7.4. Table 8.3 is the template that should be used for capturing actions if this version of the model is being applied. This captures the marketing and other strategies necessary for all appropriate qualifying, competitive advantage and productivity factors for the strategy. The example combines the factors analysis shown in Table 7.4 for enhancing the service provided by the call centre and the actions shown in Tables 8.1 and 8.2 for developing a website to help achieve an overall strategy, provide best-in-class customer service.

TABLE 8.1 Marketing actions template (critical success factors)

Action	Who responsible	Metric	Frequency	Who measures	Who sees output	Cost £
CAF 1 24/7 website						
Develop website specification	Manager customer communications	Meets customer needs	Three measures: ● Inception of project ● After initial design ● After final version	Market research dept	● Website development team	£5,000
Launch e-mail to customers	Manager customer communications	● Awareness ● Website usage	● Monthly survey of customers ● Daily	● Market research dept ● Customer service team	● Marketing director ● Marketing and customer service teams	£10,000
CAF 2						

TABLE 8.2 Other actions template (critical success factors)

Action	Who responsible	Metric	Frequency	Who measures	Who sees output	Cost £
CAF 1 24/7 website						
Build website	IT	• Critical path in the brief • Budget	Monthly updates	Marketing and IT	• Marketing and IT Directors • Manager customer communications • Development team • Marketing/IT finance managers	To be agreed
CAF 2						
CAF 3						

TABLE 8.3 Summary of actions by strategy

Strategy: Provide 'best in class' customer service

Actions	Who responsible	Metric	Frequency	Who measures	Who sees output	Cost £
Marketing actions						
Develop website spec.	1	1	1	1	1	1
Develop brief for 24/7 enhanced phone service (answered in 6 rings, 60% queries answered during call)	Manager marketing ops	2	2	2	2	2
Other actions						
Develop website	3	3	3	3	3	3
Develop plan to enhance contact centre	Manager customer services	2	2	2	2	2
Total (£)						

Key:

1: see Table 8.1 for details

2: see Table 7.4 for details

3: see Table 8.2 for details

8.2 Developing the budget

By budget, we mean the allocation of resources. This is an *input* to marketing activity. We don't mean the sales forecast, as this is an *output* metric. Unfortunately, the same term is often applied to both of these, when in fact they are radically different.

In many organizations the annual round of budget planning starts with what was spent last year, therefore leading to a repetition of the same round of activity, which over time can become increasingly divorced from the real needs of the business. We would argue that this is not the best way to address the future needs of a business in today's highly competitive markets – and this is not the way that is proposed within the Metrics model.

However, we also recognize that users of the model may have to apply it within the conventions used by their organizations. So, while the model does not absolutely require that budgets be structured differently, we advocate a structure that enables the resources necessary to achieve defined objectives to be identified, in other words the resources necessary for implementing the actions for each segment identified by applying the model, as described in the previous sections of this chapter.

The budget should therefore be structured according to the impact factors that the action is designed to address. They would be quantified by building up a picture of the action required to implement each strategy.

This approach that we describe is very different from traditional practices. It begins the process of tracking the *links* between the *use* of resources and the *effect* they will produce in the marketplace. This is in effect a zero-based or activity-based approach where the resources needed to achieve a specific goal are identified as the budget, rather than starting from the expenditure in the previous cycle. Budget categories are then defined by groups of actions, ideally according to the impact factor they are designed to address. Categories need to be reassessed annually: some will continue from one year to the next and others will not. This alone will be valuable in helping to break away from established practices unrelated to achieving precise goals.

If an activity-based approach is introduced, the agenda for the company, and the likely resources that need to be deployed to achieve goals, will become much clearer, both in terms of what *should* be the result if strategy is actioned, and also in terms of what will *not* be achieved if resources are not allocated to facilitate defined strategy. It will also make it easier to link the marketing budget with the budgets of other functions, which should also show resources allocated to those of their actions that are directed at specific impact factors. In addition, taking this 'bottom-up' approach to defining resource needs and assembling budgets, linked to achieving specific goals, should enable the marketing team to engage more effectively with other areas of the company in gaining cooperation.

Marketing, seen as an integrated activity, incurs costs of five types:

1 external marketing spend, mainly on marketing communications;

2 internal marketing department costs;

3 technology, such as CRM systems, customer databases and websites – this is a growing area of resource need and will often incur a mixture of internal and external costs;

4 leverage of internal resources of other departments, for example in developing and implementing IT projects;

5 a requirement for other departments to spend externally – again, IT projects may require investment in new technology via the IT function.

However, only the first two (and mostly the external marketing spend) are normally recognized as marketing costs, for the following reasons:

- External spend on marketing campaigns receives the most attention because of their visibility. However, as the links between campaign expenditure and business targets are not always clearly defined, marketing budgets are frequently subjected to mid-year cuts if the financial forecast looks grim.

- Internal departmental costs are generally set without much regard to planned programmes, generally in different levels of headcount.

- Leverage of other internal resources is particularly important in taking a more integrated view of marketing, as marketing engages the rest of the business in delivering against strategic impact factors. The cost of these resources is rarely quantified, as still relatively few companies operate activity-based costing: but it could be. A prime example might be the investment in a CRM system that can deliver benefits for marketing, sales, customer service and operations.

- External spend by other departments is incurred when marketing identifies an impact factor that requires new equipment, software, etc. For example, shortening delivery times might require investment in additional trucks in order to reach the target levels of performance specified as a competitive advantage factor.

Companies would be better prepared to respond to marketplace needs if they aligned budgets in other areas with the marketing plan, rather than seeing marketing requirements as 'nothing to do with us', or stealing resources, or arriving at short notice with unplanned demands, or any of the many other reasons for rebuffing marketing actions. Furthermore, not only is taking this broader view of the resources deployed by marketing more realistic, but it also positions marketing more correctly, and effectively, in the organization.

Custom and practice have led to marketing budgets being generally divided into external spend categories, such as advertising, exhibitions, print, etc, which often bear no relation whatsoever to the real goals of the business, such as increasing market share. Basing an important business process on such a weak foundation leads to budgets being treated with disrespect. As a result, budgets can be manipulated, with the consequence that companies learn nothing about whether they used their resources effectively, nor even whether they made accurate estimates of the costs of their actions.

The following section describes the process within the model for identifying the resources needed to develop and implement the actions identified as being necessary to achieve goals for a segment, and how then to compile a detailed activity-based budget.

8.3 Budget templates

The first template in this section, Table 8.4, splits the overall costs of each action recorded in the earlier templates into the external and internal components. As described above, often the only costs captured by marketing are the external costs – such as for advertising agency work, media buying and market research, and similarly for sales the costs of in-store promotions. This template also includes the internal costs for each action to enable the use of company resources to be identified and prioritized. So, for example, the costs incurred by the marketing team in developing the website brief shown in Table 8.1 would be recorded here, plus the costs for the IT team in Table 8.2. Similarly, the Benefits Dependency Network illustration described in section 8.1.1 and illustrated in Figure 8.2 would incur significant internal costs in developing the proposed intranet system, including the pilot, and training users. This template is suitable for either version of the model, as it pulls together all the actions, regardless of whether they are related to an action plan to address a single impact factor or the impact factors being addressed for a particular strategy.

The next template (Table 8.5) applies to *only the strategy-based version* of this stage and shows the summary of the impact factor costs for each strategy.

The next two templates provide the segment totals – Table 8.6 is the total for all impact factors, and Table 8.7 is the equivalent for the strategy-based version.

The final template in this section, Table 8.8, pulls together the totals for all the segments analysed via the model.

TABLE 8.4 Actions: external and internal costs

Impact factor (or strategy) ....

Marketing actions	Cost £		Other actions	Cost	
	Internal	External		Internal	External
Total					

TABLE 8.5 Budget template (strategy-based)

Strategy impact factors	Budget £ Marketing actions		Budget £ Other actions		Total budget £	
	Internal	External	Internal	External	Internal	External
Qualifying factors						
Total QFs						
Competitive advantage factors						
Total CAFs						
Productivity factors						
Total PFs						
Strategy total						

TABLE 8.6   Segment budget template (impact factor-based version)

Impact factors	Budget £ Marketing actions		Budget £ Other actions		Total budget £	
	Internal	External	Internal	External	Internal	External
Qualifying factors						
Total QFs						
Competitive advantage factors						
Total CAFs						
Productivity factors						
Total PFs						
Segment total						

TABLE 8.7   Segment budget template (strategy-based version)

Strategies impact factors	Budget £ Marketing actions		Budget £ Other actions		Total budget £	
	Internal	External	Internal	External	Internal	External
Qualifying factors						
Total QFs						
Competitive advantage factors						
Total CAFs						
Productivity factors						
Total PFs						
Segment total						

TABLE 8.8   Budget final template (all segments)

Segment	Budget £ Marketing actions		Budget £ Other actions		Total budget £	
	Internal	External	Internal	External	Internal	External
Total						

8.4 Establishing linkages

This section of the chapter is all about cause and effect. The objective is to help organizations assess what the impact is likely to be as a result of implementing the actions. However, there is no doubt that this is likely to be inconclusive. The old adage about 'Tell me which half of my marketing spend is ineffective and I'll stop spending money on it' remains to some extent true – but, by linking resource allocation to defined actions that have been identified from a detailed analysis of impact factors by segment, the overall spend should be more effectively targeted.

Marketers make assumptions, consciously or otherwise, about cause and effect in planning their actions. It is well known, for example, that a discount price promotion will produce a greater response than a coupon. Such principles were established through disciplined research and recording of data, built up and repeated over a period of years. Including a test element within marketing campaigns whenever possible (eg a control group excluded from the campaign) and ensuring that necessary data on the impact of marketing activity are captured and analysed pay dividends in identifying the actions that really work.

The cause and effect of simple promotions may be observed more readily than some of those in this model, but more systematic observation and capture will inform other decisions as well. At the least, if assumptions made about the linkages between stages in the model above were quantified and captured, then communication between marketers and others in the company would certainly be better and expectations would be clearer.

For example, a 2 per cent increase in market share for a segment may be seen by one person as a good response to an action or set of actions, while someone else may count anything less than 5 per cent as poor. Unless the linkage between the action and change can be demonstrated, such differences do not surface, leading to considerable misunderstanding and differences in perception.

Quantified linkages or gearing may be best expressed as a range rather than a single number. Then the outcome can be modelled and applied in a business case for both ends of the range, which helps managers to make better decisions about allocation of resources.

The more data that are collected and effectively analysed and interpreted, the more the organization can learn and improve. In many companies, data may be collected for marketing activity, but the quality of the recording is so poor that the same mistakes are made over and over again. Therefore, in spite of having multiple opportunities to learn, the organization has no mechanism for capturing data across different time spans and no mechanism for learning. The objective is to develop a knowledge base culture, as illustrated in Figure 8.3. Not only does this require an investment in the processes and tools to capture data and turn data into knowledge, but there must be a company culture that appreciates the value of being knowledge based in establishing and maintaining competitive advantage. Increasingly, firms invest in better data about their customers' behaviour and will test activities continually and responding in real time: the 'big data' and Marketing Automation promises.

The question is: what price should be placed on data? Owing to the much reduced cost of capturing and storing data, it is tempting to take every opportunity to collect and hold as many data as possible. But every decision has an opportunity cost, and this applies just as much to customer-related data as to other areas of the business. In addition, organizations are often faced with alternative strategies for obtaining data – they can be built up over time from contacts between the organization and its customers (internal), or the organization might be able to obtain data more quickly, but at a much higher cost, from a data vendor (external). Figure 8.4 shows an extension to the data value chain process that attempts to put a value to the business of a data item and thereby helps decide whether it is worth collecting, and which route, internal or external, is the more cost-effective.

FIGURE 8.3   The value chain of data, information and knowledge

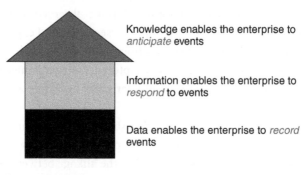

Knowledge enables the enterprise to *anticipate* events

Information enables the enterprise to *respond* to events

Data enables the enterprise to *record* events

Source: Kelly (1997)

FIGURE 8.4   Information supply chain

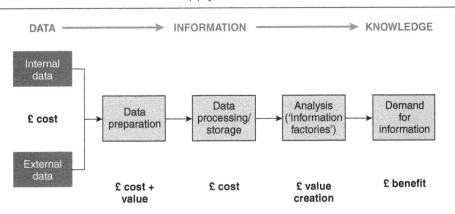

In effect, the process is all about building a business case for obtaining data, in terms of the value that data can provide. It is unusual for this value to be simply extracted from the item on its own; it is usually obtained from its association with other data items through data analysis and modelling.

The following hypothetical scenario illustrates the key points in the above model. The marketing department of a car breakdown service organization decides that retention could be improved by factoring in the number of cars in the household. This would enable a differential pricing strategy to be introduced and additional upsell opportunities to be introduced into the retention cycle. It would also help segment customer value more effectively, which would be reflected in reducing the marketing effort directed at low-value customer segments. Marketing therefore creates a business case for collecting the data by estimating the increased financial contribution to the business, comprising additional revenue and reduced costs. Against this revenue are offset the estimated costs of obtaining the data and the costs incurred in turning the data into knowledge. In this case, the business had the option of either purchasing the data from a lifestyle database company or collecting the data internally through, for example, contacts made with customers through the call centre call and revised application forms. Owing to the significant costs by either route, a test is quickly set up using a small quantity of external data. This test identifies that the figures in the business case are achievable, and the decision is taken to collect the data internally. Owing to having developed a business case, the impact on the current productivity levels of call handling can be shown to be a relatively small price to pay compared with the positive overall return to the organization. This helps 'sell' the new requirement to call handling management.

The key message is that data acquisition must be business led. The process also identifies the metrics to check whether the cost–benefit analysis forecast was in fact achieved.

In applying business case techniques, companies may find it useful to separate marketing investment for longer-term goals (eg building brand or customer equity), requiring evaluation over an extended period of time, and marketing operations costs directed at shorter-term results (eg acquiring new customers).

The points in the model where linkages can be established are shown in Figure 8.5. The term 'gearing' is used, as the objective is not simply to look for incremental uplifts in outcome, but to identify situations where a particular insight gained from the segment and impact factor analysis has a disproportionate impact on competitive advantage.

The next template in this chapter (Table 8.9) captures the expected impact of implementing the actions for the impact factors for a segment of customers. The information contained in the template covers:

- *actions (by impact factor or strategy):* as identified in the earlier analysis;
- *metric:* how the effect of implementing each action will be measured;
- *current:* what the current level of performance is, if applicable or currently known;
- *change:* what is expected to be the impact of the action;
- *segment performance metric:* which segment metric will be expected to be influenced by this action;
- *current:* the current level for this segment metric;
- *change:* the change expected in this segment metric as a result of the action being taken.

FIGURE 8.5   Metrics model with explicit linkages

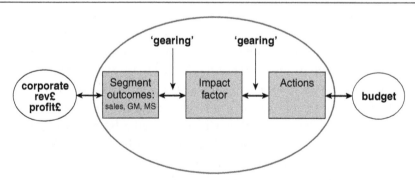

**Clarify and quantify linkage assumptions in stages
eg x% increase in CAF = y% increase in sales in
segment A**

TABLE 8.9 Expression of linkages (impact factors to segment performance)

Impact factors and actions	Metric	Current	Change	Segment performance metric	Current	Change
Qualifying factors: actions						
Improve data quality	• Visible address errors • 'Gone away' returns	10% 15%	Reduced to 4% Reduced to 5%	Customer retention	40%	+ 10%
Critical success factors: actions						
Web-based 24/7 support	• Volume visits to site	N/A	• 2000 PM (50% of segment 3 visits PM)	• Market share	50%	+ 5%
	• Reduced volume calls to call centre	N/A	• –40%	• Customer retention	40%	+ 10%
Productivity factors: actions						
Payment via CC on website	• Migration rate	N/A	• 10%	• Market share	50%	+ 5%
	• Transactions	N/A	• 300 PM	• Customer retention	40%	+ 5%
	• Revenue per customer	N/A	• As per other channels	• Segment profitability	£xxx	£xxx+
	• Cost to support/maintain	N/A	• – 50%		30% GM	35% GM

The expected impact on the segment metric will probably be an estimate agreed by the team, unless there is a previous example to provide more accurate guidance. The example shown in the template illustrates the type of information that might be included.

Under qualifying factors, the example shown is the need to improve data quality, which is considered to be below expected standards. The impact is that an unacceptable proportion of mailed items are returned by the Royal Mail marked as 'gone away' (the person the item is addressed to no longer lives at that address). Two metrics are shown to judge performance plus the current level of performance and the impact on the levels of address errors and 'gone away' anticipated by taking action. Finally, there is the metric of customer retention levels, which will be used to judge the impact at segment level, plus the current level of retention and the expected change resulting from improving data quality. Similarly, the impacts for examples of actions under competitive advantage and productivity factors are also shown. In terms of the productivity factors, the costs are expressed in terms of the favourable impact on gross margins.

A similar template (Table 8.10) can be used to record the linkages between the actions and impact factors.

TABLE 8.10   Expression of linkages (actions to impact factors)

Action	Metric	Current	Change	Impact factor	Current	Change
Marketing actions						
Other actions						

8.5 In conclusion

- Marketing should be responsible for implementing the strategies/impact factors, but this is almost always done in collaboration with all parts of the company, so all relevant actions must be identified.

- All significant internal and external actions should have costs attached to them, in terms of expenditure and/or time.

- Quantifying the assumptions made helps communication, clarification of expectations, decision making and learning. There can be no good reason for not doing so.

- Collecting data on expectations and actual outcomes does not necessarily lead to understanding cause and effect but, even so, capturing observation will help to make better predictions in the future.

- Expressing linkages should be possible, but determining the most relevant metric could be more problematic.

- In some cases the expectation is that a targeted metric will not change, but action may nevertheless be required to sustain it, for example advertising that maintains a presence in the market rather than leading to incremental sales from existing customers or new customers.

References

Binet, L and Field, P (2007) *Marketing in the Era of Accountability*, WARC/IPA, London

Kelly, S (1997) *The Fundamentals of Data Warehousing*, Wiley, Chichester

Mouncey, P, McDonald, M and Ryals, L (2004) *Key Customers: Identifying and implementing IT solutions that add value to key account management strategies*, Cranfield University, Cranfield

Peppard, J, Ward, J and Daniel, E (2007) Managing the Realization of Business Benefits from IT Investments, *MIS Quarterly Executive*, 6 (1), pp 1–17

Delivering accountability – finalizing the metrics strategy

09

> *What is important, and what is easy to measure, are not always the same thing.*
>
> **(BINET AND FIELD, 2007)**

> *Measurement is the first step that leads to control and eventually to improvement. If you can't measure something, you can't understand it. If you can't understand it, you can't control it. If you can't control it, you can't improve it.*
>
> **(H JAMES HARRINGTON, ERNST & YOUNG)**

Summary

This chapter describes how to finalize a metrics strategy, the final step in the process. This brings together the metrics from all the previous stages of the Metrics model developed in the three workshops. Key to finalizing the process is to decide those metrics that will be included and those that won't and, also, who will see the different metrics in the final list in order to develop subsets for different levels of management within the organization and for different functions and teams. The stage in the overall Metrics model process is shown in Figure 9.1 (Workshop 4).

The grey arrows within the model show the process for identifying the metrics, while the black arrows show the application of these in measuring performance, changes in the market, etc. This also provides the link back to the start point of the model process – the organization's corporate goals.

FIGURE 9.1   Marketing Metrics model process: finalizing the overall metrics strategy

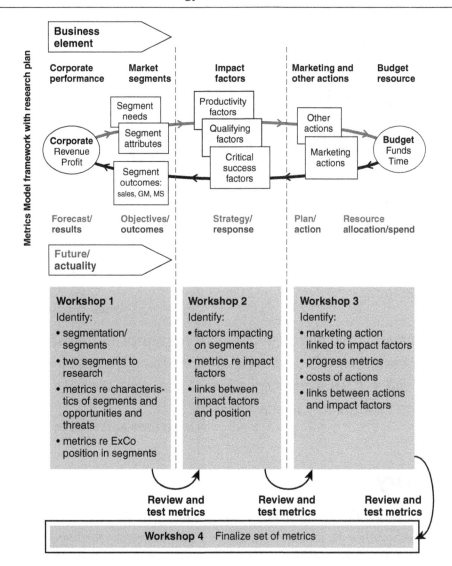

9.1 Developing metrics that matter

In compiling the final list of metrics, it is vitally important to ensure they are 'fit for purpose'. The following is a checklist of points to consider in order to develop a metrics strategy that provides reliable information for management decision making:

- Beware of spurious correlations: correlation is not the same as causation. As Binet and Field (2007) point out, correlations between brand performance and exposure to a campaign are often used as measures, but other factors may be disguising the true picture, such as seasonality.

- There is no single measure: the trend, especially for board-level data, is to reduce the number of key measures to the absolute minimum. However, there is no single 'golden' metric that on its own provides a sufficient understanding of the impact of marketing on achieving corporate goals. Each objective needs its own measure or measures.

- Don't focus on intermediary measures: the impact of marketing is too often measured through changes in 'awareness', 'beliefs', attitudes', 'intentions', etc. These are called 'intermediary objectives', as they do not tell you whether or not changes at this level have influenced actual purchasing, or retention behaviour. However, the real objective of marketing is to change people's behaviour, and therefore metrics should focus on measuring the extent to which this has actually happened. Positively influencing the intermediary measures may be a key objective of marketing activity, but if successful it should lead to action, and that is what should be at the heart of the metrics strategy.

- Be market focused: market share is a key metric in measuring the performance of marketing. However, market share within each segment is far more useful than simple share within the overall market, as this does not help assess whether the defined strategy is influencing behaviour by the groups of consumers the organization is targeting. Focusing on market share also means that the organization is taking into account trends in the market and the performance and actions of competitors. The InterTech example shown in Chapter 3 illustrates the need to focus on the position of the organization within the market rather than simply focusing on internal measures of performance such as sales and spend.

- Apply the tools: as mentioned earlier, econometrics provides a useful methodology for identifying the contribution of each element in the marketing mix. There are also methods for helping to identify groups of customers that are potentially at risk from the predations of competitors, or those of their customers that might be interested in a new supplier (eg the Conversion Model – Hofmeyr, 1990). The same applies to measuring the value of intangible assets such as brand or customer value, as described in Chapter 13.

- Market position versus market growth: some marketing expenditure is simply to retain current market position, while other expenditure is to grow market share. It is important to try to distinguish between the two and ensure that the metrics used enable this to be achieved.

- Be comprehensive: by using a tool such as the value chain described in Chapter 7, all the areas that can have an impact on delivering the promise made by marketing to consumers can be identified. From this analysis, a comprehensive, pan-organization set of key metrics can be developed.

9.2 Auditing for success

In addition to providing a method to identify the strategy, actions and metrics for each key market segment, the model also provides a useful audit process, or checklist, for organizations to ensure all the key issues have been identified and covered in developing an appropriate strategy and associated measures. A summary of the main points that should be covered is shown below. All of these points are covered in detail in previous chapters:

- Is the team developing the metrics strategy sufficiently representative and empowered to ensure that the outcomes will be actioned?
- Does the process have a senior management sponsor and support at board level?
- Which corporate goals could be influenced by marketing strategy?
- Is the definition of marketing used by the organization sufficiently broad to include all points of contact with consumers?
- Is there a detailed segmentation of the market (not just the organization's customers – the acid test here is that the segments would still exist even if your company was no longer in existence), and have the key segments of consumers been identified that the organization is most interested in within future strategy?
- Does the segmentation analysis include profiles of the relevant consumers, and has it identified their detailed needs?
- Are the company's aspirations or goals for each segment clearly defined?
- Are there strategies in place to deliver these aspirations?
- Has the company identified the baselines necessary for successfully operating in each segment (qualifying factors)?
- Does the company know what consumers expect from a market leader provider in each segment (competitive advantage factors)?
- Has the company identified how to meet market needs as efficiently as possible (productivity factors)?

- Have all the necessary actions been identified in order to deliver the strategy for each segment?
- Have all the necessary teams been fully involved in developing the actions, and are they included in their plans?
- Have the resources – internal and external – needed to deliver these actions been assessed and costed?
- Can the impact of the actions on market performance be assessed?
- Have all the necessary metrics been identified at each stage of the process?
- Does the final list of metrics identify who will see each metric and who is responsible for taking any necessary corrective action?

9.3 Bringing it all together

The core sets of metrics, and how they link together to enable the final set to be identified and agreed, are diagrammatically represented in Figure 9.2. The objective is to bring together the sets of metrics identified in the previous stages of the model, covering:

- corporate goals (Workshop 1);
- market segments (Workshop 1);
- impact factors (Workshop 2);
- actions and budgets (Workshop 3).

FIGURE 9.2   Finalizing the metrics

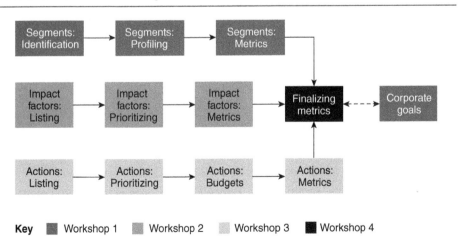

Key   ■ Workshop 1   ▨ Workshop 2   ▨ Workshop 3   ■ Workshop 4

However, before the appropriate template can be completed, there needs to be a reality check conducted on the full lists derived in the earlier stages of the analysis process. This is necessary, as the overall strategy will probably need to be phased in over time. In addition, some of the data, or metrics, might be readily available, whereas in other cases a plan to collect data and derive the metrics will be needed, for example where a new activity is part of the strategy. In some cases, it may prove very difficult to collect the data, or the level of investment required may be deemed unacceptable relative to the benefit. The information supply chain described in Chapter 8 and illustrated in Figure 8.4 can also be used to help decide whether it was worth investing in collecting data to provide a particular measure. Discussing the implications of the modern data rich world could fill at least another book. In addition to traditional sources (primary research – survey, operational data, retailer data), customers generate data online directly through your online channels and through social media. At the time of writing this book, we are at the cusp of large-scale location tracking through smart phones. One benefit from the Metric model process is that, by identifying all the necessary metrics needed to track performance over time, a more strategic approach to analytical data is enabled; rather than just gathering more and more 'because it is there', 'big data' will cost big money and intuitively, it is appealing to guide such investments with knowledge of which data really matters.

One organization used the following framework to categorize the full list of metrics:

- *'Things we are implementing'*: these are metrics that are already in place or being developed. These mainly consisted of the measures that were being used to track the performance of the business – primarily derived from market research, customer satisfaction, internal financial measures and industry data.

- *'What we know we want to have'*: these are metrics identified in the model process considered essential to monitoring key strategies and market changes that were not currently being collected. For example, while a company may monitor the market overall, the data are not collected at segment level. The necessary metrics would be developed as part of the strategy implementation process.

- *'What we don't do but probably should'*: these were metrics that, while helpful, were after detailed consideration not considered essential or worth investing resources in for the time being. Reviewing the need for these would be included as an action at appropriate stages in the future plans.

- *'What we don't know and probably won't'*: the final category covered metrics that would be either very difficult or relatively expensive to collect in terms of the value derived from undertaking the measurement. These would be the subject of further investigation, or a business case.

An alternative format used with another organization was a four-box matrix, as shown in Figure 9.3. This plots the value, or importance to the overall strategy, of implementing a metric by the level of difficulty in collecting the necessary data to generate the metric.

In the examples shown, creating consumer profiles for each segment has a high value, and would be easy to achieve – simply undertaking a cluster analysis of the results from a monthly market research survey using data already collected in the questionnaire. Also, in working through the Metrics model, measuring the impact of the overall marketing strategy on either customer or brand equity was judged an important measurement. However, measuring the impact on customer equity seems to be easier to implement than for brand equity and therefore is probably the measure to implement. In comparison, collecting the sales of a key competitor on a monthly basis is difficult, and not of major value. Maybe it would be easier to collect the data at less frequent intervals, perhaps only annually. Finally, although it will be fairly difficult to measure the impact of developing a website on customer retention, its importance suggests that this will need to be addressed in the metrics strategy.

Plotting all the proposed metrics in this way will help prioritize the metrics strategy.

The final, and key, template is shown in Table 9.1. This summarizes the agreed list of metrics for each segment, covering:

- segment metrics;
- impact factors;
- actions.

FIGURE 9.3 Taking a reality check

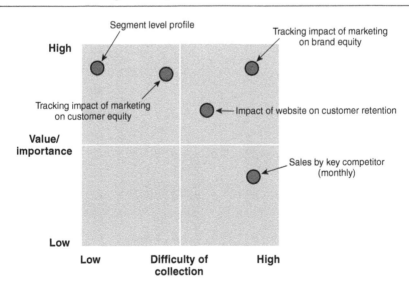

TABLE 9.1   Final metrics list

Segment title: SMEs with up to £1m TO per annum

Metric (title)	How measured/ source	Collection (now/future)	Frequency	Formula	Who measures	Who sees	Who acts
Segment metrics							
Segment size	Industry market research survey	To be collected from end April 2008	Monthly	Grossed up from sample survey data	Market research dept	Marketing director/ management	Marketing
Market share	Industry market research survey	Collected now	Monthly	Volume/value calculated from % and average weighted value per sale	Market research dept	Board (quarterly), marketing management	Marketing sales teams
Sales	Transaction data	To be collected at segment level from end Oct 2008	Weekly	Compiled from extended profile data on customers	Marketing database team	Marketing and sales management	Sales team
Impact factor metrics							
Day after order delivery (CAF)	Logistics stats	From Sept 2008	Daily	Derived from delivery stats	Logistics dept	Operations, logistics, marketing, sales, customer services management	Operations, logistics
	Customer satisfaction survey	From May 2008	Quarterly	Direct (%)	Market research dept		
	Mystery shopping	From May 2008	Quarterly	Direct	Market research dept		
Action metrics							
24/7 website	• Required standard	From implementation	• Quarterly	• Customer survey and mystery shopping	• Market research dept	IT operations, sales, marketing	IT and operations depts
	• Site visits		• Daily	• Internal stats	• Operations sales teams		
	• Orders		• Daily				
	• Costs per order		• Monthly				

For each metric, the key questions that need answers are as follows:

- *How will it be measured, and what is the source?* For example, it could be any specific market research survey, internal management information system, etc.

- *Are the data that provide the metric collected now, or will they be collected in the future?* If they are to be collected in the future, when will measurement commence?

- *When, and how frequently, will the measure be made?* For example, market share and segment profiles might be measured from a quarterly survey of consumers; average time to calls being answered from call centre data; or customer satisfaction from a monthly survey.

- *Is the metric to be a raw measure, or will it be derived or modelled from one or more data-sets?* Econometrics-based models might be used to help identify the most appropriate mix of advertising channels to use; index scores might be calculated from customer satisfaction survey data; customer equity might be constantly recalculated depending on the product mix used by customers; and market share might simply be the answer to a brand usage question in a survey of consumers.

- *Who is responsible for collecting or deriving the measure?* Establishing responsibility is vital – does this lie within the marketing team or other areas of the business, and has this responsibility been agreed?

- *Who sees the metrics?* It is important to identify who within the organization sees each agreed metric, and in what form. For example, is it an input to a balanced scorecard or board-level dashboard, or is it used only by the marketing team to measure a particular activity, such as an advertising campaign? While marketing may use a suite of metrics to measure the effectiveness of advertising and promotional campaigns, the board may see only a quarterly report on market share.

- *Who is responsible for taking action?* It is also vital to identify who has responsibility for taking action if the metric shows that one or more targets set for the strategy are not being achieved.

The example shown in Table 9.1 shows three metrics for monitoring the changes at *segment* level: the overall size of the segment, the market share of the company and main competitors, and sales volumes. Market share is the one shown that is reported at board level (quarterly).

One *impact factor* example is shown – next-day delivery, identified as a competitive advantage factor for this segment. This shows that responsibility for corrective action lies outside the marketing team, whereas the measurement process is split between the internal logistics team (delivery statistics) and externally conducted market research (customers' view of the service) commissioned by the market research department. This is because, while the logistics team measures orders leaving the warehouse, it does not measure the performance of the third-party delivery company from a customer perspective.

Finally, one key *action* is shown – introducing website ordering to support the next-day delivery service. Again, this is split in terms of who measures and who needs to take corrective action.

This final list should be used as the master list, feeding into other existing management information reports, such as balanced scorecards, as mentioned above. Key to finalizing the metrics strategy is the need to define those who should be exposed at board level – this is a key reason why the Metrics model process needs a senior manager as sponsor, preferably at board level.

Obviously, this will always be an iterative process, as the strategies and actions defined at any given moment in time will need to be updated to ensure continuing competitiveness in terms of market needs and actions of competitors, and to remain in tune with changing company priorities.

References

Binet, L and Field, P (2007) *Marketing in the Era of Accountability*, WARC/IPA, London

Hofmeyr, J (1990) The Conversion Model: A new foundation for strategic planning in marketing, 3rd EMAC/ESOMAR symposium, Athens, Greece

Why data quality can make or break accountability

10

Information systems are like buildings. Some are elegant, functional, integrated and low maintenance. Others are jerry-built amalgams of bits and pieces that have been added on in a haphazard fashion.

When we speak of poor data quality it is often understood only to mean inaccurate data, or missing data or inconsistent data. But very often the data failures of organisations have their roots in a failure to understand the value of data.

(KELLY, 2006)

Summary

The two quotes above are from the chapter entitled 'Achieving an intelligence capability' in Kelly's book and provide two key reasons why organizations fail to effectively manage the flows of data available within an organization, or a market, and turn them into knowledge. The 'big data' challenge is to separate important signals from the noise 'Infobesity', more data than we can digest, is a condition that requires strategic level attention, if the root causes are to be addressed. Challenges created by new, increasing flows of data are not new – as anyone, including one of the authors of this book, who lived through the initial customer data revolution in the 1980s, when computing power was limited and expensive and analytical software was in its infancy, would testify to. 'big data' has increased the complexity, but the issues Kelly described remain at the heart of the challenge – and the responsibility for failure lies at board level, at the very top of the organization.

This chapter describes why organizations need to develop a company-wide data management strategy, championed at board level, as a key building block in achieving accountability. Data that are 'fit for purpose' are a vital foundation for marketing strategy and in ensuring that the Metrics model provides an accurate picture of the market and in measuring the performance of the organization in meeting its goals.

The final section of this chapter describes how to develop a data strategy to underpin the Metrics model, and why this is a vitally important foundation if the marketing strategy is to be successful and performance in achieving goals is to be accurately measured. This has become an increasingly important issue in marketing, owing to the increasing use of technology applications such as customer databases, data warehouses and CRM systems.

10.1 The importance of data quality

One of the key challenges faced by marketers in developing an effective metrics strategy is to ensure that the quality of the data used as a source for the measures is appropriate to provide reliable information.

A data quality workgroup consisting of members of the Cranfield Marketing Measurement and Accountability Forum (MMAF) identified the following as constituting 'best practice' in data management to support marketing strategy:

- An enterprise-wide data strategy is essential in achieving high levels of data quality. Marketing strategy is often supported by data managed in other parts of the business, for example in operational areas such as customer service centres, underlining the importance of having an enterprise-wide strategy.

- Earlier research undertaken on data management at Cranfield by one of the authors (Mouncey and Clark, 2005) indicates that a company-wide strategy is still a rare situation.

- Data need to be collected with the wider needs of the enterprise in mind, rather than being collected for a single purpose (as is often the case).

- Data definitions (metadata) need to be consistent.

- A business case for data quality is essential to identifying and quantifying the real costs and lost opportunities.

- Data quality needs to be 'owned' by business units, not IT.

- Overall data strategy needs to be 'owned' at board level and made the responsibility of a dedicated team.

- 'Soft' and 'derived' data are becoming increasingly important in developing competitive advantage, and pose particular challenges within a data management strategy.

- Data quality must be viewed as an iterative issue, requiring constant attention, its own defined metrics framework, continual investment and regular auditing.

- Communication is an essential component within a data management strategy to ensure commitment.

The case for developing an effective data management strategy for marketing is described in the following sections.

10.2 Are data the weakest link in your marketing strategy?

The Cranfield research study (Mouncey and Clark, 2005) on data management strategies referred to above found that practices within organizations were polarized. In some organizations data management was defined as the weakest link in their strategy, in others their core strength. The following quotation underlines the importance of good data governance practices within one area that has grown to be of significant importance for marketers in recent years and required large-scale investment in new processes, hardware, software and capabilities within many companies – customer relationship management (CRM): 'Managers wishing to fail at CRM or sabotage a CRM project need look no further than "Data" to find the weakest link in the CRM project.' This quotation from *Carving Jelly*, a guide to CRM project management by Nick Siragher (2001), is equally appropriate to any investment in marketing activity, especially as CRM systems and associated databases have become increasingly important sources of information to measure the performance of marketing.

Taking marketing communications as an example, one of the key reasons why entries to the IPA Advertising Effectiveness awards fail to impress the judges is that the evidence to link expenditure on advertising to any impact on business results is either lacking or deeply flawed. The quality of the data used to support the case is also often suspect (Institute of Practitioners in Advertising, 2006).

The above quotation from Siragher also implies that some employees may have a hidden agenda and see this as a way to frustrate or derail the ambitions of their organization, or may be seeking to justify or defend a course of action that does not in reality represent a good investment for the enterprise's scarce resources. In either case, it underlines the need to ensure that the strategy being developed by marketing has the full support of all other areas of the organization that are necessary to implementation. This commitment also needs to be at all levels in the organization.

A meaningful data management strategy to support marketing activity must not simply focus on one area, such as customer-related data. It is not uncommon for the aims within a marketing plan to be frustrated by bad practice in data management within other parts of the organization. The following real-life case study illustrates how the poor management of data, in this case within the manufacturing division, can increase costs and create an uncompetitive situation in a B2B marketplace. In this example this led to increasing difficulties for the marketing and sales teams in achieving their goals in a particular geographic market.

MINI CASE STUDY

A leading international engineering company manufactured components that had several part numbers, depending upon either the final assembly process they were used for, or the identity of the customer. As a result, it was often difficult to track where a particular component was made. In one case, all orders for a particular part number were traditionally processed through the UK factory, but in reality the component was made in Germany. A Belgium subsidiary used this component in a final assembly for local customers, but found that their price to customers had become uncompetitive. Analysis eventually identified the problem. The Belgium factory ordered the component from the UK factory (I day); the UK factory then passed the order to the UK warehouse (2 days). The UK warehouse ordered the component from the factory located in Germany (2 days). The German factory fulfilled the order to the UK warehouse by truck (5 days), and then the UK warehouse shipped it to the UK factory (2 days), followed by a further trip over to Belgium (3 days). At the time, no one could see the full journey from order to delivery, only the stage that applied to them. By integrating product codes and source data in the data warehouse, the component could then be sourced direct from Germany across the border to the Belgium factory, leading to a cut in delivery times from 15 to 5 days and a significant reduction in distribution costs. This led to a more effective marketing and sales strategy, based on competitive pricing and improved delivery times.

Sometimes, a whole market can be transformed by a new entrant with an innovative vision of data management that can create a step-change in the relationships between suppliers and customers. Take the case of GHX's arrival in the medical supply market (Mouncey, McDonald and Ryals, 2004). Historically, each manufacturer of a particular medical product would sell direct to hospitals and clinics, or to specialist intermediaries. Mostly these transactions also took place off-line, using paper catalogues produced by each supplier. However, many hospitals had more than one source for particular products and as each manufacturer used its own description and numbering, the inventory lists needed to manage medical supplies were extremely lengthy and confusing. This led to many incorrect orders, slow delivery times, large numbers of returns, high costs, withheld payments and lots of heated discussions when things went wrong! None of this was good for the relationships between suppliers and hospitals (or for staff and potentially, patient care) as meetings tended to focus on errors and delayed orders, rather than on new ideas and more collaboration. GHX came into this chaotic marketplace with a radical, but highly practical, solution. They set up as an intermediary between the manufacturers and hospitals, but they developed a single electronic catalogue of products where each product, no matter who manufactured it, was given a common description and stock number. Also, the whole order process was put online. Figures 10.1 and 10.2 illustrate the process.

FIGURE 10.1   'Many-to-many' e-marketplace: GHX

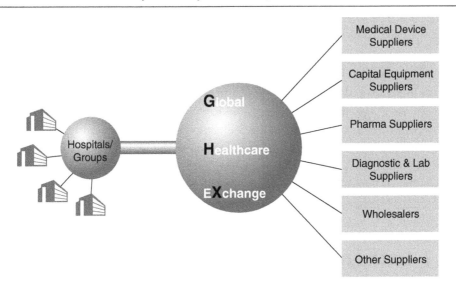

SOURCE: GHX

FIGURE 10.2   GHX electronic catalogue creates standards

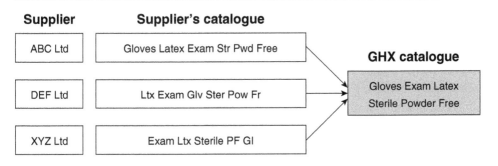

FIGURE 10.3   GHX – the benefits

'Hard' measures

- Reduction in order errors (60% reduced to nil)
- Reduced resources (order taking/processing)
- Reduction in product returns
- Consolidated orders (16 orders per wk reduced to 2)
- Reduced no. of suppliers
- Reduced debtor days (funded by suppliers)

'Soft' measures

- Reduced conflict in supplier customer relationship
- Improved customer service
- Increased 'face to face' meetings
- Broader/deeper key account relationship relationship
- Opportunities for collaboration (eliminate centralized purchasing)

As you can see from Figure 10.3, this created immense benefits for all stakeholders.

This innovative, data-led, solution has provided error-free transactions, improvements in cash flow, major cost savings and removed immense frustration from the process of ordering and supplying medical supplies. Most importantly, the trust between customers and suppliers improved leading to the manufacturers being able to develop collaborative-level key account relationships with hospitals, enabling discussions to be strategically focused on identifying new opportunities for innovation in products and services, instead of 'fire-fighting' day-to-day operation issues.

10.3 Data and competitive advantage

When responsibly managed and creatively used, data to support and facilitate marketing-related activities (including sales and customer service activities – as contained in the definition of marketing used in this book) can provide organizations with significant differentiation from competitors and transform their relationship with the marketplace. However, by failing to develop and implement effective strategies for data management, organizations are likely to underachieve within their sector and suffer from higher, and costly, levels of customer churn. Their ability to accurately measure outcomes and progress in achieving goals will also be significantly compromised.

The availability of data to support, facilitate and measure the impact of marketing has grown exponentially in the past decade. Sean Kelly (2006), a leading expert on data management in marketing, describes today's world as the era of 'data wars', where the competitive success of organizations is increasingly dependent upon their data management competencies in supporting marketing. Kelly has also described the rise of 'information intermediaries', as illustrated in Figure 10.4, organizations within the overall demand/supply chain that have recognized the competitive advantage of customer-related data as a key weapon in controlling marketplaces. For example, in the FMCG sector, a retailer with a sophisticated customer loyalty programme can decide to charge its suppliers for access to this valuable store of data, thereby potentially limiting suppliers' knowledge of customers and the market, or increasing the cost of being able to access the data. This has obvious implications for organizations that rely on intermediaries for access to end-users and their ability to identify segments in the market and collect data about them and their needs. In Kelly's view, it is very difficult for a single organization to effectively exist on both sides of the dotted line (see Figure 10.4).

The availability of data on customers and the granularity of the data, coupled with the opportunities to use the data to create differentiated value propositions for different types of customer, were highlighted within a further Cranfield research report (Clark, McDonald and Smith, 2002). Understanding the data flows available to an organization is a key factor in identifying, firstly, viable marketing-related strategies for an organization and, secondly, the most appropriate strategies to adopt.

One energy company believes that data quality creates a differentiation from competitors, especially as its strategy is based on creating a single view of the customer. For example, customer services can resolve queries at the first call.

FIGURE 10.4   The rise of the intelligent intermediary

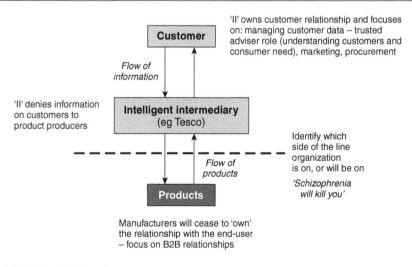

Adapted from Kelly (2006)

A leading engineering company identified that, owing to multi-numbers for the same part plus difficulties in identifying the geographic source of a product, order delivery times and distribution costs, and therefore prices, had become uncompetitive. By integrating product codes and source data in the data warehouse, the part could be sourced direct to the customer, leading to a cut in delivery times from 15 to 5 days and a significant reduction in distribution costs.

10.4 Data literacy

English (1999) provides ample evidence of the cost, often highly significant, to organizations of poor data management. It is not simply that organizations have no, or an inadequate, strategy for managing their data; it is much more fundamental than that. It is as if these organizations suffer from poor data literacy, a type of black hole within their culture – and data literacy is a prerequisite for marketing in today's world. For example, poor quality of data was cited by respondents within a survey conducted by Strathclyde University for the Institute of Direct Marketing (IDM) (Mouncey *et al*, 2002) as the key factor that inhibited the value and application of their customer databases. Any organization that has substantial numbers of customer records that cannot be included within marketing programmes because of data quality issues, or that are inaccurate, leading to poor targeting, is sacrificing substantial future flows of revenue – rather like having half the production line out of action, or the shop shut at times of peak demand. An illustration of the cost to an organization of poor data quality is given in section 10.10. Records that are inaccurate or lack key data items lead to dissatisfied customers, inappropriate offers being made, and invalid metrics, and could potentially contravene the fourth principle within the UK Data Protection Act 1998 requiring personal data to be both accurate and, where necessary, up to date.

10.5 Challenges to data integration

In addition to struggling with data quality issues, organizations also quickly discover that the allied challenge of integrating data captured through a disparate range of sources also creates numerous problems. For example, how can (if at all) data collected through traditional market research surveys, a rich source of customer profiling and the essential 'why' (attitudinal and behavioural) information, be combined with the narrowly focused transaction records commonly the main basis for a customer database? How can all that be analysed alongside that which customers post on social media sites, videos they upload and SMS messages they leave with the firm?

What are the legal and ethical boundaries that organizations face when attempting to integrate personal-level data obtained from a variety of internal and external sources? The challenge increases exponentially as organizations implement increasingly complex multichannel strategies, particularly if real-time information becomes essential. Organizations also tend to forget that data are generated through business processes, and process mapping therefore needs to be a key competency in the marketing data strategy toolbox.

A report on data management strategies (Information Age, 2005) included a comparison between the mobile phone manufacturer Nokia and Barclays Bank. The report cited the 120 separate databases within Nokia containing customer data – 'a patchwork built up by its different divisions for their own purposes (legitimate) as the company has grown at breakneck speed'. The structure includes, for example, individual data marts for:

- analysing the performance of mobile operators;
- tracking third-party resellers;
- logging end customers who registered their product.

Overall the situation had led to high levels of data duplication, effort and confusing multiple versions of the truth! It means that Nokia had problems answering such questions as:

- How many active customers are there (rather than phones shipped)?
- Who are the most profitable customers and what are their profiles?
- How loyal are Nokia customers?
- Which sales are primarily for business use?

Barclays, on the other hand, took three years to solve similar problems by building an enterprise data warehouse to improve the interaction with its 12 million customers. This led to a saving of £10 million in its annual marketing budget by improved targeting. Barclays also claims other economies, as there are fewer systems to support or maintain – estimated as around £1.1 million per mart within a large organization (including software licences).

The objectives for an enterprise warehouse were cited as:

- a single version of the data;
- a single view of the customer;
- improved data quality (one source for cleansing and ensuring accuracy);
- accessibility by users throughout the organization;
- a quicker response to changing business needs;

- more frequent updates;
- an enhancing of regulatory compliance.

These are all issues faced by many organizations.

Data quality issues simply become magnified when data integration projects are attempted, leading to potentially severely flawed decision making and contact strategy, and major challenges in accurately measuring the performance of marketing.

10.6 Creating a business case (return on investment) for data quality

A further dilemma faced by organizations is that they have no real framework for identifying the return on investment (RoI) for the data that they hold or need. While individual items of data can be stored at relatively low cost, to this must be added the more substantial ongoing investment in collecting or acquiring the information, and keeping it up to date. Organizations need a framework that can identify the core data essential to achieving their business goals (including performance measurement), and that also enables them to demonstrate the added value created by the data. Tools such as the information supply chain or the Benefits Dependency Network, described in Chapter 8, can also be used to help organizations build a convincing business case to address this issue. The logic of the BDN suggests that the data alone does not generate RoI, but that they enable the implementation of other strategies that do. The monetization of investments that create capabilities that enable ambitious strategies is a perennial issue for IS research (Goh and Kauffman, 2005).

Corporate priorities can play a major role in addressing data quality issues. For example, a leading international manufacturer based in the UK was able to establish the real contribution to the overall business of accurate data once finance realized the importance of the data warehouse as a key source of management information and managed it as a company-wide strategic asset. This example underlines the impact of different data standards within an organization. As finance wanted to use the data to provide accurate and up-to-date information to help improve the operational management of the business, they introduced more stringent requirements to those previously applied for marketing purposes.

10.7 Creating insight

Organizations increasingly talk about customer (or consumer) insight instead of market research, but unless there is a structured approach to knowledge management, real insight will be extremely difficult to achieve in practice. Customer segmentation is a key tool in deriving insight, but this needs to be tailored to the data available to the organization, the market sector, and to be multidimensional. In some sectors, such as travel and personal electronic devices, a customer-managed segmentation may be more appropriate. Some firms have moved beyond this and into the mass customized zone – practising one-to-one or segment-of-one marketing. However, some of the biggest challenges facing any organization developing a segmentation-led strategy include a lack of data, the level of granularity relative to that necessary for decision making, and the poor quality of available data.

Some insight data can be defined as *hard* (readily factual) data (eg name and address, transaction details) and others as *soft* data, such as attitudes and behaviour. Data captured through internal financial systems are usually *hard* data, whereas traditional survey research-based data are classed as *soft*. Most customer databases and data warehouses contain primarily *hard* data. A third category used to support marketing needs is *derived* data generated through modelling, such as trend and propensity used both inbound and outbound for marketing analysis. Similarly, despite pleas from leading exponents of the customer equity concept, there is as yet no recognized accounting methodology that allows the customer base, and the knowledge held about it, to be treated as some form of capital asset, in the same way that brands can be valued on a company balance sheet.

Key data for most organizations include data that can identify the customer, together with some form of transaction information. Typical customer-related data that are critical to marketing are shown in Table 10.1. The primary type of each data item is shown by an 'X', and subsidiary types, used to create the derived data, by 'y'. This indicates the importance of, firstly, analytical/modelling tools and associated competencies in order to create the derived variables and, secondly, 'soft' data in gaining a comprehensive picture of customers.

One leading IT company also divides data by appropriateness: *static* – how well the data provide an accurate description of a customer; and *dynamic* – whether the data are suitable for predicting future behaviour, and whether the data match the strategic future needs of the organization.

TABLE 10.1   Categories of data

Data	Hard	Soft	Derived
Customer contact details	X		
Geodemographic code			X
Segment	y	y	X
Sales/transactions (all channels/products)	X		
Product/service usage	X	X	
Payment methods	X		
Retention/churn	X	y	
Loyalty	y	y	X
Contacts (and reason) (all channels)	X	y	
Campaigns	X	y	y
Satisfaction		X	X
Channel preference	y	y	X
Profile	y	y	X
Acquisition source/cost	X		
Current value/profitability	y		X
Future value/profitability	y	y	X

10.8 Technology and Information Systems

Information Systems facilitate data capture, hold data, and provide the tools with which to extract value and deploy the knowledge. Customer data, the database platforms, data warehouses and integration systems, tools and deployment technologies are all now key components within the core infrastructure of many organizations. These tools require constant investment in order to keep them up to date – best practice data management is a complex, enterprise-wide, iterative journey rather than a one-off, functional project, with data at the core. But 'garbage in, garbage out' will be the result unless data quality issues are addressed as part of the overall strategy.

Data need to be viewed as a key corporate asset if the continual investment in the necessary infrastructure and application tools is to be readily accepted at board level. The data asset therefore needs a long-term strategy all of its own.

10.9 Success factors

Evidence from the rich databank compiled by QCi, a then subsidiary of the Ogilvy Group, comprising audits of over 5,000 companies using their CMAT benchmarking tool (Woodcock, 2000) clearly indicates however that, despite the undoubted importance of information, technology and processes, the three key factors that make the difference within customer-related strategy are to do with the people (culture, training, etc), measuring what happens, and the customer management practices devised by the organization. QCi advise that these three should be the priority for attention, and that these should be developed to support the overall business model – not the other way round. They conclude that: 'Companies who manage customers well using sensible, observable, well-implemented business practices are likely to be best-in-class performers. Conversely, companies who do not set up good customer management practices are likely to be poor performers' (Mark Say, QCi).

A global survey of 600 CIOs and IT directors undertaken in 2001 by PricewaterhouseCoopers posed six questions that CEOs need to consider in deciding whether the organization is paying sufficient attention to data issues and at the right level within the company structure:

- Have we suffered significant problems, costs or losses in any area because of data quality?
- In two years' time will more of our business depend on automated decisions and processes based on electronic data?
- Are we paying sufficient attention to data issues at board level?
- Who is ultimately responsible for the quality of our data?
- Do we have a data management strategy – or just a series of fragmented policies?
- Do we trust the quality of our own data – or of anyone else's?

The same survey showed that effective data management had led to the following important benefits for companies interviewed:

- reduced processing (59 per cent of companies interviewed);
- increased sales through improved prediction (35 per cent);
- winning a significant contract (32 per cent);
- increased sales through better analysis (43 per cent).

10.10 Identifying the cost of poor data quality

As illustrated earlier on in this chapter, many organizations have to date either under-estimated the importance of data quality or failed to address this as an enterprise-wide issue. As described earlier, a survey of companies commissioned by the IDM (Mouncey *et al*, 2002) found that data quality was the top mentioned barrier that limited the role of the customer database, even in those organizations claiming to be gaining high value from their database.

According to QCi, 39 per cent of organizations have no data quality standards in place, and 56 per cent have no capability for tracking whether their data quality is improving or not. QCi have several examples within their 'Data Roll Call of Shame' that illustrate the consequences of inadequate standards of quality:

- In a mailing of 20,000 mugs, 5,000 were returned as undelivered or 'gone away'.

- A holiday company specializing in holidays for women did not include a title field in their file sent to a mailing house, which inserted a default of 'Mr'.

- Counter staff at a bank used the name field to flag customers whom they suspected of fraud by adding '(Care fraud)' after the surname. As the direct marketing team were unaware of this practice, a mailing was sent out including letters addressed to customers with '(Care fraud)' printed after their name.

These types of errors will inevitably have impacted on customer retention and other revenue streams and have incurred additional costs in rectifying the problems. In addition, there are also likely to have been negative consequences for brand image – more of an issue today because of the rise of 'culture jamming' (Lawes, 2007) through blogging on the internet.

Similar problems also occur in the public sector – owing to an incorrect look-up table, court offenders were sent letters requesting payments for the wrong offence.

In terms of personal data held about customers, examples such as those above could lead to these organizations having breached the Data Protection Act 1998 principles covering accuracy and the holding of up-to-date personal data. Privacy Laws & Business, an advice service on data privacy, believe from their survey data that many leading organizations are failing to take this legislation seriously enough, with a significant minority transferring personal data to third parties without the permission of the data subject (Privacy Laws & Business International, 2004).

The cost to business of inadequate data quality is high – some experts put this as being between 15 and 25 per cent of operating profit (Cooper and Murray, 2004).

The following example, based on a real calculation made in the late 1990s, may not be up to date but provides a graphic illustration of the revenue lost as a result of poor data quality. Table 10.2 shows the predicted loss of revenue in two categories (future sales of the core product, cross-/upsell opportunities) from the inability to contact customers through direct mail methods for three reasons:

- 'Gone away' markers attached to the record – records suppressed for mailing owing to mail having been returned by the Royal Mail marked as 'No longer at this address' (ie no up-to-date address for that customer).

- 'Do not mail' markers – records suppressed because of Mail Preference Service markers, other requests not to mail, or poor internal processes that lead to such markers being applied for other non-related reasons.

- Missing or incorrect data items – markers indicating that key personal identifiers or product holding details are missing from the records, or records known to contain inaccurate data or suspected of being incorrect.

TABLE 10.2   The cost of poor data quality

Value of lost gross revenue	Number of customers		
	1,000	100,000 (revenue over one year)	1 million (revenue over five years)
	£	£	£
Sales of core product	80,000	800,000	4,000,000
Lost cross-/upsell opportunities	4,000	400,000	2,000,000
Total lost revenue	84,000	1,200,000	6,000,000

Rigby and Ledingham (2004) underline the point that perfect data comes at a cost – in terms of processes, systems and the actions that may be necessary to respond to the data. The extra accuracy may deliver little or no real incremental added value to either the company or its customers. They describe why a leading global printer equipment manufacturer opted for real-time information to stem a growing tide of customer dissatisfaction with the service provided by its call centre. The article describes the impressive results in terms of increased call centre productivity, lower training costs, reduced call waiting times, lower product returns, and increased insight into customer needs and behaviour that can be used to target customer communications more effectively. The key point is that the pay-off could be measured and that the benefits were more widespread than initially anticipated. This article also includes a framework for identifying the true value of information and addressing the key questions:

- How good is the information?
- What is it good for?
- What are the costs (of keeping/putting it right)?
- Which business results matter most (and therefore where are accurate data vital)?

10.11 Data management strategy

The Gartner Group, which has published several estimates of CRM project failure rates, has cited ignoring customer data as the number one reason for the failure of CRM investment (Nelson and Kirby, 2001), echoing the quotation from Siragher (2001) earlier in this chapter. The survey conducted by PricewaterhouseCoopers (2001) mentioned earlier found that only 40 per cent of 'traditional' (excluding dotcoms) organizations had a formal and board-level approved data strategy, and 57 per cent of boards only occasionally, rarely or never discussed data issues.

According to QCi (QCi Assessment, 2002), organizations implementing CRM tend to invest heavily in technology without sufficient investment in data management. Out of the 260 best practices covered by the CMAT audit process used by QCi to audit organizations' customer management capabilities, no fewer than 140 required evidence of the effective management and use of customer data (Foss *et al*, 2002). Organizations are acquiring increasing quantities of data, but the objectives for doing this are often unclear and, in addition, the problem of how to maintain the data is not being adequately addressed. The result is what QCi call 'data chaos'. Based on their in-company assessments, 'best practice' customer-focused companies:

- have recognized the implications of EU data privacy legislation and are improving the accuracy and understanding of the data they hold;

- are increasing the visibility of customer-related data and making it accessible to customer-facing staff, business partners and intermediaries;

- are displaying a more trusting and mature attitude towards their customers by increasing the visibility of customer data, thus enabling these customers to gain a measure of control over their relationship with the organization and maintain the information held about them (usually resulting in a higher level of accuracy).

Only 9 per cent of the organizations assessed through the CMAT audit process in 2002 had developed effective business cases for customer strategies that would enable progress to be tracked over time. This has major implications for the extent to which issues to do with data are recognized and actively addressed within the overall strategy – what gets measured gets managed.

A key problem facing organizations is that existing processes and data are fragmented and uncoordinated across and between traditional business silos or functions – sales, marketing, customer service, call centres, retail outlets, websites, etc. Front-office and back-office systems are not effectively linked together. For example, the call centre support system may not be directly linked to the customer database and therefore agents are denied access to contacts and transactions through other channels – or these updates are not sufficiently frequent to provide a 'real-time' picture. Local systems may be designed to meet purely local needs. In addition, organizations are often dependent upon 'legacy systems' as key sources of data, where the processes and definitions used for data may be poorly documented.

The key question is the extent to which organizations have strategies for data management in place that can help resolve these types of issues and support the overall marketing strategy. The evidence from earlier research investigating customer-focused strategies indicates two fundamental factors that lead to data quality issues inhibiting progress: 1) Any strategy for data tends to lag behind the decision to implement customer strategies (Mouncey and Clark, 2005). 2) A comprehensive, enterprise-wide data strategy is rare. QCi believes, for example, that few organizations (4 per cent in 2002) have an enterprise-wide information strategy or plan.

Data to support marketing may be sourced from many different points within the organization. Data may also be obtained from external sources, such as business partners or information providers (eg research agencies, advertising/media agencies). Overall, this diversity creates problems of ensuring consistency, integrating the different feeds, and overcoming resistance from data owners and conflicting business objectives across the enterprise. Company mergers and acquisitions cause further problems in confidently identifying individual customers through problems with integrating data from different systems and data management regimes.

10.12 Why an enterprise-wide approach to data management is vital

Issues that arise in this situation can include the metrics that drive operational units, such as customer service/contact centres, where any emphasis on productivity metrics conflicts with requirements from other areas of the business in either updating existing customer data or collecting new data items. These issues can be resolved only either by having an enterprise-wide strategy for data, where everyone understands the importance of accurate and comprehensive data in achieving business goals, or where there is a process in place that requires a cost–benefit case to be made, identifying the enterprise-wide opportunities that particular data might provide – and then measuring the results.

A case study based on a leading telecommunications company (Reid and O'Brien, 2005) describes the outcome where inadequate processes and data quality issues had not been addressed, leading to the initial attempt by the organization to build a single customer view as having 'failed to model anything close to a real-world customer entity'. The authors conclude that:

- Organizations should not assume that data held in dispersed databases will be of a similar format.

- Data from secondary sources may be out of date.

- Organizations need to engender a culture where data are viewed as being for the greater good of the whole enterprise rather than for the exclusive use of a business unit or in a single operational process.

For example, within the organization where the emphasis in strategy is focused on customer retention, owned within part of the sales and marketing team, difficulties could be experienced whenever this team tries to gain the support of other teams who collect and process customer data – such as the call centres. In an Asian company, where strategy hinges on the accuracy of the data collected within a questionnaire completed in-store by new customers (Mouncey and Clark, 2005), there are specially trained customer service staff within each shop who help ensure that the necessary information is obtained, by focusing on the subsequent benefits that can be enjoyed by customers and their households. Despite this emphasis, there are still residual data quality issues.

Within an international telecommunications company, the responsibilities for customer strategies have been devolved into the business units, and there is no longer a board role with this title. However, despite there having been a senior champion in the past, the initial strategy did not lead to a truly 'data literate' culture across the constituent parts of the overall business unit. To help address this 'black hole', an information management steering board was formed with the responsibility for creating a corporate data strategy covering this business (Mouncey and Clark, 2005).

External pressures can sometimes act as a catalyst for change, especially if the pressure comes from an industry regulatory body. For example, despite the emphasis on the customer within a leading UK mutual financial services organization, marketing has historically been carrying the metaphorical torch for data quality as a group-wide issue. However, the changing external regulatory framework for the industry sector as a whole is now driving data strategy on to the corporate agenda. New standards for integrating and reconciling data have been introduced, and the increased requirement for ensuring quality may well lead to a main board member having data strategy added to his or her portfolio of responsibilities.

10.13 Developing an enterprise-wide information strategy

English (1999) describes one method to assess the current state of information management within an organization and the associated criteria for measuring progress, the Information Quality Management Maturity Grid, adapted from the methodology for assessing quality management devised by Philip Crosby. This is illustrated in Table 10.3.

This methodology maps five stages in information strategy maturity against six measurement criteria, describing the factors for each cell within the matrix. Such a framework can help senior management identify the current position, develop an effective strategy and then measure progress towards the defined goals. Definitions or rules need to be agreed for factors such as:

- accuracy (including the level of confidence);
- matching/integration;
- updating;
- archiving;
- discarding;
- compliance (with any sector regulations or legislation);
- fit with business goals;
- setting markers covering usage.

TABLE 10.3 Information Quality Management Maturity Grid

Measurement categories	Stage 1: Uncertainty	Stage 2: Awakening	Stage 3: Enlightenment	Stage 4: Wisdom	Stage 5: Certainty
Management understanding and attitude	No comprehension of info quality as management tool. Blame IT/admin.	Recognize a problem; unwilling to allocate resources.	Learning about quality management: more support and help.	Understand absolutes of IQ management; recognize personal role.	IQ essential activity.
IQ organization status	Emphasis on correcting bad data; quality hidden within departments.	Main emphasis still on correcting bad data.	Structure for IQ exists and advising applications.	IQ management reports to CIO; full involvement with business areas.	Main focus is prevention.
Information quality problem handling	'Firefighting'; no definitions; blame culture.	Short-term ad hoc 'fixes'; no long-term thinking.	Problems faced and resolved openly and communicated.	Early identification of issues; open participatory culture.	IQ problems prevented except in exceptional situations.
Cost of info quality as % of revenue	Reported: No Actual: 20%	Reported: 5% Actual: 18%	Reported: 10% Actual: 18%	Reported: 8% Actual: 10%	Reported: 5% Actual: 5%
Info quality improvement actions	No organized activities or understanding could be organized.	Trying obvious short-term efforts.	Implementation of structured IQ programme; issues understood.	Beginning to optimize solutions.	IQ improvement the norm.
Summation of company info quality posture	'We don't know why we have problems with IQ.'	'It is absolutely necessary to always have problems with IQ.'	'Problems being resolved through IQ improvement and management commitment.'	'IQ problem preventation is routine.'	'We know why we don't have IQ problems.'

SOURCE: English, 1999

FIGURE 10.5   The planning cycle

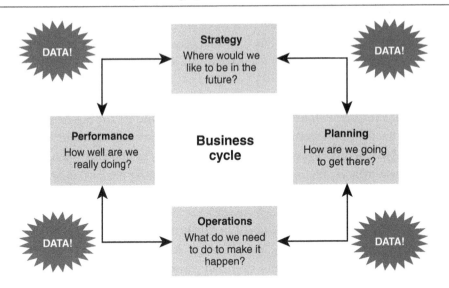

Within one leading energy company, 'data' are viewed as an integral part of the corporate planning cycle, as illustrated in Figure 10.5.

A process like this moves data quality to the top of the corporate agenda by establishing a clear link between data quality and its vital role in achieving strategic goals. This process helps reduce the risks to marketing strategy, as data quality is viewed as a strategic issue for the whole organization.

10.14 Data governance

Developing a strategy for data management is only the starting point. The continuing challenge is to ensure that the agreed policy and defined processes are adequately actioned throughout the organization at an operational level. As a key part of their strategy, organizations therefore need to audit formally the extent to which information is being effectively managed to support marketing strategy, identify the gaps, develop an improvement plan and measure progress over time. Without this they will be unable either to pin down the costs of poor quality or to quantify the benefits that will flow from a programme of improvement. This analysis will also help scope the budget necessary to achieving the level of quality required to achieve business goals. Where data are critical to measuring the performance of key business functions, the board could agree to this responsibility being given to the internal audit function.

Defining what is meant by data quality is a key issue. 'Fit for purpose', rather than absolute quality, should be the aim. For example, some gaps and inaccuracies may be acceptable within a data-set used for modelling, but the standard would need to be much higher where transactions data and records of customer contact history, through all channels, are used in real time to support a service call centre or a self-service website.

'Fit for purpose' may also be defined by needs to meet regulatory requirements (eg Basel 2 requirements within financial services organizations) and legal requirements (eg European data protection legislation – keeping data accurate and up to date; meeting subject access requirements; being able to differentiate between SMEs and domestic customers or differentiate personal data from non-personal data held about business contacts, etc; safety legislation, such as being able to contact car owners to recall vehicles to rectify safety defects, etc). According to a survey conducted by Privacy Laws & Business International in 2004, many organizations are failing to take data privacy issues seriously, and QCi (QCi Assessments Ltd, 2002) found that only 37 per cent of the companies they had assessed had adequate plans in place to meet the requirements of the 1998 Act. Finally, 'fit for purpose' considerations also apply to the issues affecting the capture of source data and the user situation. For example, the competence of employees involved in the capture of data and those who have access to it needs to be taken into account.

Data quality also covers the need to ensure that critical data items are identified and appropriate strategies are developed to ensure that any deficiencies are addressed. A US insurance company (Pula, Store and Foss, 2003) identified that 'roof year' (the date that a new roof is put on a building) was a key data item in assessing risk within buildings insurance. Subsequent analysis of its database showed that:

- Seven per cent of records contained a null value for this item.

- Many records held 'default' years – 1900 or 1908.

- Nearly two-thirds of values were for 1997 as a result of a major data file conversion in that year, as any record with a null value or a roof year equal to the building's date of construction was assigned the 1997 default to ensure policyholders were not penalized because of incorrect information.

- There were varying and inconsistent business rules for assigning a 'roof year'.

- There was an assumption (proved wrong) that the system introduced in 1997 was built and maintained to a higher quality in terms of data than earlier systems. In fact, it was discovered that no data cleansing of source files for the new system had been undertaken as part of the migration process.

Similarly, the data quality programme at the Bank of Scotland (Clark, 1998) discovered that a very high proportion of customers were shown as being the same age as the century. This was due to 1900 having been used as the default for this field if the date of birth was unknown!

Other examples of poor data definitions include 12 different spellings of the colour 'beige' (Automobile Association roadside services database) and 37 reasons for cancelling an insurance policy (Pula, Store and Foss, 2003)!

An energy supplier has implemented a data quality audit process with the following objectives:

- to develop a data quality scorecard and supporting framework;
- to explain clearly the methodology so it can be replicated;
- to answer the key question: 'How accurate is the information held about customers?';
- to produce a detailed data quality audit report, including data quality metrics and business rules;
- to assess the cost to the business of data quality issues;
- to describe clearly the methodology behind the costing model;
- to document recommendations and the value to the business of improvements;
- to provide a framework to support the data governance strategy and input to future work programmes;
- to identify and highlight the value of 'quick wins'.

The scorecard covers: completeness, conformity, accuracy, consistency and duplication. The governance strategy is managed within the customer insight team, with commitment at board level and from senior finance management. A specialist consultancy undertook the initial data quality audit, with a remit as a partner in achieving, and embedding, best practice within the organization. The strategy has created a much more open and transparent approach to discussing data issues – not just about applications. It has enabled data flows to be identified within the company, and the impacts caused by inadequate data quality. Workshops are used to identify priorities, including the cost and revenue implications.

This is against a background within the company where there was a perception that data quality was poor, but with no responsibilities for addressing the problem, no policies, no impact assessments and no clear understanding of the costs to the business of poor data quality. In addition, there was the probability that the situation infringed legal and regulatory frameworks. The strategy is now firmly positioned to identify and communicate the cost to the business of poor data quality, especially from a customer relationship perspective. Communication is a vital part of the strategy, together with a 'no blame' approach, engendering a passion to improve and engagement across all parts of the business through a cross-functional flexible approach.

The leading international manufacturing company described in section 10.6 has also included data quality in its scorecard and board-level dashboards as part of its corporate performance management strategy. As mentioned earlier, board-level interest in data quality was fuelled by finance taking over the responsibility for the company's data warehouse.

A key initial step in the quality process is to audit all the ways that the organization collects particular types of information, for example auditing the processes for collecting information from new customers or prospects – application forms, call centres, websites, and third parties such as agents, retailers, business partners, data providers, etc – to ensure that a common format for collecting core customer details is in place. One organization found that basic data on customers were recorded in 32 sources, but there was no consistent approach to the format used, for example sometimes collecting full forenames but on other occasions only one or more initials, recording date of birth in some sources but age in others, and treating some data as optional in one business area and essential in others.

A further step in the overall audit process is to ensure that checks are regularly undertaken to ensure that agreed standards are being adhered to and that processes deliver the required level of quality. For example, a leading mutual organization commissioned a market research agency to undertake a survey of members to assess the accuracy of data held about them prior to demutualization in order to estimate the likely extent to which voting papers would be received by only those entitled to vote. The results of this survey could have been used as evidence if any member had challenged the validity of the voting process. Regularly auditing customer data in this way should be part of a best-practice data management strategy.

Particularly in the early stages of implementing strategy, there needs to be a dedicated data quality team. Within a telecommunications company interviewed in earlier research (Mouncey and Clark, 2005), this responsibility was a defined role within the central customer insight team, which reports to the marketing director. An engineering company has 'data champions' in all its business units round the world. These are not data specialists; generally they are experienced managers in a variety of roles, but with a common appreciation of how good-quality data are an essential foundation to creating an efficient, well-managed business.

The responsibility for defining and implementing a data strategy must be business unit owned, rather than being left to the IT department. The same applies to any team put in place to manage data quality – this must represent business interests and be managed from a business perspective. The tools described in this and other chapters are designed to be used by business units. The IT specialists will play an important role in supporting the business units to achieve their goals, and have tools and solutions available to help facilitate the implementation of the agreed data strategy. In addition, the data quality programme must be business led. The key criteria for the data quality business case should include:

- productivity improvements (eg shorter-duration phone calls);
- reduced costs (eg reduced errors in the order process, fewer complaints to resolve);
- increased revenue (eg cross-/upsell, improved customer lifetime value);
- reduced customer churn.

Proving the business case for the improved quality of information over time may also be incorporated into the measurement of the incremental value generated by marketing activities. For example, Vauxhall Motors measured the incremental effectiveness of its overall CRM programme (Boothby, 2002) by having a representative control cell of 10 per cent of the overall customer and prospect base who received no communications from the company. Control samples could also be applied to measuring the value of improved data management processes in terms of the impact on revenue, customer satisfaction and image.

References

Boothby, K (2002) Vauxhall Motors: Engineering profitable long term customer loyalty, *Interactive Marketing*, 4 (4)

Clark, K (1998) Case study: The Bank of Scotland, Data Quality 98 (conference presentation), London

Clark, M, McDonald, M and Smith, B (2002) *Achieving Excellence in Customer Relationship Management*, Cranfield School of Management, Cranfield

Cooper, J and Murray, D (2004) *Adopting Best Practice in Data Quality*, Institute of Direct Marketing, Teddington

English, L P (1999) *Improving Data Warehouse and Business Information*, Wiley, New York

Foss, B, Henderson, I, Johnson, P, Murray, D and Store, M (2002) Managing the Quality and Completeness of Customer Data, *Journal of Database Marketing*, 10 (2)

Goh, K H and Kauffman, R (2005) Towards a Theory of Value Latency for IT Investments in Hawaii, IEEE, pp 1–9

Information Age (2005) *The Effective IT Report 2005*, Information Age, London, February

Institute of Practitioners in Advertising (2006) *Advertising Works 14*, pp xi–xvi, Institute of Practitioners in Advertising, London

Kelly, S (2006) *Customer Intelligence from Data to Dialogue*, Wiley, Chichester

Lawes, R (2007) Culture Jamming: A new, researchable consumer trend, Proceedings of the Market Research Society Conference, Brighton, March

Mouncey, P and Clark, M (2005) *Data: The Weakest Link or the Core Strength in CRM Strategy?*, Cranfield University School of Management, Cranfield

Mouncey, P, Tzokas, N, Hart, S and Reslender, R (2002) Core Strategic Asset or Just a Tactical Tool: How UK companies view the value of their customer databases, *Interactive Marketing*, 4 (1)

Mouncey, P, McDonald, M and Ryals, L (2004) *Key Customers: Identifying and implementing IT solutions that add value to key account management strategies*, Cranfield University, Cranfield

Nelson, S and Kirby, J (2001) *Key Reasons Why CRM Fails*, Gartner Group, Stamford, Connecticut

PricewaterhouseCoopers (2001) *Global Data Management Survey*, PricewaterhouseCoopers, London

Privacy Laws & Business International (2004) *E-news*, April, www.privacylaws.com

Pula, E N, Stone, M and Foss, B (2003) Customer Data Management in Practice: An insurance case study, *Journal of Database Marketing*, 10 (4)

QCi Assessment (2002) *State of the Nation*, QCi Assessment Ltd, London

Reid, A and O'Brien, D (2005) Creating a Single View of the Customer for CRM Strategy: A case example, *Interactive Marketing*, 6 (4)

Rigby, D and Ledingham, D (2004) CRM Done Right, *Harvard Business Review*, November

Siragher, N (2001) *Carving Jelly*, Chiltern Publishing, High Wycombe

Woodcock, N (2000), Does How Businesses Are Managed Impact on Business Performance?, *Interactive Marketing*, 1 (4)

The book so far has described an approach to marketing accountability that incorporates strategy, risk and long-term competitiveness. We propose an integrated and comprehensive model and a pragmatic method for its operationalization. Despite what we hope you agree is its completeness, there are a number of important emerging trends that complement the model outlined in this book. We have asked some of our collaborators to provide specialist support in addressing them and we present them as complements to the core model. Each should be appreciated as standalone topic pieces, highly relevant to marketing accountability, but not necessarily integral to our measurement model and process in all instances.

- Chapter 11, written by Stan Maklan and Hugh Wilson of Cranfield, deals with customer management strategies that are increasingly popular: CRM and customer experience. Our research suggests that the starting point for customer experience is multichannel marketing, the integration of all of the emerging channels into a holistic customer experience (eg physical location, internet, mobile devices, social media sites).

- Chapter 12 is written by Robert Stratton of MarketShare, a specialist analytics firm with an extremely impressive advisory board of leading academics in 'big data' and market analysis. It writes about trends in social media analysis. Most firms are spending increasing sums on this new media but likely struggling to understand how to assess it with respect to other opportunities. As one of the authors of the book likes to ask: 'How much is a like really worth?'

- Chapter 13 is another co-authored topic piece between Stan Maklan and David Haigh, Founder and CEO of Brand Finance. David is one of the world's most respected figures in area of brand valuation and a leading authority on the topic. Malcolm McDonald is a Board member of Brand Finance.

Assessing the effectiveness of customer strategies

11

STAN MAKLAN AND HUGH WILSON

Cranfield University

So far, we have explored accountability through the lens of traditional product-based marketing strategies. Marketing's origins are in helping firms identify and satisfy customers' needs and wants at a profit. The strategies for achieving that objective have traditionally been via creating bundles of product, service and emotional attributes that customers prefer to competitors' offers. Measuring marketing accountability is therefore an exercise in determining the extent to which the firm uses its customer knowledge to create more insightful market segmentation, responds with the appropriate portfolio of offers (products, services) and communicates its offers in a compelling fashion. And if one looks at many of today's most respected companies, such strategies are highly successful and associated with superior financial performance: Apple, BMW, Samsung, Coke.

However, over the past 20 years, an alternative logic has emerged to complement the above. Companies can see their business as a network of relationships, and their role is to apply know-how and insight to harness agile supply chains and generate long-term value for their best customers. The theoretical underpinnings to this approach consist of relationship marketing and service-dominant logic, wherein all value is co-created with customers (Vargo and Lusch, 2004).

While this holistic view has many components, we will focus on the customer end of that network: how firms assess the effectiveness of their customer strategies. Operationally, there are three key management processes that define customer strategy: customer relationship management (CRM), customer experience management (CEM, sometimes referred to as CXM), and multichannel management (MCM). Running a business to generate long-term customer value has profound implications for measurement and accountability.

11.1 Customer relationship management – measures

The core managerial activities of relationship marketing is to treat different customers differently (Peppers and Rogers, 1994). Managers grade their customers by a combination of profitability, risk or attractiveness and create strategies for maximizing the contribution of each customer. For some customers, it means reducing the cost to serve, while others require added investment in new services. Managers need to accumulate data at the level of individual customer inclusive not only of revenue, but real cost-to-serve and be ready to create models of long-term customer behaviour.

Armed with this data and some modelling skill, managers can estimate a customer's lifetime value (CLV) as a net present value of all future purchases, minus the total cost to serve, of an individual customer. Pfeiffer (2011) provides a simple formula for calculating CLV as a function of annual margin ($ M) multiplied by the customer's expected tenure: itself a function of retention rate (r) and the per period discount factor (d).

$$CLV = \$ \ M \ (r \ / \ 1+d-r)$$

The above model does not explicitly recognize the cost of acquiring a customer and we would add such cost (AC) to make the model more complete:

$$CLV = \$ \ M \ (r \ / \ 1+d-r) - AC$$

Hence CLV is the net present value of all future free cash flows attributable from a single customer. Adding up all the CLVs across the current and potential customer portfolio generates a firm's Customer Equity (CE), the net present value of all future free cash flows attributable from the firm's customer base, which is the value of its customer base. This is the customer flip side of Brand Equity (BE) and valuation approaches discussed elsewhere in this book for assessing the value of the firm's marketing assets (Chapter 13).

Therefore strategies to improve relationship marketing effectiveness include:

- Increasing revenue through cross-selling or up-selling
- Reducing the cost to serve (improve margin) through more intelligent use of channels and pricing
- Reducing defection (increasing retention)[1]
- Reducing the cost of acquisition through more targeted marketing, social media, word of mouth.

CRM systems have evolved over the past 20 years to provide the operational capability to cross- and up-sell more effectively. Advances in analytics permit firms to make offers more likely to be accepted by customers and improve retention through identifying behavioural patterns associated with future defection and intervene to retain customers before they defect. But perhaps the most popular use of the new CRM systems is to aggregate all data about individual customers and provide access to that data across all points of contact between the customer, the firm and its customer-facing partners. This integration across channels can increase revenue, reduce defection, but above all, it offers imaginative ways to reduce the cost to serve. We discuss channel integration and measures of its effectiveness further in this section. In addition, managers are experimenting with more sophisticated pricing algorithms that offer the possibility of differential pricing based on customer behavioural patterns, time of purchase and channel.

Pfeiffer acknowledges that the simple CLV model has limitations. It assumes a constant margin and retention rate over the lifetime of the customer. Margins vary as do defection rates. Moreover, once a customer leaves, they are lost for good in this formula. In reality, customers come and go (always a share) and lost for good has been challenged by academics who suggest more sophisticated and realistic modelling of switching (Rust, Lemon and Zeithaml, 2004). However, for many companies, merely understanding simple CLV would represent a major challenge as companies' cost accounting systems rarely capture individual cost-to-serve.

If one looks at a business as a function of its offers and segments, the decisions made will relate to optimizing the portfolio of goods and services, improving product profitability and gaining share. Looking at a business as a series of individual CLVs will focus management attention on identifying and retaining profitable customers, making unprofitable ones cheaper to serve and increasing revenue among customers with the potential to buy more.

11.2 Customer satisfaction and experience

Underpinning relationship marketing strategies must be a premise that for some customers, obtaining that which they need through relationships can be more advantageous than merely buying through the market at low prices (Thompson *et al*, 1991). Where the solution sought is complex, requires considerable tailoring or development of specific new solutions (Williamson, 1981), trust reduces the cost of acquiring or monitoring the solution and its delivery (Morgan and Hunt, 1994), it might 'pay' to work with trusted suppliers over an extended period of time. Thus, there is a link between customers' observed (or stated) behaviour and intermittent factors that cannot be observed directly (Gupta and Zeithaml, 2006). Perhaps the most important and tested of these is intermittent factors is customer satisfaction. It has been linked empirically with the value of the firm (Anderson, Fornell and Agnar, 2004), improved cash flow and lower risk (Gruca and Rego, 2005), RoI and market share (Anderson, Fornell and Lehmann, 1994). The mechanisms linking satisfaction to financial performance are varied but perhaps the most cited is the work of the management consultant, Reichheld (1996), whose work links satisfaction to loyalty, loyalty to purchases, margin and recommendation. Essentially, if you are satisfied with the supplier, you are more likely to buy from them again and recommend them to others.

11.2.1 Customer satisfaction

Satisfaction is universally used in business and has many advantages. Firstly, it is intuitively appealing: who would want customers NOT to be satisfied? Therefore it is understood at all levels across the firm. Secondly, it is very easy to gather the data and measure. Most firms use a simple five item scale question: the mathematics could not be simpler. The data can be trended, it can be assessed at the level of the firm, business unit, each offer, each service encounter. What is lacking is a universal formula for linking increases (or decreases) in satisfaction with market and financial outcomes. The academic literature has quantified the relationships for specific situations or companies suggesting that each firm must model levels of satisfaction against targeted outcomes. The modelling will not be as simple as merely collecting satisfaction scores as outcomes depend on many factors (the quality of the offer, competitors' activities, price relative to the competition, economic health, consumer confidence) and its impact is really felt in real time – one must build in a time delay between, for example, a fall in customer satisfaction and a decline in revenue. This is further complicated by an observation that the (negative) impact upon revenue is more pronounced where satisfaction is falling than where it is rising.

11.2.2 Net Promoter Score

Closely aligned with satisfaction is a measure that has proven enormously popular in practice: Net Promoter Score (NPS). NPS measures potential word of mouth, the strength of the customer's belief as to the quality of your offer. Reichheld (2003, 2006) maintains that the best predictor of customer behaviour and stock market price with respect to customer strategy can be found in that one measure alone and that it is superior to customer satisfaction.

NPS is typically calculated by asking customers how likely they would be to recommend the firm, offer, service on a zero to 10 scale. Subtracting all answers through six from the answers nine and ten generates a net promoter score. The simplicity of the 'one number you need to manage your business' has proven extremely popular and the authors see almost universal use of the measure among providers of consumer services.

The data supporting the claims however, has yet to be submitted for peer review. Renowned loyalty scholars (Keiningham *et al*, 2007) tried to replicate Reichheld's study and did not find that promoter score outperforms traditional measures of customer satisfaction in predicating performance. Instead, the authors find the results of NPS and satisfaction to be similar, which is perhaps unsurprising.

11.2.3 *Customer experience and its measure*

More recently, service-marketing scholars have rediscovered an old idea: people desire experiences more than they do products and services; the latter are a means to an end. This notion, perhaps first introduced by economists in the 1930s is very much aligned to the modern notion of a service-dominant logic wherein customers create value when they use the goods and services that they buy. Companies don't create value, they just create offers that are experienced by customers. Experience is defined as customers' perceptions of all encounters with the provider pre, during and post purchase; it includes functional and emotional attributes and occurs across customer touchpoints or channels (Klaus and Maklan, 2012; Lemke, Clark and Wilson, 2011). Customers have jobs or goals and have experiences on the way to achieving them. They seek suppliers who will help them realize their goals quickly and effectively. If value is truly created in this way, then experience should be a better predictor of customer loyalty, recommendation and overall engagement with the supplier.

Measuring customer experience is in its infancy at the time of writing this book. Early work posits that experience can be measured as a multi-item scale that predicts customer repurchase, satisfaction and recommendation (Klaus and Maklan, 2012). Unlike with satisfaction or NPS, the amount of work required to create and measure the scale is considerable, nor do we believe that there will be a universal scale applicable across all industries and contexts. It is possible that each firm will need to measure experience commensurate with its customer strategy and positioning. However it does hold the promise of being potentially a better predictor of repurchase and recommendation than satisfaction.

11.3 The multichannel challenge[2]

In preliminary explorations of customer experience practice, the first step for most firms is channel integration. Indeed, this is the lesson of CRM implementation too.

The starting point for the execution of almost any customer strategy is to provide customers with a seamless experience across all touchpoints with the company in order to improve service, close more sales and reduce the cost to serve. There is a need in both B2B and B2C markets for more proactive and sophisticated metrics to track the journey taken by our customers as they traverse today's complex multichannel route to market, and to understand this journey both from the customer's perspective and from the firm's. To do this, marketing and sales professionals need to refresh their metrics in four areas, which form the subject of the following sections:

1 *Breaking down measures of marketing and sales effectiveness by the stages of the buying cycle.* With an essentially stand-alone channel such as a traditional direct sales force, we can measure how well the channel contributes to market share by monitoring its rate of conversion of leads to customers, and hence its cost of acquisition. But, if the role of the channel is to take the customer on to the next step in the buying cycle and hand them over to a different channel for the purchase itself, we need to monitor more specifically the conversion efficiency and the cost of moving the customer along that specific step. So the whole buying cycle might involve several efficiency ratios and corresponding costs.

2 *Implementing marketing measurement techniques across a wider organizational base,* such as the units responsible for sales and CRM (which, intriguingly, is often under separate control from either marketing or sales). These techniques, which cover both situations where the individual customers are known and can be tracked and those where they can't, include control groups and econometric modelling.

3 *Managing the overall return on investment holistically across channels.* Measuring channel effectiveness in isolation – the profitability of the website, the sales force, the retail store or the call centre – is meaningless if the customer hops between several channels during the sales process. Holistic measures such as the overall expense-to-revenue ratio are therefore needed.

4 *Bringing multichannel metrics into the boardroom.* How can a multichannel marketing and sales organization develop a single set of metrics for regular review by the marketing director or indeed the board?

11.4 Breaking down conversion metrics by the buying cycle

It is good practice to develop staged metrics to evaluate the efficiency of the sales process at each stage of the buying cycle, and many organizations do this to a greater or lesser extent. Figure 11.1 shows an example for the call centre channel, taken from a British Gas service centre that also has a cross-selling role. The process and the metrics that support it are focused on this issue of cross-selling efficiency.

But metrics design becomes more complicated when multiple channels are involved in the customer relationship. To illustrate this, we will discuss a high street chain's website. Earlier to market than most of its competitors, it began with the typical dot-com vision of a 'pure-play' internet channel. Customers would be recruited via banner advertisements and paid search to the website, where they would place their order, which would then be fulfilled via a delivery from a store. But it soon discovered that this single-channel model was flawed. It calculated soon after launch that the cost of acquisition was £1,600! Clearly, much needed correcting. With some help from communications and the specialists, it calculated the ratios shown in Table 11.1 to help it analyse what was going wrong. (Data and strategy details have been amended to protect confidentiality.)

This breaking down of conversion metrics by the stages of the buying cycle was essential for the company to diagnose what was going wrong, and to evaluate the various possible solutions. The company found that more careful placing of adver-tisements and paid search made some difference to the locatability/attractability

TABLE 11.1   Efficiency of a banner ad campaign

Ratio	Calculation	Notes
Awareness efficiency (aware customers/target market size)	40,000 = 20% 200,000	Banner ad campaign increased this metric from 15% to 20%. Cost £50,000.
Locatability/attractability efficiency (visitors/aware customers)	3,000 = 7.5% 40,000	3,000 unique visitors to website during campaign (from 1 million page impressions). Cost per visitor £16.
Contact efficiency (active visitors/visitors)	600 = 20% 3,000	600 visitors stayed beyond home page.
Conversion efficiency (purchasers/active visitors)	30 = 5% 600	30 purchases from click-throughs from banner ads. Cost per purchase £50,000/30 = £1,600.
Retention efficiency (repurchasers/purchasers)	Not known	Not known at time of evaluation.

FIGURE 11.1 Tracking conversion ratios: British Gas

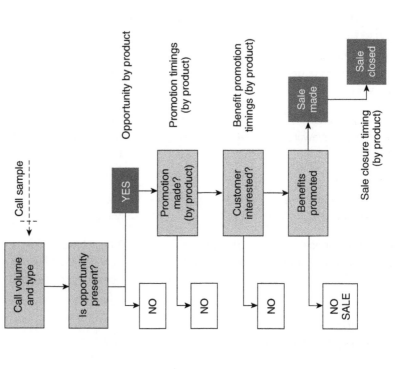

Process

Calls analysed through remote monitoring following process shown.

Opportunity definition

For the purpose of this exercise an opportunity was defined as being:

Any call where the customer currently holds less than a full complement of products/services and is likely to benefit from further British Gas products and services.

An opportunity generally exists within a call where the CSE has built rapport with the customer and 'earned the right to sell' through provision of quality service.

The resolution of certain types of complaint calls may also provide an opportunity.

Non-opportunity calls

The customer has called to make a complaint and it is clear that any sales promotion is likely to cause further damage to the customer relationship with British Gas.

Certain calls cannot be promoted on, eg third party, deceased, etc.

Data collection

An electronic data capture form was developed and used.

ratio but not enough. Its promotional emails to the customers of a related business (being careful to ensure that the email came from the business on whose website the customers had already registered, to avoid accusations of spamming) provided a much better ratio, as did its reciprocal arrangements with other online retailers with complementary product ranges, providing links to each other's sites in one case and a co-branded site in another.

Most successful of all, though, was offline promotions. The company made a big difference at virtually no cost – except considerable political perseverance by the internet division's chief executive – through prominent displays of the website address on stationery, store signs, vehicles and so on. It tried handing out promotional leaflets in shopping centres, finding this a much more cost-efficient approach than online advertising. And it tried offline press advertising (with a promotional code offering a discount on first purchase, to ensure trackability). For the first time, it could compare advertising costs online and offline, as it had worked out the impact of its banner ads not just on sales but also on awareness levels.

The company also paid attention to achieving a higher conversion rate once leads had been generated. Some simple changes to the home page improved the contact efficiency, while continuing usability testing ensured that customers weren't needlessly lost through user interface glitches.

The resulting strategy involved a mix of promotional approaches, and is constantly evolving. This strategy involved much closer working between channels than the company had initially anticipated. Therefore the company began to develop cross-channel conversion metrics, which can be annotated on what we call a channel chain diagram, as shown in Figure 11.2.

Figure 11.2 shows what channels are available for each stage of the customer relationship, supplemented by lines indicating the common routes from one channel to another. On the whole, customers who first spot an item in the store will continue to buy it from there. But, as we mentioned earlier, the company was surprised to discover that, of those customers who looked at an item on the website and went on to buy it, only a quarter did so online, the rest going into their local store.

This presents the problem of tracking this cross-channel customer behaviour. How can the impact of a paid search campaign with a search engine be measured if it is as likely to generate traffic to a store, salesforce or call centre as to a website? How can the impact of a direct mail campaign be tracked if it generates website traffic as well as direct responses? We will discuss some of the ways of disentangling the effects of multiple marketing and sales initiatives next.

FIGURE 11.2   Channel chain and metrics – high street chain

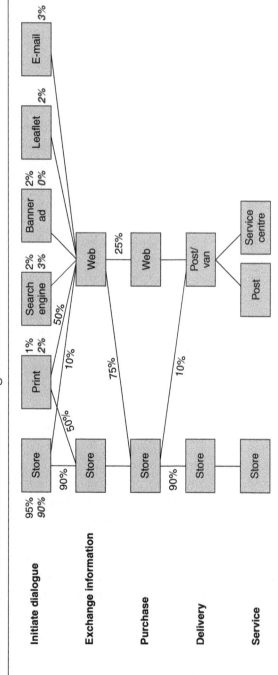

Note: The top figure by each box shows the percentage of current business initiated by the medium.
The bottom figure in *blue italics* shows a future target. Figures against lines: 50% from 'Print' to 'Web',
for example, means that 50% of the leads from print advertising then find out about the product from the web.

11.5 Tracking cross-channel behaviour

How can we measure the impact of multiple sales and marketing initiatives that cut across multiple channels? There are two broad cases to consider.

a *Where the individual customer's journey can be tracked.* The ideal approach is to follow the individual customer or prospect as they hop from one channel to another. Techniques for observing the customer as they channel-hop include: different telephone numbers on different advertisements; special web pages as different entry points to a website depending on the promotion; coupons and special offer codes linking to a specific advertisement; asking website visitors to register; and so on. At US mobile telephony business Nextel, callers are tracked as they pass through all stages of any transaction whatever the voice channel. This enables their response to dealing with an automated channel – as opposed to an agent – to be monitored and Nextel to put in place appropriate strategies for both high- and low-value customers. Loyalty cards, and the B2B equivalent of encouraging customers to identify themselves and register whatever the channel, can also be extremely useful here. By integrating loyalty card data across both stores and the web, Tesco can track when someone has browsed online and then purchased the same product in the store.

b *Where the individual customer cannot be identified.* The problem with many situations, though, is that we cannot directly tell what stimuli the customer is responding to, or what channels they have looked at prior to purchase. Here, such methods as econometric modelling that look at the impact of overall spend across different channels or media may be the only option.

The relevant techniques to support these different situations have flourished in pockets of marketing practice – such as direct mail and television advertising – for quite some time, but their usefulness extends far beyond these areas. We will therefore explain the basics of two approaches, control groups and econometric modelling, and illustrate their applicability to the evaluation of multichannel effectiveness.

11.5.1 Control groups

A very useful technique for measuring the RoI of individual activities within a complex multichannel route to market is control group measurement or experimental design (Almquist and Wyner, 2001). Control groups or control cells are used to track the impact of any specific activity over and above all the general noise the customer may hear. They are used to identify the specific impact, for example, of a direct mailshot. Instead of mailing all of the target customers, a subset of the customer base or control group is set aside at random and not mailed, with the remaining action group receiving the mailing. The only difference between the action and control groups is the receipt of the mailing, so any difference in the two groups such as different purchasing rates can be attributed to the mailing (once random variation has been accounted for statistically).

As an example, a retailer evaluated the impact on sales of a new customer magazine for its loyalty card holders. It compared the performance of the mailed customers with a control cell who were not sent the mailing. The results, shown in Table 11.2 (with amended figures and some figures omitted to protect confidential data), showed a significant increase in sales in the mailed group.

The company also wanted to know whether an email campaign to the loyalty card holders was effective. So it subdivided its customers further, one group receiving emails as well as the magazine and another receiving just the magazine. Another control cell analysis, teased out the additional sales that were being generated by the email campaign as against the magazine alone. When compared against the costs of media production, mailing and emailing, this analysis enabled the company to conclude that both the magazine and the email campaign were well worth maintaining.

Sometimes, a campaign or set of activities naturally falls into a sequence of stages, in which case a multi-stage control group design can be used. A B2B service provider tracked the effectiveness of a direct mail campaign by looking both at the effect on an initial mailing, and also at the incremental effect of a follow-up mailing, as illustrated in Figure 11.3.

While the technique is mostly applied to marketing activities such as direct mail and different home page formats, it is equally useful (and much under-used) for assessing different sales channels. British Telecom's Major Business Division used control groups to evaluate the effectiveness of a pilot programme introducing desk-based account managers. The action group had a small team of desk-based account managers supporting field-based salespeople, while the control group continued to use just field staff. The experiment found that the action group had a considerably lower cost of sale and achieved higher customer satisfaction, as well as generating incremental revenue (Wilson, Street and Bruce, 2008).

Another example of the use of control groups to evaluate the success of a whole programme is General Motors' 'Dialogue' multichannel CRM initiative. General Motors set out to build long-term relationships with prospects through direct mail, emails and magazines, constantly tailoring these communications by asking for customer data on expected car renewal date, models of interest and so on, and then handing on a warm lead to a dealer. By setting aside a control group who were not included in this programme, General Motors were able to assert with some confidence that their pilot programme with the launch of the new Vectra generated over 10,000 additional car sales.

TABLE 11.2 Control cells – customer magazine impact

Customer behaviour before and after the mailing period was analysed to understand the impact of the magazine mailing

	Performance pre-mailing*		Performance post-mailing*		Increase over pre-mailing* period (%)		Out-performance of mailed members
	Mailed members	Control cell	Mailed members	Control cell	Mailed members	Control cell	
Active members							+6.8
Spend							+23.7
Visits							+7.4
Transactions							+15.1
Average transaction value							+11.8
Average spend per visit							+16.8
Average spend per member							+19.8

* Pre-mailing period is 25 Sept 2002 to 13 Nov 2002. Post-mailing period is 20 Nov 2002 to 9 Jan 2003.

FIGURE 11.3 Multi-stage control groups

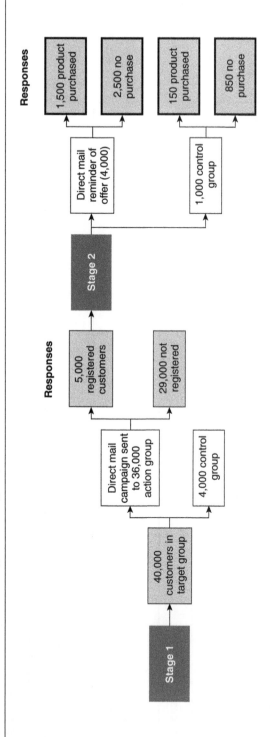

11.5.2 Econometric modelling

When trying to disentangle the effect of several different marketing initiatives, another approach is to look simultaneously at the impact of all of them through econometric modelling. This uses the statistical technique of linear regression to tease out the relative impacts of several 'independent variables', such as advertising spend across a number of media, on a 'dependent variable' such as sales. Used extensively to evaluate the efficacy of TV advertising, the technique can be used across a range of other applications.

As an example, a major website used the technique to evaluate its promotional spend across a number of media. Values for a range of independent variables, such as promotional spend in TV, radio, newspapers and online, were entered for each month over the last few years, along with the dependent variable of the number of visitors to the website that month. (So this example shows that econometric modelling can be applied to any stage of the sales process and not just the bottom-line sales figure.) Independent variables were also entered for such other factors as the level of competitive advertising – see Figure 11.4.

A statistical package then separated the impact of these various variables and produced the conclusions shown in Table 11.3. This showed that each pound of advertising spend was generating 2 visitors from television advertisements and 4 from online spend, but 5.5 from radio and 13 from press advertisements (while competitor advertising spend had a negative effect, as one would expect). The company naturally adjusted its spend towards greater weighting on press coverage.

FIGURE 11.4   Variables in an econometric modelling study

Variables:

■ **Own advertising**

- TV
- Radio
- Newspapers
- Online

■ **Competitor advertising**

■ **Seasonality**

- Days of the week
- Months of the year
- Weather

■ **Events**

- Christmas holidays
- Bank holidays
- Queen's Jubilee

■ **Market growth**

TABLE 11.3   Econometric modelling to assess media effectiveness

Channel	Unique users	Half-life	Unique users per £ spent
TV	12,000,000	10 wks	2
Radio	250,000	1 wk	5.5
Press	3,000,000	3.5 wks	13
Online	1,200,000	3 days	4
Competitor activity	−1,000,000	5 wks	–

We believe that this technique, which is in use mainly in some FMCG markets, could be much more widely applied to other sectors, and in particular that it offers the potential to evaluate the effectiveness of some multichannel campaigns that cannot otherwise be properly assessed. It does require a fair amount of historic data, though, which often rules it out.

11.6 Assessing the overall performance of the route to market

Techniques such as control groups and econometric modelling, then, can be invaluable for assessing the contribution of specific activities. But how can we assess the overall performance of the multichannel route to market?

The British Telecom pilot of the introduction of desk-based account managers, which we referred to earlier, is a good example of how to do this in a holistic way, as it incorporated not just revenue and profit measures but also customer satisfaction and employee satisfaction ones.

But there is one metric that deserves some specific further attention: how to measure the profitability or contribution of marketing channels. It is common for organizations to track channel performance, and to reward channel management, on the basis of the contribution of each channel, typically measured in terms of revenue minus channel expenses – or, to put it another way, the expense-to-revenue ratio of expenses as a percentage of revenue.

This works well if each channel operates independently, but if more than one channel is involved in the purchase process the measure is clearly imperfect. If the high street chain's website that we discussed earlier generates four times as much revenue for the stores as it takes online, then its overall contribution to the business is clearly greater than its own expense-to-revenue ratio would suggest.

There are two ways round this problem. The first is to allocate a financial value to the leads being passed to another channel – the approach we discussed in section 11.2. But it may prove impractical to track all of this channel-hopping behaviour in detail. Another interesting approach adopted by BT and IBM among others is therefore to focus on overall expense-to-revenue ratio not for a single channel but for a group of customers irrespective of channel.

Figure 11.5 illustrates this for BT Business, the part of BT Retail that sells to small and medium-sized companies. BT calculates the expense-to-revenue ratio for each channel – field sales, desk-based sales, two categories of intermediary and BT.com – comparing these with benchmarks representing a best-practice organization. But it focuses primarily on the overall expense-to-revenue ratio across all channels (shown

FIGURE 11.5   Expense-to-revenue ratio – BT Business

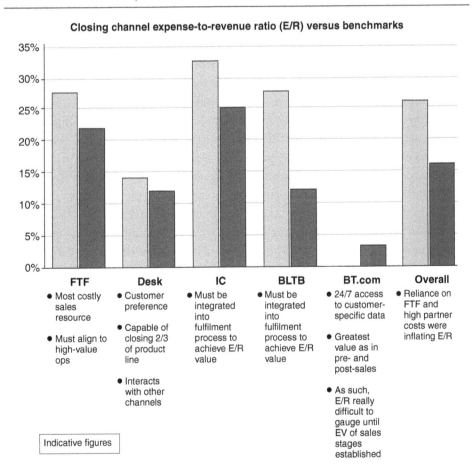

Closing channel expense-to-revenue ratio (E/R) versus benchmarks

FTF	Desk	IC	BLTB	BT.com	Overall
● Most costly sales resource	● Customer preference	● Must be integrated into fulfilment process to achieve E/R value	● Must be integrated into fulfilment process to achieve E/R value	● 24/7 access to customer-specific data	● Reliance on FTF and high partner costs were inflating E/R
● Must align to high-value ops	● Capable of closing 2/3 of product line			● Greatest value as in pre- and post-sales	
	● Interacts with other channels			● As such, E/R really difficult to gauge until EV of sales stages established	

Indicative figures

at the right of Figure 11.5). By targeting sales managers on this overall ratio for the set of accounts for which they are responsible (as well as on account revenue, of course), the managers are motivated to make sensible use of lower-cost channels and to get the channels working together effectively, while leaving them empowered to work out exactly how this can best be done in each account. Because profits ultimately come from customers and their lifetime value, this represents one of the most successful models we have seen for motivating behaviour in sales channels that aligns with the organization's interests.

11.7 Metrics for the multichannel boardroom

We have seen that, particularly where the organization is structured around channel silos, ways must be found of ensuring that the channel barons who head them up are motivated to act in the best interests of the customer and the company, rather than maximizing the sales and minimizing the costs of that particular channel. This means developing a single set of metrics for the multichannel route to market as a whole.

At this point one might ask: 'So what is the best top-level set of metrics for a multichannel company? What metrics should the boardroom be seeing?' Unfortunately, this is a bit like asking what is the best car: it all depends on whether you are a family of four with a dog looking for the right vehicle for the weekend, or an image-conscious single person looking to impress. If what you measure is a key lever for achieving strategy, then good metrics sets are as individual as the strategy itself – and no one ever tells us that their strategy is identical to that of the competition. So there is no way round the time-consuming process of determining the right metrics for the circumstances. Although the end result we are looking for is a reasonably parsimonious set of key measures to steer the customer-facing parts of the business by, to arrive at this important choice correctly takes a fair amount of work.

If we can't present a universal answer, then, we can at least give an idea of how to ask the question. We will give a flavour of what is involved by describing the development of a top-level metrics set for a multichannel retailer, using a well-oiled IBM process for the development of balanced scorecards, which we have found in Cranfield to be an effective, pragmatic approach. This example is a fictional one, albeit based on a composite of our experience of several multichannel organizations.

11.7.1 Understanding cause and effect

This well-established company comes from a bricks-and-mortar background, but over the last few years has added a transactional website as well as traditional catalogue-based home shopping. It has also diversified into different store formats. While its target segments vary in their price sensitivity, its positioning can be broadly described as differentiated rather than price focused. Its switch to a multichannel strategy was accordingly driven by the desire to provide a convenient set of options covering a range of purchase situations, and thereby to increase share of wallet, rather than by any hope of reducing costs through a switch to lower-cost channels.

The IBM process draws on long experience of the systems thinking tradition that provides the best underpinning to metrics design. It first involves the creation of a driver tree showing cause-and-effect relationships between the objectives of the multichannel strategy and the key drivers influencing them. Developed over several workshops with a small team of managers, the driver tree is illustrated for the retailer in Figure 11.6. This tree is clearly much too complex to use on an everyday basis, but this complete picture of potential measures provides a necessary precursor to selecting a manageable subset for a multichannel balanced scorecard.

The model begins with the key objectives of the multichannel strategy, towards the right-hand side of the diagram. For this retailer, these are primarily focused on customer satisfaction and revenue generation and protection: for example, increasing 'share of wallet' by extending the product line and the range of shopping occasions, as well as increasing customer market share through improved geographical coverage. The retailer also set an objective of 'sweating the existing assets': for example, it makes more sense in terms of return on capital to serve home-shopping customers through existing stores rather than invest in dedicated picking centres. This formed part of the small area of the network concerned with cost (at the top of the tree): we would expect a price-focused retailer, by contrast, to have a particularly well-worked cost-focused branch.

The overall financial objective is of 'multichannel contribution', a measure of revenue minus direct product costs and costs of running the channels. The company considered the use of customer lifetime value here, but concluded that this would leave flighty, low-spending 18-year-olds at the top of the pile, and anyone much over 45 at the bottom, and result in excessive 'robbing today to get tomorrow'.

As well as the objectives themselves, the model includes the key drivers of these objectives, which are defined as variables with a high impact on one or more objectives and over which the organization has high influence. Their direct or indirect impact on the objectives is shown with lines on the driver tree. (Where a driver impacts on several different variables, all but one of its appearances in the chart are shown in brackets.)

Some of these drivers relate directly to the customer experience, such as 'Customer time to achieve purpose', which in the case of placing an order is around 5–10 minutes for an experienced web customer, as against 20–25 minutes to place a telephone order. Others are enablers of this experience, such as IT integration, a crucial influence on such variables as the customer's perception of an integrated experience across channels, and the quality of the company's integrated view of the customer.

FIGURE 11.6 Driver tree – multichannel retailer

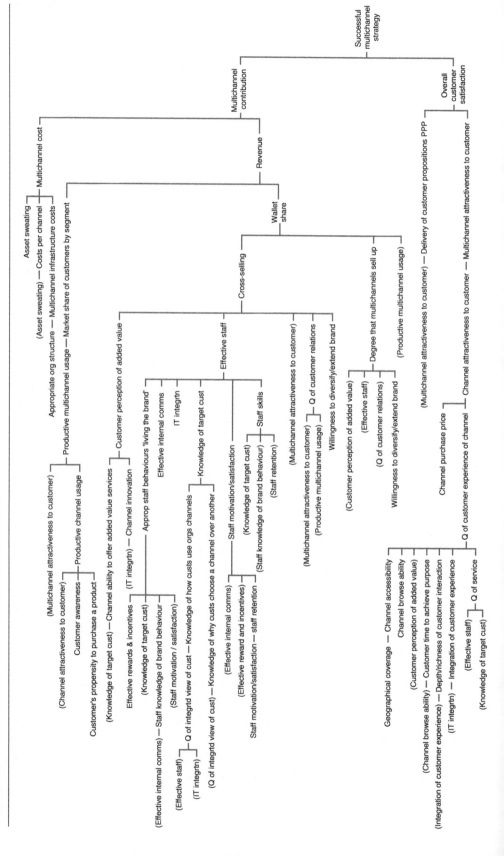

The often long and painful process of IT integration also, perhaps surprisingly, aids with channel innovation rather than being in tension with it. One of the reasons why Tesco.com pulled ahead of its rivals was that, from an early stage, its loyalty card data were integrated across channels. This enabled greater personalization on the website, as customers could pick from a list of their previous in-store purchases as well as their online ones, and spend loyalty points through either channel – service innovations that key competitors took some time to match.

11.7.2 *Choosing key metrics for a scorecard*

This driver tree looks complex, and generally they are. The fact is, though, that success-ful multichannel strategies depend on many factors, relating to people, processes, tech-nologies and customer perceptions as well as products and physical assets. And this complexity needs to be understood if we are to choose the right metrics to follow.

But, if we were to routinely track every variable on the tree, we would be in danger of creating a measurement industry and burying ourselves in complexity. And, what's more, this complexity of metrics would be quite unnecessary. At its simplest, if A influences B, which in turn influences C, it will probably suffice to measure just A, or perhaps A and C. So by adopting this kind of thinking we need to define a sensible subset of the variables to steer our strategy by. We want a small list or scorecard that will, with sufficient confidence, enable us to track progress towards our strategic objectives. How will we know if we've got the scorecard right? If the directors responsible for channels to market will willingly link half their salary to it!

Broadly, this choice involves making a selection of variables which:

- Cover the tree horizontally, incorporating a mixture of objectives and their drivers. The drivers are important because they show why the objectives are – or aren't – being achieved. They can also act as an early warning system: a decrease in staff satisfaction may not show up in the financials for some months or even longer.

- Cover the tree vertically, so important branches of the tree (such as the branches relating to 'Effective staff' and 'Quality of customer experience of channel') are represented.

- Can be viably measured.

The scorecard for the retailer is shown in Figure 11.7. This example scorecard di-vides into the standard sections of 'Results', 'Core processes', 'Customers and stake-holders' and 'People and knowledge' – though these are not set in stone. Many of its items might equally appear in a single-channel organization, for example revenue, customer satisfaction, price and staff satisfaction. Others, though, reflect the multi-ple means by which customers deal with this company.

FIGURE 11.7   Multichannel scorecard for retailer

Results (6)	Customers and stakeholders (5)
• Revenue • Multichannel contribution • Degree multichannel sells up • Costs per channel • Degree of sweating assets • Multichannel infrastructure costs	• Overall customer satisfaction • Customer propensity to defect • Customer propensity to purchase • Customer perception of added value • Integration of customer experience
Core processes (3)	**People and knowledge (4)**
• Productive multichannel usage • Price (relative to competitors/other channels) • Quality of integrated customer view	• Staff satisfaction • Appropriate behaviours 'living the brand' • Willingness to diversify/extend the brand • Knowledge of target customer

Consider, for example, 'Degree multichannel sells up' in the 'Results' quadrant. A major driver of profitability in the low-margin retail sector is the proportion of sales of higher-margin products, such as Tesco's Finest range. So a key benefit of new channels sought by this retailer is increasing this proportion – through higher-margin top-up shops on the internet, for example.

This emphasis on upselling contrasts, for example, with much of retail financial services, where, because of the high cost of customer acquisition, cross-selling can be the key to getting more lifetime value from the customer. First Direct say that those of their customers who use both online and telephone channels have double the number of product holdings of those who only use the telephone – and have lower defection rates too. The retailer of our example also considers cross-selling vital, but has decided to focus on upselling, as it believes it has more scope for improvement in this area.

Defection rates are an issue for this retailer, too, so early warning of the customer's propensity to defect is polled regularly and included in the scorecard. Another vital customer measure is their perception of added value – whether they feel the multi-channel proposition provides something that they want or need that they cannot get from the previous model. Amazon's recommendation facility based on past purchases is a case in point.

Achieving a channel mix that provides this added value and increased customer revenues is not cheap, however. From new formats such as metropolitan mini-stores to heavy investment in its web channel and supporting logistics, our retailer has been incurring significant capital expenditure as it rolls out its channel strategy, as well as ongoing maintenance costs to keep this infrastructure up to date. To keep an eye on this, the 'Results' quadrant includes a measure for 'Multichannel infrastructure costs'. These can of course go down as well as up, through outsourced or consolidated call centres, for example. In the case of loyalty cards we are seeing movement in both directions, some retailers outsourcing to save costs, while conversely Tesco bought its key supplier dunnhumby.

'Productive channel usage', a key variable driving market share, needs some explanation. With an essentially stand-alone channel such as a traditional direct sales force, we can measure how well the channel contributes to market share by monitoring its rate of conversion of leads to customers, and hence its cost of acquisition. But, if the role of the channel is to take customers on to the next step in the buying cycle and hand them over to a different channel for the purchase itself, we need to monitor more specifically the conversion efficiency and the cost of moving the customer along that specific step. So the whole buying cycle might involve several efficiency ratios and corresponding costs.

11.8 Steering by the stars

Measuring the effectiveness of marketing and sales was never easy, and today's multichannel, multimedia world makes it even more complex. Techniques such as control groups and econometric modelling are not new, but their application throughout the buying cycle, across multiple channels and outside the control of marketers within areas such as sales is comparatively immature. With a bit of forethought, marketing campaigns and changes to the sales approach can be evaluated rigorously – a great bonus when the case for a wider roll-out of a new approach needs to be made.

One company is currently using control groups, for example, to assess whether a field-based sales force or a call centre is more appropriate for various categories of sale. By allocating 1,000 leads at random into two piles, one going to the sales force and one to a call centre, the company will soon have clear data to confirm or if necessary modify the managers' intuition. Meeting the accountants halfway has to be better than retreating behind the half-truth that the value of a happy customer cannot be measured.

Metrics are of course only the beginning, and we need a proper process for developing multichannel strategy in the first place. For such a process, the reader is referred to Wilson, Street and Bruce (2008). But, if our channel decisions are to be more rational than those we saw in the dot-com boom, the choice of metrics plays a crucial role. Most organizations have reasonably developed metrics for individual channels, but extending this metrics set to allow for today's channel-hopping customer requires some fundamental rethinking. It is essential, however, if we are to steer by the stars and not by the light of passing ships.

Notes

1   Reducing defection also reduces the risk as measured by the variability of cash flow hence retention strategies both increase revenue and reduce the discount rate providing a double impact on CLV.

2   We acknowledge with gratitude the contributions to this material from members of the Cranfield Customer Management Forum and, in particular, five current and former consultants at IBM: Rod Street, Matt Hobbs, Jennifer Love, Mike Bazett and Ian Bowden.

References

Almquist, E and Wyner, G (2001) Boost Your Marketing RoI with Experimental Design, *Harvard Business Review*, October, pp 135–51

Anderson, E, Fornell, C and Lehmann, D (1994) Customer Satisfaction, Market Share and Profitability: Findings from Sweden, *Journal of Marketing*, **58**, pp 53–66

Anderson, E W, Fornell, C and Agarwal, S (2004) Customer Satisfaction and Shareholder Value, *Journal of Marketing*, **68**, pp 172–85

Gruca, T S and Rego, L L (2005) Customer Satisfaction, Cash Flow, and Shareholder Value, *Journal of Marketing*, **68** (3), pp 115–30

Gupta, S and Zeithaml, V (2006) Customer Metrics and Their Impact on Financial Performance, *Marketing Science*, **25** (6), pp 718

Keiningham, T L, Cooil, B, Andreassen, T W and Aksoy, L (2007) A Longitudinal Examination of Net Promoter and Firm Revenue Growth, *Journal of Marketing*, **71**, pp 39–51

Klaus, P and Maklan, S (2012) EXQ: A Multi-Item Scale for Assessing Service Experience, *Journal of Service Management*, **23** (1), pp 5–33

Lemke, F, Clark, M and Wilson, H (2011) Customer Experience Quality: An exploration in business and consumer contexts using repetory grid technique, *Journal of the Academy of Marketing Science*, **39** (1), pp 846–69

Morgan, R and Hunt, S (1994) The Commitment-Trust Theory of Relationship Marketing, *Journal of Marketing*, **58** (3), pp 20–38

Peppers, D and Rogers, M (1994) *The One-to-One Future*, Piatikus, London

Pfeifer, R (2011) *Customer Lifetime Value*, **44**, pp 1–9

Reichheld, F F (1996) *The Loyalty Effect*, Harvard Business School Press, Boston

Reichheld, F F (2003) The One Number You Need to Grow, *Harvard Business Review*, **81** (12), pp 46–54

Reichheld, F F (2006) *The Ultimate Question: Driving good profits and true growth*, Harvard Business School Press, Boston

Rust, R, Lemon, K and Zeithaml, V (2004) Return on Marketing: Using customer equity to focus marketing strategy, *Journal of Marketing*, **68** (1), pp 109–27

Thompson, G, Frances, J, Levacic, R and Mitchell, J (1991) *Markets, Hierarchies and Networks*, Sage, London

Vargo, S and Lusch, R (2004) Evolving to a New Dominant Logic for Marketing, *Journal of Marketing*, **68** (1), pp 1–17

Williamson, O (1981) The Economics of Organization: The transaction cost approach, *American Journal of Sociology*, **87** (3), pp 548–77

Wilson, H, Street, R and Bruce, L (2008) *The Multichannel Challenge: Integrating customer experiences for profit*, Butterworth Heinemann, Oxford

Social media: metrics and measurement

12

ROBERT STRATTON, VICE PRESIDENT ANALYTICS

MarketShare

Social media: an introduction

Interpersonal communication is increasingly recognized as an important source of information for consumers, both through offline word of mouth and online social media. Social media refers to the various platforms that facilitate social interaction in virtual communities and networks. Although much of the current interest in social media is focused specifically on social networking sites, the impact of online social interaction extends into the mainstream web through, among others, virtual game worlds, blogs, consumer review sites such as TripAdvisor and collaborative projects such as Wikipedia (Kaplan and Haenlein, 2011). Social media has had a broad and significant impact on online behaviour; including consumer's search, community formation, content creation and sharing (Kietzmann *et al*, 2012).

Assessing the value of marketing without considering the impact of word of mouth and social media can lead to suboptimal strategic decisions for marketers (Zubcsek and Miklos, 2011). Similarly, attempting to measure the impact of social media without measuring the other forms of marketing will result in incorrect assessments. From the marketer's perspective, introducing and distributing information into the social media ecosystem can serve a number of different possible objectives, including customer relationship management, customer service provision, branding and promotion. Once introduced, this information may travel widely through peer-to-peer sharing. Brands are also seeking to engage in specific campaigns to generate offline and online word of mouth. In addition, other content or commentary about the brand – either positive or negative – may be originated by consumers and circulate without any input or control on the part of a company. In all of these contexts, marketers face a challenge in understanding the nature and level of distribution of this content, and how it affects other metrics such as brand perception, customer satisfaction and sales.

12.1 How social media differs from other media channels

Although there are relatively established techniques for tracking and measuring the impact of other media, social media has some unique characteristics. Instead of managed content that is produced and approved by the advertiser, a very diverse array of messages about a brand may be transmitted around the social network at any time, and may be repeatedly modified by other users. Understanding the nature of these messages, particularly on a mass scale, can be problematic. In addition, messages transmitted in social media may be originated by an advertiser or by other parties – treating these differently may be important because in many cases a message shared by another consumer might be expected to be more trusted and therefore more significant than a message shared by an advertiser.

The circulation achieved by content in social media is not managed by a broadcast strategy or measured by a single audience research system, and so assessing the reach and frequency of the circulating content is not as straightforward as in other media. Rather than the traditional media impression or GRP there is a vast range of currencies used to describe exposure and consumer responses used across different sites – understanding what these mean in terms of the effectiveness of delivery can be difficult.

12.2 Social media metrics

Social media metrics can in general be classified into one of four broad categories:

1 The type and sentiment of the content.
2 Delivery – the number of times the content has been seen by users.
3 User responses to the content.
4 Properties of the users in contact with the content.

12.2.1 Type and sentiment metrics

Social media content is usually in the form of text, image or video. The meaning that can be extracted from content is maximized when it is processed and analysed by a trained analyst, but given the array of diverse content produced, cost considerations mean that in practice automated solutions are often used. The type of content found in social media can be problematic for automated processes to accurately classify – much of it is very context specific, for example a tweet in reply to another tweet, or incorporates heavy abbreviation or slang.

FIGURE 12.1 Social media metrics

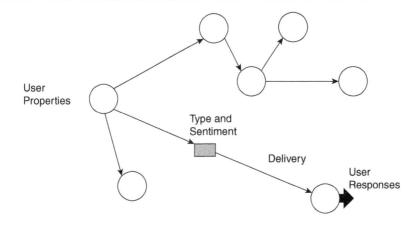

User
Properties

Type and
Sentiment

Delivery

User
Responses

Some of the simpler automated approaches involve scoring the overall sentiment of the sentence or phrase by assessing the combined positivity of the words used, while more advanced approaches use Natural Language Processing. The end output of a content scoring exercise is usually a classification for each piece of content that scores its sentiment towards a particular brand or subject mentioned in the content, for example positive or strongly positive.

12.2.2 Delivery metrics

Some individual sites offer reach and frequency figures, but with a multi-site campaign these figures are not additive. In principle it is possible to estimate the cross-site reach and frequency of a particular event using surveys based on individual level site usage, but there may still be exceptions because the users involved may be a distinct subset of the survey, therefore disproportionately active across a subset of sites. In the absence of consistent cross-site reach and frequency data we find that the most useful metric for a harmonized data-set is the number of impressions delivered – the number of times each piece of content has been viewed. This can be aggregated across sites, and can usually be split into impressions delivered directly by the advertiser and impressions from content shared by other users.

12.2.3 User response metrics

Social media sites often provide a way for users to respond to content, and many of the metrics available refer to actions that users have taken in response to the delivery of a particular piece of content. Some common examples are 'likes', 'shares', 'comments', and 'downloads'. The responses available to users differ across platforms, and some content specifically asks users to respond in a particular way, so it's difficult to interpret these responses as a reflection of content quality.

12.2.4 User properties

User properties are metrics that describe characteristics of the social media user. These include things such as physical location, preferences – perhaps measured through likes or subscriptions to pages, and influence – often measured through network size and the number of times a user's content is re-shared. Although they are potentially of great interest to advertisers, in practice the low coverage and disparate nature of the metrics provided across sites make them difficult to interpret systematically.

12.2.5 Metric reliability

With any social media metric, it is important to consider the reliability of the underlying data. Privacy settings and technical factors such as API limits mean that the total coverage of the data available may be incomplete. In addition, some of the data under consideration may have been created by bots or fake users. Some of these problems can be reduced by using the proportion of total content that is reflecting a particular sentiment, rather than total volume.

12.3 Measuring the effects of social media

As a prerequisite for any measurement exercise, data needs to be collected across a range of categories including market conditions, competitive activities, marketing actions, consumer response, and business outcomes, as well as the social media metrics described above. Even when data has been assembled across all of these areas, care must be taken in interpreting the role of social media in creating business outcomes. Social media metrics may act as a proxy for general word of mouth – changes in the level of conversation in social media may be highly correlated with changes in the level of offline conversation – but because online conversation is more trackable, the role of social media may be overstated if analysed in a simplistic manner. In addition, although certain social media metrics may be found to be highly correlated with an end outcome, the correlation may not always justify the interpretation that social media has 'caused' the outcome. In any process there may be one or more causal factors and a series of 'enabling' factors.

Although social media may be a causal factor in some circumstances, there are other non-causal roles that it may also play. For example, when content from another medium, such as a TV ad, is being shared within a network it may be thought of as enabling the TV campaign to achieve a higher circulation. When multiple users share an existing interest or sentiment, social media may enable them in forming a community. In other cases, social media activity may be jointly determined with or caused by the outcome. For example, a consumer may post about their intention to buy a new car, in which case the post and the subsequent purchase are both caused by the intention. Later they may share their experience of using it, in which case the post is caused by the sale.

12.3.1 Developing hypotheses and models

Given the differing roles that social media may be playing, the first step in an evaluation exercise is to create context-specific hypotheses about how a particular social media metric is thought to relate to an end outcome. Once the hypotheses have been developed, there are two broad approaches to measuring the impact of social media that can be used to test them. One method is based on data attribution and the other on model-based inference.

12.3.2 Traditional attribution methods

Traditional attribution methods use digital linkages in web tracking data to partially track the sequence of online advertising exposures and actions that a user took before visiting or making a purchase on a website. These methods work on the assumption that other influences, except for those that were digitally trackable, were irrelevant to the outcome action. For example, if a social media user clicks on a link which takes them to the advertiser's website, the social media link alone is considered to explain the visit. Equally, if a social media user searches for something a connection has shared with them, then clicks through from search, the role of social media in creating the sale is lost. One additional feature of the data attribution approach is that only outcomes that take place in trackable online environments, such as a company's website, can be taken into account.

12.3.3 Social media as a complex system

Measuring this relationship between external forces in the broader environment and internal forces in social media requires a particular type of modelling approach that can represent complex systems. Social media acts as a complex system when higher level collective behaviour such as rumours and cascades emerge from interactions between individuals. The relationship between the inputs and outputs in a complex process can be extremely non-linear, so the indirect model needs to be able to recreate

FIGURE 12.2   The modelling approach

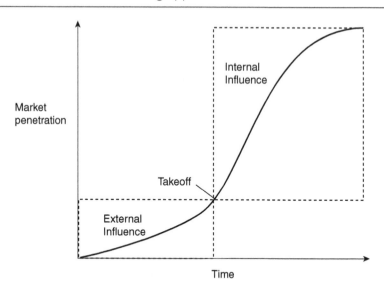

the dynamics of social media that lead to these non-linearities. These might include the structure of the user network, the ways in which new content enters the network, user sharing mechanisms and outcome user behaviours.

Various studies have reviewed the strengths and weaknesses of different modelling approaches for these purposes and find simulation-based methods to be a useful tool (Said, Thierry and Alexis, 2001; Peres, Muller and Mahajan, 2010). Social media simulation methods work from the bottom up, using a representative, software-based social network. Watts and Dodds, among others, have used these methods to investigate indirect network phenomena, testing the assumptions behind Katz and Lazarsfeld's 'two step flow' theory of information exchange (Watts, 2007). Other studies have looked at the role of how cascade effects develop in online social networks.

Social simulation models can be customized for specific situations using appropriate network types. For example, a regular or small world network (Watts, 1998) could be used, or a topology that recreate the characteristics of a specific social media platform (Cha *et al*, 2010). As well as different network types, appropriate interaction processes can also be represented – if the main dynamic that needs to be modelled is content sharing, an epidemiological framework could be used in which infected users share content with susceptible users. Alternatively a more generic social pressure process, like that proposed by Bass (1969), can be represented – in this framework each user perceives and responds to the percentage of adopters in his immediate network

12.3.4 Modelling social media with simulations

In a typical implementation, a population of software entities is created, with each entity representing a social media user and each iteration of the model representing a time period. The users are able to perceive external factors, which are introduced over time based on the real historic data collected.

The users are arranged in a network, and each has a threshold for sharing content with other users. Any user's likelihood for sharing is based on the combination of external factors the user perceives, the characteristics that the content contains, the number of times a piece of content is delivered to them, and the originator of the content. Each user has the ability to take a number of actions, such as liking, sharing and commenting, depending on the application.

There are two main groups of elements that affect the model's internal dynamics: the facts that exist outside of the model, such as advertising and economics; and the facts that are contained within it, like social network structure and social sharing mechanism. The internal structure of the model can make quite a difference to the model's output – for example using a small world network structure, with a mixture

FIGURE 12.3   Indirect effects

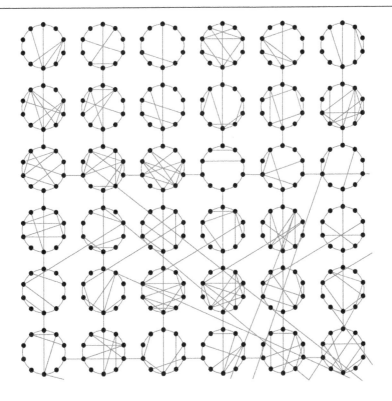

of short paths connecting most of the individuals within each clique and longer paths connecting the cliques, trends emerge locally among the immediate group and are later propagated more widely through the longer paths. A simulated user may therefore feel evidence of increased social pressure where multiple contacts in their network are performing the same actions, for example 'liking' the same post or the same comment.

The simulated user's sensitivities and behaviours are calibrated using optimization methods until the aggregation of user actions reflects the metrics observed in the real world.

12.3.4 Making social media accountable

Accountability of social media can be measured via a three-stage approach that equates with methods used for other channels:

1 Harmonizing the available social media metrics into a common currency and creating summary metrics that integrate disparate content.

FIGURE 12.4   Internal and external influences

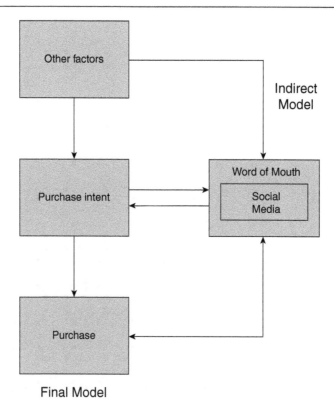

2 Feeding these harmonized metrics into a modelling framework that can untangle the internal dynamics of social media, providing insights on how to maximize viral sharing, and separating the unique impact of social media from its mediating and amplifying role for other external factors.

3 Measuring social media in a holistic framework that takes account of other relevant factors in the market, including other marketing activity and other forms of social interaction.

12.3.5 Modelling-based attribution approaches

Originally developed and patented by MarketShare, modelling-based attribution is the use of predictive analytic models as simplified representations of the real world that can be calibrated against empirical data and used to answer questions about how the world is working. In the social media context, the model might use a statistical or computational representation of the broader business process to help marketers answer questions about social media's effects. The modelling approach can typically consider a wider range of online and offline factors – evaluation of social media may be more accurate if it takes account of these interactions with other factors rather than treating it in isolation. The other relevant factors may include marketing touch points across media and sales channels, and elements that may be part of the broader consumer environment – such as price promotion, shelf space, and location.

12.4 Indirect effects

FIGURE 12.5 A small world network

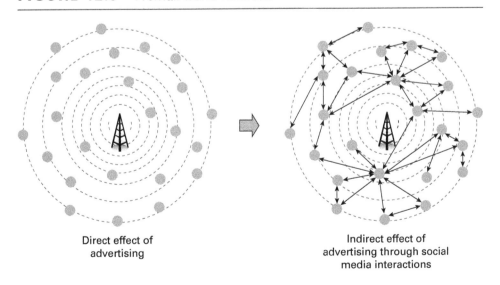

Direct effect of
advertising

Indirect effect of
advertising through social
media interactions

In order to create and test these hypotheses it is useful to develop an intermediary model that can represent the interrelationships between social media and the wider world. The purpose of the intermediary model is to achieve two things. Firstly, it can help to identify the social media activity that was caused by external factors – meaning that the importance of social media itself won't be overstated in the final evaluation. Secondly, the intermediary model can help marketers understand which of their activities were successful in driving viral sharing in the network.

12.4.1 Relating social media to end outcomes

While MarketShare's indirect model described above can tell us the proportion of social media exposures that are attributable to other factors, and how external instruments can be used to maximize viral sharing, marketers are also interested in the impact of social media on outcomes such as consideration and sales.

Since we have already controlled for the elements of social media that are more difficult to model with equations, more conventional econometric models can help to disentangle the contribution of social media to an end outcome from the other effects present in the market. Equation-based models are comprised of variables, typically selected to be representative of the target phenomenon, and a functional form that represents the relationship between them. The equation might take a number of forms, both linear and non-linear. Because marketing factors tend to work multiplicatively with each other with the marketing effort in any given channel increasing the impact of other channels, a multiplicative equation form is usually most appropriate. The parameters of the models are then solved through regression.

These equations and their parameters can help to separate the effect of influences in the market, identifying the contribution of the main factors and the timescales over which they act. Once we know the incremental value that each bit of activity is adding to the end outcome we can calculate the return for the spend involved in running the activity. In social media, some of the activity will involve no spend. The return on social media can then be compared with the returns from other candidate marketing instruments.

References

Bass, F M (1969) A New Product Growth Model for Consumer Durables, *Marketing Science*, **15**, pp 215–27

Cha, M, Haddadi, H, Benerenuts, F and Gummadi, K (2014) Measuring User Influence in Twitter: The million follower fallacy, ICWSM, online, 17 February 2014

Kaplan, A M and Haenlein, M (2011) Two Hearts in Three-Quarter Time: How to waltz the social media/viral marketing dance, *Business Horizons*, **54** (3), pp 253–63

Kietzmann, J H, Silvestre, B S, McCarthy, I P and Pitt, L F (2012) Unpacking the Social Media Phenomenon: Towards a research agenda, *Journal of Public Affairs*, **12** (2), pp 109–19

Peres, R, Muller, E and Mahajan, V (2010) Innovation Diffusion and New Product Growth Models: A critical review and research directions, *International Journal of Research in Marketing*, **27** (2), pp 91–106

Said, L B, Thierry, B and Alexis, D (2001) Multi-Agent Based Simulation of Consumer Behaviour: Towards a new marketing approach, *International Congress on Modelling and Simulation Proceedings*

Watts, D J and Dodds, P S (2007) Influentials, Networks, and Public Opinion Formation, *Journal of Consumer Research*, **34** (4), pp 441–58

Watts, D J and Strogatz, S H (1998) Collective Dynamics of 'Small-World' Networks, *Nature*, **393** (6684), pp 440–42

Zubcsek, P and Miklos, S (2011) Advertising to a Social Network, *Quantitative Marketing and Economics*, **9** (1), pp 71–107

Assessing the value of market assets

DAVID HAIGH AND STAN MAKLAN

13.1 Background

As the financial discourse began to dominate managerial thinking, the marketing community responded by adopting both its language and concepts. Marketing management was (is) continually challenged to demonstrate the value of its spending, particularly the large amounts directed to advertising. In the heady days of 1960s growth, advertising was a magic elixir, not far off the dot.com euphoria of the late 1990s. Spending was not scrutinized rigorously or systematically, but to be fair to managers of that era, at that time, the 'right' campaign could yield enormous returns and there were many untapped opportunities. As market growth slowed, however, operating boards subjected marketing spending to more thorough examination and rightly asked: what do we get for all this spending?

This raised a fundamental question that is still often debated: how to assess marketing spending between immediate sales revenue and investment for long-term gain. Should the costs associated with advertising and promotion be expensed in the period that they occur, or capitalized and expensed subsequently against future income? International accounting standards generally ask companies to expense marketing costs as they occur, yet there is strong evidence that building strong brands and improving customer relationships takes many years but provides even more years of benefit. This creates a serious mismatch between expense and revenue realization with the consequence that it encourages companies to cut marketing expenditure when they need to make a difficult profit target, because such cuts boost profit immediately while only affecting revenue in the future. Few firms really know how much future income is put at risk by cutting marketing expenditure and the timing of those impacts. With that level of uncertainty about the future, marketing leaders have been under pressure to 'defend' their budgets for decades. A considerable amount of academic and managerial time and effort has been devoted to estimating the impact of marketing spending over time and many companies have developed sophisticated models to reduce the uncertainty around the return on marketing expenditure/the future cost of cutting spending.

To enhance the quality of this discussion, academics leverage key concepts from financial and accounting disciplines and call it 'equity'. Core to accountancy best practice is the principle of matching revenue to expense. In this context, marketing academics sought to apportion and match marketing expenditure between the immediate and longer-term revenues that strong brands and customer relationships generate. This is made operational through financial theories wherein the value of the market asset, be they based upon brands or customer relationships, is determined by the estimated cash flows generated by that asset over time and discounted to a present value by a risk-adjusted rate. Where the estimate of cash flows, and their timing, is accurate and the rate at which that is discounted accurately reflects the risks, the net present value of the market asset reflects its economic worth to the firm and its shareholders. This conceptualization of brands and customer relationships as economic assets was a real breakthrough. Sophisticated organizations can now value the equity in their brands and relationships and how that equity varies with different marketing strategies and levels of marketing support. Moreover, by using the concepts and language of finance, marketing's arguments can be more credible and persuasive. In the next sections we will show how these concepts have been operationalized in the context of brands and customer relationships, how they relate to each and how one can use the equity concept with the Accountability Model. We will also end with a cautionary note about the limitations of this approach.

13.2 The limitations of traditional accountancy

Traditional accounting focused on tangible assets, including working capital, plant, equipment, land and buildings. Intangible assets were ignored and accountants treated any excess value arising on acquisition as 'goodwill'. Then, towards the end of the 20th century, it became apparent that the 'goodwill' values arising were so high the issue had to be addressed.

A recent Brand Finance plc analysis of the world's 127 markets reveals the scale of the problem (Figure 13.1). The 'Global Intangible Finance Tracker 2013' study analysed 56,000 companies with a total enterprise value of $57 trillion. The study revealed that 50 per cent of all enterprise value is made up of intangible assets. Only a small proportion was disclosed and explained in published accounts.

FIGURE 13.1   Global enterprise value over time

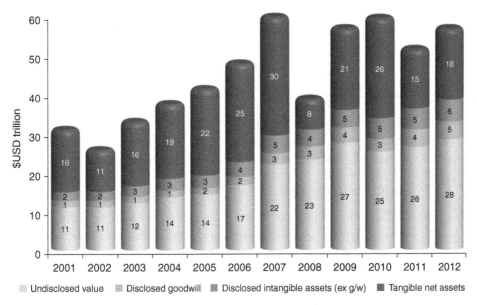

SOURCE: Brand Fiance plc 2013

However, accountants are being forced to react to this rapid rise in the value of intangible assets. As Baruch Lev, Professor of Accounting and Finance, Stern School of Business, NYU (Webber, 2006), has commented:

> In the past few decades, there has been a dramatic shift, a transformation, in what economists call the production function of companies – the major assets that create value and growth. Intangibles are fast becoming substitutes for physical assets.

13.3 Valuation of market assets

An obvious solution to this gap between 'real' shareholder and that which is captured by traditional accounting is to capitalize the real value of intangible assets. For historical reasons, putting the 'brand-on-the-balance-sheet' has been the focus of this discussion. Companies have long been active in their acquisition of brands, and forthright in their statements about the rationale for some major acquisitions: the desire to acquire the target firms' brands. Consider the consolidation of firms in the global confectionary market and consumer goods. Kraft did not buy Cadbury's for any secret recipe or unique manufacturing know-how; it acquired brands for which it paid a premium on the estimate that as part of its global business, it could generate future cash flows in excess of the debt incurred. It is precisely such forms of acquisition that acted as a catalyst of debate about capitalizing the value of these brands rather than writing them off at acquisition time or amortizing over time. Brand valuation grew from an audit perspective into a distinctive practice due to the unique nature of brands as assets. In 2010, the ISO agreed principles for valuing brand financially under ISO10668. In 2013 there was a move to look again and update this standard.

13.3.1 What do we mean by 'brand'?

The starting point of brand valuation must be to define what is meant by a brand.

The term is used differently by different people. In our experience there are three different concepts, all of which are sometimes referred to as the 'brand'.

13.3.1.1 A logo and associated visual elements

This is the most specific definition of brand, focusing on the legally protectable, visual elements, used to differentiate one company's products and services from another to stimulate demand for those products and services. The main legal elements covered by this definition are trade names, trademarks and trade symbols.

In order to add value, trademarks and trade symbols need to carry 'associated goodwill' acquired by providing high-quality products and by giving good service over a long period to add value. For trademarks and trade symbols to go on conveying value to licensee's high-quality products and good service need to remain associated with the trademarks or trade symbols.

There are two broader definitions of brand which are frequently used by academics and practitioners.

13.3.1.2 A larger bundle of trademark and associated intellectual property rights

Under this definition, 'brand' is sometimes extended to encompass a larger bundle of intellectual property rights. Marketing intangibles such as domain names, product design rights, trade dress, packaging, copyrights in associated colours, smells, sounds, descriptors, logotypes, advertising visuals and written copy are sometimes included in the wider definition of 'brand'.

Many of these legal rights can be registered or protected in different trade classes and territories. If registered or legally owned, such rights can be traded, transferred, sold or licensed. When licensing a brand, an agreed bundle of these rights is usually included in the legal agreement between the licensor and the licensee.

Some commentators have interpreted the intellectual property rights included in the definition of brand very widely indeed. In fact, tangible as well as intangible property rights have been referred to as integral components of brands. Some argue that the Mercedes brand would be incomplete if it were separated from the other tangible and intangible assets used to build Mercedes products.

The reason that some argue a larger bundle of intangibles should be included in the definition of brand is because consumer loyalty is created over a long period by many touch points and consumer experiences. This '360-degree' experience may require the presence of any or all of the unique intangibles noted here to maintain brand quality and integrity.

Protagonists of a more holistic definition of brand ask whether the Mercedes brand would command such fierce loyalty and price premium without the benefit of Daimler Benz design, engineering and service. Similarly they argue that the Zantac brand would be incomplete without the Ranitidine patent. The Guinness brand would not be Guinness without the genuine recipe and production process. This more holistic view is consistent with the opinion that brand is a much broader and deeper experience than either the 'logo and associated visual elements' or even the full range of 'brand and relationship intangibles' referred to here.

13.3.3.3 A holistic company or organizational brand

The determination of which intellectual property rights should or should not be incorporated into the definition of brand often leads to the view that brand refers to the whole organization within which the specific logo and associated visual elements, the larger bundle of 'visual and marketing intangibles' and the 'associated goodwill' are deployed.

A combination of all these legal rights together with the culture, people and programmes of an organization all provide a basis for differentiation and value creation within that organization. Taken as a whole they represent a specific value proposition and they create stronger customer relationships.

Based on these three definitions, for the purposes of this chapter we refer to the first definition as 'trademark'. The second definition we refer to as the 'brand'. The third definition is the 'branded business'.

13.3.4 The process of brand valuation

ISO 10668 specifies principles and good practice for brand valuation; the Committee rejected the notion of specifying a precise methodology that would be followed slavishly across the world in all contexts. So individual brand valuers must respect the principles outlined and interpret them in a way relevant to the task at hand. One of the world's principle specialist brand valuation firms is Brand Finance and it offers a core method that it has used globally for some time and its own definition of brand equity that it uses for its valuation purposes.

FIGURE 13.2   Brand Finance approach

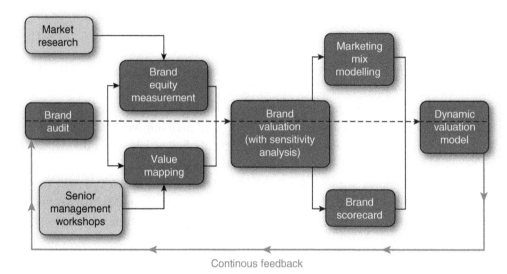

Continous feedback

SOURCE: Brand Finance plc, 2008

13.3.4.1 The brand audit

Before any brand and intangible asset valuation can take place an in-depth study into the current situation of the branded business is necessary. This includes an understanding of the:

- quality of brand management;
- existing products and channels to market;
- new product development plans;
- current pricing strategy;
- current distribution strategy;
- key competitors in current and potential areas;
- available market research;
- available financial data;
- key ratios and assets employed analysis;
- information on licensing strategy; and
- brand registration and ownership.

Based on the brand audit one can form an initial impression of the overall strength and weaknesses of the branded business as well as an understanding into the potential opportunities and threats within the industry.

The brand audit forms part of the initial phase of understanding the brand equity drivers of the branded business.

13.3.4.2 Brand equity measurements

The Brand Finance method, common with other brand valuers, assesses brand equity less from the consumer cognition and affect perspective, instead it estimates the measures of outcomes that affect financial performance.

A classic example of how brand equity translates into better financial performance can be seen in the cola market. In blind tests Pepsi Cola consistently outperforms Coca-Cola in terms of consumer taste preference. But when Coke branded packaging is revealed, initial preference completely reverses. Branding persuades consumers to behave irrationally, adding value to otherwise functionally identical products and services. Thus, strong brands with high 'brand equity' possess the ability to persuade people to make economic decisions based on emotional rather than rational criteria.

13.3.4.3 How to measure brand equity?

A Brand Finance's Brand Value Added® (BVA®) drivers of demand analysis reveals the major drivers of demand, and brand's performance relative to competitors against each driver. The analysis is divided into two areas, namely: drivers' importance/brand contribution, driver performance/sensitivity.

FIGURE 13.3   The financial effect of brand equity on each stakeholder group

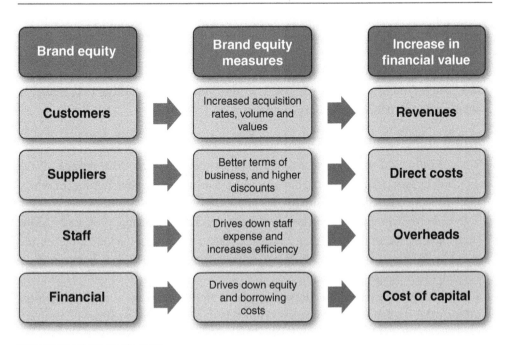

SOURCE: Brand Finance plc, 2008

Driver importance/brand contribution – involves identifying the key drivers of demand by different segments and determining the brand contribution to each driver.

This helps brand manager's answer the following questions:

- Which drivers have most influence on overall 'brand preference'?
- Which ones can we influence?
- Where should we focus our communication?
- What brand image adds to the business?
- What is the argument for additional investment in the brand?
- Where does image have a strong influence and where should the organization focus?

Driver performance/sensitivity – involves determining how a brand performs compared to competitors on key drivers of demand and determining the elasticity of each attribute.

This helps brand manager's answer the following questions:

- Where are we performing poorly versus competitors?
- What should we emphasize?
- Where do we need to improve?
- How can we understand the impact of changing the customer rating on a particular attribute on overall 'brand preference'?
- What is the sensitivity of changes in customer behaviour (and hence business performance) to changes in brand preference?

Based on this analysis one can determine the elasticity of changes in brand preference and changes in customer defection and acquisition, which will ultimately influence financial performance of the branded business.

13.3.4.4 Value mapping

It is not only vital to have an understanding of the drivers of value among all the stakeholder groups of a business but also to have a sufficient understanding of where value is being created in the entire value chain of the branded business.

In order to help understand this, one can undertake a value mapping study. Value mapping is a process of developing a thorough understanding of the key resources and assets in the business together with an appreciation of the linkages between these through the business value chain.

Value mapping is based on data collected during the brand audit and management and/or other stakeholder interviews. From this data the project team will establish a value map of the business, which should be presented in a conceptual framework

FIGURE 13.4   Brand value mapping (retail fuel)

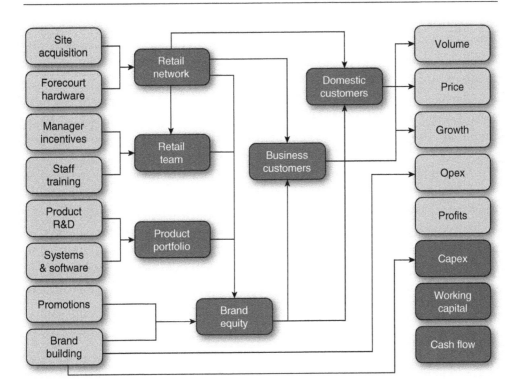

SOURCE: Brand Finance plc, 2008

highlighting what key resources and assets of the branded business are driving, for example, volume, price or growth of the entire business (Figure 13.4).

Value mapping becomes an excellent tool at the start of any valuation to identify key tangible and intangible assets in the business and ultimately guides the valuation, scorecard and/or dynamic modelling process.

13.4 Brand valuation and sensitivity analysis

The brand audit, brand equity measurement analysis and value mapping analysis provide in-depth insights into the entire branded business from which valid assumptions can be made in the brand valuation model. A brand valuation model is a framework that allows for optimal resource allocation and strategy selection across all market segments.

There are two critical questions to answer in brand valuation. The first is exactly what is being valued? Are we valuing the trademarks, the brand or the branded business?

The second important question is the purpose of the valuation. An important distinction can be made between technical and commercial valuations.

Technical valuations are generally conducted for balance sheet reporting, tax planning, litigation, securitization, licensing, mergers and acquisitions and investor-relations purposes. They focus on giving a point in time valuation that represents the value of the trademarks or of the brand as defined above.

Commercial valuations are used for the purposes of brand architecture, portfolio management, market strategy, budget allocation and brand scorecards. Such valuations are based on a dynamic model of the branded business and aim to measure the role played by the brand in influencing the key variables in the model.

We recommend that the starting point for every valuation – whether technical or commercial – should be a branded business valuation. This provides the most complete understanding of the commercial context of the brand.

A branded business valuation is based on a discounted cash flow analysis of future earnings for that business discounted at the appropriate cost of capital. The value of the branded business is made up of a number of tangible and intangible assets. Trademarks are simply one of these and 'brands' are a more comprehensive bundle of trademark and related intangibles.

There are a number of recognized methods for valuing trademarks or brands as defined here.

One can look at historic costs – what did it cost to create? In the case of a brand one can look at what it cost to design, register and promote the trademarks and associated rights. Alternatively, one can address what they might cost to replace. Both the historic cost method and the replacement cost method are subjective but we are often asked to value this way because courts may want to know what a brand might cost to create.

It is also possible to consider market value, though frequently there is no market value for intangibles, particularly trademarks and brands.

Generally speaking the most productive approach to brand valuation is to employ an 'economic use' valuation method, of which there are a number.

Firstly there is the price premium or gross margin approach, which considers price premiums or superior margins versus a 'generic' business as the metric for quantifying the value that the 'brand' contributes. However, the rise of private label means that it is often hard to identify a 'generic' against which the price or margin differential should be measured.

Economic substitution analysis is another approach – if we didn't have that trademark or brand what would the financial performance of the branded business be? How would the volumes, values and costs change? The problem with this approach is that it relies on subjective judgements as to what the alternative substitute might be.

The difficulties associated with these two approaches mean that the two most useful 'economic use' approaches are the 'earnings split' and 'royalty relief' approaches.

Under a 'royalty relief' approach one imagines that the business does not own its trademarks but licenses them from another business at a market rate. The royalty rate is usually expressed as a percentage of sales. This is the most frequently used method of valuation because it is highly regarded by tax authorities and courts, largely because there are a lot of comparable licensing agreements in the public domain. It is relatively easy to calculate a specific percentage that might be paid to the trademark or 'brand' owner.

Under an 'earnings split' approach one attributes earnings above a break-even economic return to the intangible capital. This involves four principal steps. The first is an appropriate segmentation of the market to ensure that we study the brand within its relevant competitive framework. The second step is to forecast the economic earnings of the branded business earnings within each of the identified segments. These are the excess earnings attributable to all the intangible assets of the business. The third step is to analyse the business drivers research to determine what proportion of total branded business earnings may be attributed specifically to the brand. The final step is to determine an appropriate discount rate based on the quality and security of the brand franchise with both trade customers and end-consumers.

Regardless of which method is used, the valuation usually will require a sensitivity analysis in which one flexes each of the assumptions made in the analysis one at a time to demonstrate the impact changes in each variable has on the overall valuation. However, this is a simple mechanical exercise intended to show which assumptions the valuation is most sensitive to. The valuer's dilemma lies in trying to determine which of the key assumptions is most likely to change and how, which is where all the brand audit data and brand equity measures becomes significant.

In our experience, it is very important to express the final valuation number in context. This means explaining exactly what has been valued, using what method, and what the key insights are as to the influence of the brand on the key operating variables of the business. This emphasizes the importance of developing a valuation model that is presented in a user-friendly manner to help management make crucial decisions around marketing and branding strategy objectively and with a high degree of financial rigour.

One way in which one can effectively express a valuation model in a simple format to help answer key marketing and branding investment decisions is a brand scorecard.

13.4.1 Academic definitions of brand equity

The popularization of Brand Equity is often attributed to David Aaker (1991, 1996) who conceptualizes it as comprising of four dimensions (loyalty, perceived quality, associations and awareness) assessed with 10 measures he derived from research. In operationalizing his measures, he added a fifth characteristic: market behaviour.

TABLE 13.1 The Brand Equity Ten

Dimension	Measures
Loyalty	Price premium
	Satisfaction / loyalty
Perceived quality/Leadership	Perceived quality
	Leadership (measured by scales)
Association/Differentiation	Perceived value
	Brand personality
	Organizational associations
Awareness	Brand awareness
Market behaviour	Market share
	Price and distribution indices

SOURCE: Aaker, 1996

Aaker acknowledges that it would be helpful if all of these measures could be captured in a single metric that is widely understood and credible but acknowledges the difficulties in determining which of the above are more important, how they could be weighted, combined and against which benchmarks should brands be measured. Clearly, Reichheld's Net Promoter Score (Reichheld, 1996), claimed by the author to be the one number you need to manage your business, is much simpler to manage.

Brand Equity (BE) is generally inferred, measured through proxies rather than directly observable. There are numerous measures and renowned academics (Agarwal and Rao, 1996) compared the effectiveness of 11 different measures. Some measure BE through a focus on incremental cash flow attributable to the brand (Ailawadi, Lehumann and Neslin, 2003); for example identifying how much more do consumers pay for branded cola versus retailers generic offers and multiplying that by some measure of volume. Others look at the value of the brands to the firm's total intangible worth and use stock market measures to help infer the BE. Yet others have demonstrated that BE generates customer acquisition, profitability and retention (Simon and Sullivan, 1993). Research often focuses on individual consumers and tries to isolate their preferences or utility not explained by price, promotion or other so-called objective measures. This is part of a broader range of research that focuses on customer mindset: that is relating BE to customer preferences, beliefs, affective responses and the like.

There are a number of commercial providers of such measures, each with its own brand identify and formula, but all consider the attributes associated with a brand and its salience to the target market believing that these influence customer behaviour and hence future revenue streams. The major models include: Milward-Brown's BrandZ, Research International's Equity Engine, IPSOS's Equity*Builder and Young and Rubicam's Brand Asset Valuator (BAV); the last is perhaps most used for academic research. In addition to BE measures, we discuss separately the valuation of the brand, which is also driven by discounted cash flow analysis. Each method for estimating BE or brand value is based on certain assumptions, estimates about how one isolates the cash attributable to the brand versus all other elements of the business strategy. The broader one defines brand (the brand is everything with which the customer interacts) the harder it is to isolate the value of the brand from the value of the firm.

The direction of all this research is to show how sensitive the value of the firm is to changes in measured BE. Where this relationship can be demonstrated, companies can value accurately the worth of further brand building, or the risks of withdrawing support and reducing BE.

13.4.2 Customer equity

The locus of marketing research and practice over the past 20 years has shifted from product brands to customer relationships and more recently – customer experience. Using a similar logic to BE, those that believe that business strategy should concentrate on customers rather than offers, developed a stream of research around customer equity (CE). The logic is identical but instead of considering the value of the firm as all its risk adjusted future cash flows arising from sales of products and services, CE measures the discounted cash generated by customers (or segments thereof). While both market assets should generate the same value of the firm (Ambler and Roberts, 2006), assessing marketing effectiveness with CE will focus insight and decision making on identifying the best customers as opposed to the best offers. This may be more useful for service marketers who often struggle to effectively differentiate and brand at the product level, eg bank accounts, mobile phone tariffs, auditing service. Service marketers tend to create relationships with customers based on the promise of future service quality and support hence need to identify those customers for whom such promises are most valuable and willing to pay for them.

CE is built upon aggregating the lifetime expected future purchases of each customer, the Customer Lifetime Value (CLV): the latter representing the risk adjusted expected cash flows from a customer related to the relationship (Farris *et al*, 2006). The cash flows are a function both of the revenue attributable to that relationship and the differential cost to serve of the customer. There are many decisions that managers need to make when determining CE. For example, how does one allocate purchases to the relationship per se and even more discussed in the literature, what assumptions does one make about retention. A simple assumption is based on cohorts, often by year. Every year, one recruits so many customers and they will defect at a certain rate per annum, over time the customer base is comprised of what is left from every cohort. This is called the 'lost-for-good' approach. Another calculation of LTV is made on the assumption that once recruited, the firm will have 'always-a-share'. Empirical observations suggest that customers are rarely gone forever; they return and spread their purchases among a changing repertoire of brands over time. One might buy a VW car once, repeat, then try a BMW, then a Honda and then return to VW. Such complex patterns of consumer behaviour can be modelled to some extent with more sophisticated formulae (Dwyer, 1997; Berger and Nasr, 1998; Blattberg, Malthouse and Neslin, 2009). In addition to considering revenue choices, many firms struggle to determine the true cost of serving individual customers. Most accounting systems are cost-based systems that allocate fixed costs across business units, not to individual customers based on their differential cost to serve. Activity Based Costing (ABC) has been heralded as the answer to this problem, but firms find it hard to implement in practice.

13.4.3 Brand equity (BE) or customer equity (CE): which to use?

BE and CE are two heads of the same market asset coin (Ambler and Roberts, 2006) but this does not stop adherents of either BE or CE from stating their case vigorously. Both metrics account for risk through the differential discount rates assigned either to different brands or customer groups. Hence both trade off income, cost and risk; determinants of shareholder value ultimately. As identified above, neither is straightforward to estimate, both require judgement and choices.

The discussion of market asset equity started with a defence of consistent advertising to support brands, that is, long-term value of brand building. The discussion remains unresolved with marketing normally asking for more investment and the board not confident of what the RoI will be.

Measuring CE will focus managers on recruiting more profitable customers, those less prone to defect and those that buy more of the firm's offer. Drilling down into defection will identify sources of customer dissatisfaction, service failures, channel inconsistencies and inadequate direct communication. Customer satisfaction has been shown to improve business performance and the market valuation of the firm (Anderson, Fornell and Rust, 1997; Anderson, Fornell and Agarwal, 2004). Looking at the customer as the central unit of analysis should encourage managers to consider which other needs the firm can fulfil for its best customers, thus continually improving the offer and building ever more loyal customers. The links between loyalty and profitability are well published (Reichheld, 1996; Keiningham *et al*, 2007; Liu, 2007), hence leading academics argue that managing for CE better directs the firm's resources and efforts over time (Blattberg and Deighton, 1996; Rust, Lemon and Zeithaml, 2004).

We believe that the choice between brand and customer equity as the key measure is largely dependent on both the firm's strategy and the nature of the market. A low-cost airline, for example, will not incur the costs of differential customer marketing and retention management, hence CE is not a relevant measure. Low-cost airlines want high awareness for their offer, routes and policies such that customers immediately flock to its website when they have definite travel plans. All customers have the same cost to serve because low-cost airlines operate an inflexible customer service policy and customers asking for special services are charged for them. A mobile phone operator, however, can differentiate between heavy data and phone users on large contracts who incur even higher costs through global travel and young people who use their phone for low-value text messages domestically. The tremendous difference between lifetime value of individual phone users suggests a strategy of maximizing the CLV of the former group while reducing the cost to serve of the latter.

13.4.4 *Implications for marketing accountability*

The concept of looking at the equity created by marketing is highly consistent with all three levels of the accountability framework, but particularly at level two.

It is a 'level one' construct by design, estimating the equity value of the market asset: customer or brand. It is sensitive to revenue, cost and risk. Some suggest that marketing directors be measured and rewarded for improving such equity as a way of aligning the trade-offs that they must make to shareholder wealth. While the idea has intuitive appeal, Ambler and Roberts (2006) note that changes to discounted cash flows reflect poor forecasting as much as they do good stewardship. If I am a marketing director of a mature business in a flat market and create innovative programmes to generate, for example, 6 per cent real growth per annum and forecast with 100 per cent accuracy, year on year as I grow well in excess of the market, I am not seen to create brand or customer equity. That is because in year zero, I forecasted perfectly. If my forecasting is poor, I have a much better chance of creating (or destroying) equity. Clearly this is not the desired outcome of aligning shareholder value with marketing measurement. As the professors title their article – Beware of the Silver Metric, all metrics have unintended consequences.

At level two, it links activities to outcomes in a sophisticated manner. A relationship marketing programme can clearly be linked to CLV and CE as forward indicators of success. Similarly, BE can help assess the quality of the product market segmentation, the effectiveness of portfolio strategy and the quality of individual marketing mixes. Both BE and CE are forward-looking measures so they should be sensitive to changes in marketing strategy. For example, excellent brand management should demonstrate increases in affinity and purchase intent, the future value of which is capitalized by BE in advance of the revenue actually being generated. Similarly, taking excessive cost out of the business will damage customer satisfaction and

CE measures will predict a large fall in shareholder value well before customers defect in large numbers.

References

Aaker, D (1991) *Managing Brand Equity: Capitalizing on the value of a brand name*, Free Press, New York

Aaker, D (1996) Measuring Brand Equity Across Products and Markets, *California Management Review*, **38** (3), pp 102–20

Agarwal, M and Rao, V (1996) An Empirical Comparison of Consumer-Based Measures of Brand Equity, *Marketing Letters*, **7** (3), pp 237–47

Ailawadi, K, Lehmann, D and Neslin, S (2003) Revenue Premium as an Outcome Measure of Brand Equity, *Journal of Marketing*, **67**, pp 1–17

Ambler, T and Roberts, J (2006) Beware the Silver Metric: Marketing performance measurement has to be multidimensional, *Marketing Science Institute Working Paper Series*, 06-113, pp 1–13

Anderson, E, Fornell, C and Agarwal, S (2004) Customer Satisfaction and Shareholder Value, *Journal of Marketing*, **68**, pp 172–85

Anderson, E, Fornell, C and Rust, R (1997) Customer Satisfaction, Productivity, and Profitability: Differences between goods and services, *Marketing Science*, **16** (2), pp 129–45

Berger, P D and Nasr, N I (1998) Customer Lifetime Value: Marketing models and applications, *Journal of Interactive Marketing*, **12** (1), pp 17–30

Blattberg, R C and Deighton, J (1996) Manage Marketing by the Customer Equity Test, *Harvard Business Review*, **74** (4), pp 136–44

Blattberg, R C, Malthouse, E C and Neslin, S A (2009) Customer Lifetime Value: Empirical generalizations and some conceptual questions, *Journal of Interactive Marketing (Mergent, Inc.)*, **23** (2), pp 157–68

Dwyer, R (1997) Customer Lifetime Value to Support Marketing Decision Making, *Journal of Direct Marketing*, **11** (4), pp 6–13

Farris, P, Bendle, N T, Pfeifer, P E, Reibstein, D J (2006) *Marketing Metrics: 50+ metrics every executive should master*, Wharton School Publishing, Upper Saddle River, New Jersey

Keiningham, T L, Cooil, B, Aksoy, L, Andreassen, T W and Weiner, J (2007) The Value of Different Customer Satisfaction and Loyalty Metrics in Predicting Customer Retention, Recommendation, and Share-of-Wallet, *Managing Service Quality*, **17** (4), p 361

Liu, Y (2007) The Long-Term Impact of Loyalty Programs on Consumer Purchase Behavior and Loyalty, *Journal of Marketing*, **71**, pp 19–35

Reichheld, F (1996) *The Loyalty Effect*, Harvard Business School Press, Boston, Mass

Rust, R, Lemon, K and Zeithaml, V (2004) Return on Marketing: Using customer equity to focus marketing strategy, *Journal of Marketing*, **68** (1), pp 109–27

Simon, C and Sullivan, M (1993) The Measurement and Determinants of Brand Equity: A financial approach, *Marketing Science*, **12** (1), pp 28–52

Webber, A M [accessed 31 July 2014] New Math for a New Economy, *Fast Company* [online] http://www.fastcompany.com/38859/new-math-new-economy

APPENDIX 1
Econometrics

BRYAN FINN AND DAVID MERRICK

Business Economics Limited

A1.1 What is econometrics?

Econometrics is the application of statistical techniques to the study of economic relationships. It uses data to quantify the relationship between a set of variables that describe an economic system. Econometrics is a widely used technique across a range of businesses. In particular, it is used as an aid to decision making in marketing, where it provides the methodology for marketers to make predictions about the impact of marketing activity on a company's sales, profitability and shareholder value.

A1.2 How is econometrics carried out?

In our experience, many organizations collect substantial amounts of data about their business – often at considerable expense – but these data are not always analysed fully and consequently do not play their full role in informing business decisions. Econometrics is one technique that can assist evidence-based decision making.

At heart, the concept is simple. Econometrics allows you to test which variables (called 'independent variables' or 'drivers') have a significant effect on a variable in which you are interested (called the 'dependent variable'). For example, the dependent variable may be sales volume, and the independent variables may include price, advertising, bank holidays, the weather, competitor prices, competitor advertising, public relations events, economic indicators, etc.

Not only is econometric analysis able to tell you which of a long list of possible drivers is important and which is unimportant, but for those that are important it is able to quantify the magnitude of their impact on the dependent variable in which you are interested. This ability to select the significant variables and to quantify the magnitude of their impact enables a predictive model to be constructed. This can then be used to explore scenarios for various decisions that can be made by the business and sensitivities to external factors beyond the control of the business.

In order to do its work, an econometric analysis needs to look at variations in the dependent and independent variables. Unlike the case with other types of statistical analysis, these variations are not usually planned as controlled experiments in an econometric analysis but just happen as a result of changing circumstances and the reactions of the business to the environment in which it operates. The types of variation that are analysed fall into two main categories: 1) variations over time (called 'time-series analysis'); and 2) variations at a point in time between different groups or categories (called 'cross-sectional analysis'). These two forms of variation can, of course, be combined in a single analysis, sometimes called 'panel data analysis'.

Although powerful and widely used, econometrics is a specialist subject. Large organizations may well have a dedicated in-house team to carry out econometric analyses. Smaller organizations usually outsource this type of analysis to consultancy firms.

There are a number of other techniques that marketers can use to quantify the impact of their activities, in addition, or as an alternative, to econometrics. These include conjoint or 'trade-off' analysis, which interprets market research on how consumers value various product or service attributes, including price; statistical control experiments where comparisons are made between the behaviour of consumers, some of whom have been exposed to a marketing stimulus and others who have not; and judgemental modelling techniques, which rely on management and expert experience to quantify key marketing relationships.

A1.3 Examples of what econometrics can do

Econometrics is of interest to business in general and marketing in particular because it provides a rational and often insightful framework for decision making. A few examples of marketing issues on which it is frequently applied are:

- demand forecasting;
- evaluating the effectiveness of advertising, promotions and other marketing activities;
- identifying key drivers of market changes and trends;
- quantifying price sensitivities;
- identifying and quantifying the impact of competitor behaviours.

FIGURE A1.1   Actual sales compared to model predictions

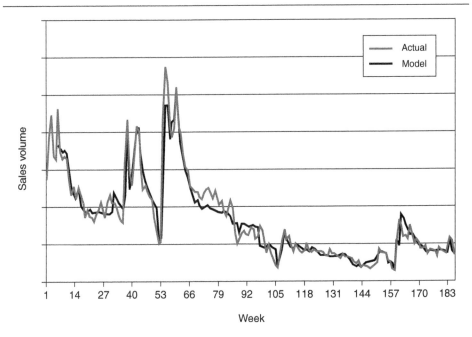

A number of detailed statistical tests are available to test the validity and reliability of an econometric model in order to have confidence that it can be used as a reliable basis for planning and decision making. In addition, however, we can look at how well the model is able to describe the existing data. A typical comparison between the model predictions and actual sales volumes is shown in Figure A1.1.

However, econometrics can do more than just provide an equation that can be validated against historic data and used to prepare estimates for the future. It can also break out the various factors that have contributed to variations in the past and thereby provide insights and understanding. A simple example in which sales are broken down between base demand, demand created by TV advertising and demand created by direct mail is shown in Figure A1.2. This shows the extent to which TV advertising and direct mail campaigns have contributed to sales over the period.

FIGURE A1.2   Impact of promotional activity on demand

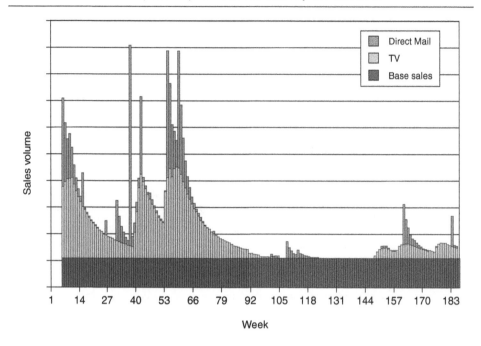

A1.4   Summary and conclusions

Econometrics is a powerful technique that is able to inform business decisions by providing evidence-based analysis. The analytical techniques required are specialized but, even so, are widely used because of the insights that they are able to provide. Of course, in order to deliver robust conclusions, econometric analysis relies on good data being available. Often the data are available but, when this is not the case, asking what data would be needed for an econometric analysis can be a valuable prompt for improved data capture.

APPENDIX 2
Seven important business questions marketers need to know the answers to

A2.1 How many units do you need to sell to break even?

A typical question, you must be able to answer when introducing a new product. The break-even point is the number of units sold where you neither make a loss or profit.

You have been given the following demand forecast by your marketing department for a product. The data includes the sales units, sales revenue and the total costs for three forecasts.

Forecast	Low	Medium	High
Sales Units	20,000	60,000	80,000
Sales Revenue £	2,000,000	6,000,000	8,000,000
Total Costs £	4,100,000	5,300,000	5,900,000

To derive the break-even point you need to:

- calculate the variable cost of making the product;
- derive the fixed costs;
- calculate the contribution per unit; and
- calculate the break-even point.

A2.1.1 Variable cost per unit

The variable cost is the additional cost of making a unit. This can be calculated by looking at the change in the total costs between two output levels.

	Sales Revenue £	Total Costs £	Sale Units
High	8,000,000	5,900,000	80,000
Low	2,000,000	4,100,000	20,000
Difference	6,000,000	1,800,000	60,000

Dividing the change in costs by the change in units gives the variable cost per unit. In this example £1,800,000 divided by 60,000 = £30 per unit.

A2.1.2 Fixed costs

Total cost is the sum of fixed costs plus variable costs. If we know our total costs and variable costs it is now possible to derive fixed costs by changing the subject of calculation.

For 80,000 units the total costs are £5,900,000 and the variable costs are £2,400,000.

Total Costs = Fixed Costs + Variable Costs, hence
Total Costs – Variable Costs = Fixed Costs.
£5,900,000 – £2,400,000 = £3,500,000
Fixed Costs = £3,500,000.

A2.1.3 Contribution per unit

Contribution is the difference between the selling price per unit and the variable cost per unit.

Every unit sold we generate £100 of revenue and costs £30 in variable costs, therefore each unit sold generates £70 in contribution. Every unit sold provides a contribution to cover the fixed costs.

A2.1.4 Break-even point

The break-even point is the level of sales where the product makes neither a profit nor a loss. To calculate the break-even point, the total fixed costs are divided by the contribution per unit.

In this example, £3,500,000 divided by £70 = 50,000 units.

A2.2 How much should I mark up a product to make my target profit margin?

The total cost of making product Ultra is £80 and the company wants to make a profit margin of 20 per cent. The profit margin is calculated by dividing profit per unit by the selling price per unit. Therefore if the company wants to make a 20 per cent margin, then how much should be added to Ultra's cost to achieve the target margin?

Mark-up is the amount added to the full cost to give the selling price. The following formula can be used.

Ultra's selling price per unit = Full cost/(1–target margin percentage)

Target margin percentage expressed as a decimal

£80/(1–0.2) = £100

The selling price for a unit of Ultra will be £100 and it will generate £20 in profit, which is a profit margin of 20 per cent.

A2.3 How do I calculate an expected monetary value?

You have been given the following demand forecast by your marketing department for product Phoenix.

Forecast	Low	Medium	High
Probability	0.3	0.6	0.1
Sales Revenue £	2,000,000	6,000,000	8,000,000

For each forecast multiply the sales revenue by its probability to give an expected value. Add up each expected value to give a wighted average for the product.

Forecast	Sales Revenue £	Probability	Expected value £
High	8,000,000	0.3	2,400,000
Medium	6,000,000	0.6	3,600,000
Low	2,000,000	0.1	200,000
Total		1.0	6,200,000

The expected sales value for Phoenix is £6.2 million.

A2.4 How much is my customer's future value worth to my organization?

You can estimate the future value of a customer by calculating a customer's lifetime value.

1 Estimate the length of the customer relationship in years.
2 Estimate future customer revenue per annum.
3 Estimate future customer costs per annum.
4 Calculate customer profitability per annum.
5 Apply the company's weighted average cost of capital to calculate the present value for each year.
6 Add up each year to calculate the customer lifetime value.

Year	20X1	20X2	20X3	20X4	Total
Revenue £m	1.3	1.5	1.9	2.4	7.1
Cost £m	0.6	0.7	1.0	1.4	3.7
Profit £m	0.7	0.8	0.9	1.0	3.4
WACC 10%*	0.909	0.826	0.751	0.683	
Present Value £m	0.64	0.66	0.68	0.68	2.66

* Obtained from present value tables

If the Alpha Stores continues to be a customer for the next four years then the company will have a lifetime value of £2.66 million.

A2.5 How do I calculate my cash to cash cycle?

Marketers need to know the answers to the following working capital questions:

1 How many days inventory does their company hold?
2 How long do our customers take to pay us?
3 How long do we take to pay our suppliers?
4 How long is our cash to cash cycle?

You have been supplied with the following data for three companies from the same industrial sector.

Company	Alpha	Beta	Delta
Average Inventory £	225,000	200,000	125,000
Cost of Sales £	1,000,000	750,000	500,000
Average Accounts Payable £	250,000	175,000	175,000
Average Accounts Receivables £	625,000	1,000,000	750,000
Sales (Credit) £	2,500,000	2,500,000	2,500,000
Purchases (Credit) £	500,000	400,000	375,000

The following working capital ratios can be calculated using the following formulas.

	Working Capital Ratio	Formula
a	Inventory holding days	365/(Cost of Sales/Average Inventory)
b	Accounts receivables days	(Average Accounts Receivable/Credit Sales)*365
c	Accounts payables days	(Average Accounts Payable/Credit Purchases)*365
d	Cash to cash cycle days	a + b − c = d

Working Capital Ratio	Alpha	Beta	Delta
Inventory holding days	82.1	97.3	91.3
Accounts receivables days	91.3	146.0	109.5
Accounts payables days	182.5	159.7	170.3
Cash to cash cycle days	–9.1	83.6	30.4

Alpha has the best cash to cash cycle as it has 9.1 days when it can invest cash to earn interest before paying its creditors. Beta has a liquidity gap of 83.6 days and will need to find short-term finance to provide liquidity, eg an overdraft.

A2.6 How do I calculate return on capital employed, net asset turnover and earnings before interest and tax?

Return on capital employed is a key profitability ratio and can be used to compare alternative returns when investing capital. The ratio takes the earnings before tax and interest from the Income statement and the total net assets from the Balance Sheet. Earnings is divided by the total net assets and then multiplied by 100 to calculate the percentage. In the following figure £4 million divided by £15 million then multiplied by 100 = 26.7 per cent. The shareholders can now compare the ROCE percentage with alternative investment opportunities such as the return from a bank.

ROCE can also be derived by calculating the Total Net Asset multiple and then multiplying it by the EBIT percentage. In the example below, the Total Net Asset multiple is derived by taking the Sales Revenue figure from the Income Statement and dividing it by the value of the Total Net Assets from the Balance Sheet. In this example it equates to 1.334, which means for every £1 of total net assets £1.334 of sales is generated. The EBIT percentage is calculated by dividing EBIT by Sale Revenue and multiplied by 100 to give a percentage. In the example below, £4 million divided by £20 million then multiplied by 100 equals a 20 per cent EBIT. Therefore the ROCE percentage = 1.334 * 20 = 26.7 per cent.

FIGURE A2.1

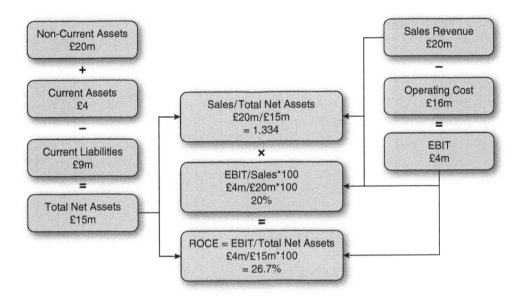

Marketers need to ask themselves where can they have a positive impact on Net Asset Turnover and EBIT.

A2.7 How do I calculate the payback period?

Concert plc is considering investing in three mutually exclusive improvement projects. The initial data collection and data analysis has been partially completed and is contained in the following three tables:

Project Year	Red Net Cash flow £	Yellow Net Cash flow £	Green Net Cash flow £
0	−10,000,000	−10,000,000	−10,000,000
1	4,000,000	2,500,000	1,300,000
2	3,000,000	2,300,000	1,600,000
3	2,500,000	2,200,000	2,000,000
4	1,500,000	2,200,000	2,500,000
5	1,000,000	2,200,000	3,000,000
6	600,000	2,200,000	4,000,000

Project Year	Red Net Cash flow £	Red Yellow Cumulative Net Cash flow £
0	−10,000,000	−10,000,000
1	4,000,000	−6,000,000
2	3,000,000	−3,000,000
3	2,500,000	−500,000
4	1,500,000	1,000,000
5	1,000,000	2,000,000
6	600,000	2,600,000

Red will pay back the £10 million between year 3 and 4. An apportionment is made between the years, which assume cash is received equally over the year. Red needs to recoup £0.5 million at the end of year 3; in year 4 £1.5 million is expected. Therefore an apportionment is made 0.5/1.5 *12 = four months. Red will recover the £10 million after three years and four months.

Yellow takes four years and 4.36 months to pay back, while Green takes four years 10.4 months to recoup the £10 million. Red has the shortest payback period.

INDEX

NB: page numbers in *italic* indicate figures or tables